Just Capitalism

Just Capitalism

A Christian Ethic
of Economic Globalization

Brent Waters

WESTMINSTER
JOHN KNOX PRESS
LOUISVILLE • KENTUCKY

Published by Westminster John Knox Press
Louisville, Kentucky

16 17 18 19 20 21 22 23 24 25—10 9 8 7 6 5 4 3 2 1

Book design by Sharon Adams
Cover design by Eric Walljasper

Library of Congress Cataloging-in-Publication Data

Names: Waters, Brent, author.
Title: Just capitalism : a Christian ethic of economic globalization / Brent Waters.
Description: Louisville, KY : Westminster John Knox Press, 2016. | Includes
  bibliographical references and index.
Identifiers: LCCN 2016009464 (print) | LCCN 2016013315 (ebook) | ISBN
  9780664234300 (alk. paper) | ISBN 9781611646917 ()
Subjects: LCSH: Capitalism--Religious aspects--Christianity. |
  Globalization--Religious aspects--Christianity.
Classification: LCC BR115.C3 W38 2016 (print) | LCC BR115.C3 (ebook) | DDC
  261.8/5--dc23
LC record available at http://lccn.loc.gov/2016009464

♾ The paper used in this publication meets the minimum requirements of the American National Standard for Information Sciences—Permanence of Paper for Printed Library Materials, ANSI Z39.48-1992.

Most Westminster John Knox Press books are available at special quantity discounts when purchased in bulk by corporations, organizations, and special-interest groups. For more information, please e-mail SpecialSales@wjkbooks.com.

To Jerre and Mary Joy

Contents

Preface

To propose a Christian ethic of globalization requires coming to terms with free market capitalism, because a globally integrated economy is inconceivable without its underlying capitalist principles. Hence the admittedly equivocal title of this book. Readers may think that it's just *capitalism*, and Christians should learn to make the best of this situation; or they may think that it is *just* capitalism, and it can be ordered in certain ways to promote Christian moral convictions. Although I have nothing against the former orientation—Christians, after all, are enjoined by Scripture to be as wise as serpents—it is the latter approach that I use in this book. My principal contention is that globalization is the only credible means at present for alleviating poverty on a global scale. Consequently, a well-ordered global capitalism is compatible with such core convictions as a preferential option for the poor and promoting human flourishing. To be naively anticapitalism is thereby to effectively opt against the poor and diminish human flourishing. Therefore, an ethic of globalization necessarily entails a defense of capitalism.

For many Christians, the world "globalization" often provokes strong negative reactions. It is frequently blamed for such ills as unemployment, exploited workers, illegal immigration, political instability, poverty, income inequality, global warming, and many other items could be added to the list. For many critics, globalization has come to serve as convenient bogeyman to blame as the principal source of suffering and material depredation throughout the world.

There are two principal causes underlying this disdain. First, it is often assumed that economic exchange in general is a tawdry affair, and the creation of affluence and wealth in particular is invariably ill-gotten gain.

ix

The Christian moral tradition seemingly supports these assumptions. The bulk of Christian moral teaching on riches and material possessions has tended to be deeply suspicious, and at times unambiguously condemnatory. And there were good reasons for this suspicion and condemnation. For roughly the first eighteen centuries of Christianity, economies were based predominantly on the ownership of land, agriculture, and extraction of raw materials and precious metals. These economies were essentially zero-sum; one became wealthy at another's expense. To hoard possessions or consume more than was needed was tantamount to impoverishing or harming those in need.

Modern economies, however, are based on productivity and exchange, and are therefore not zero-sum. Wealth or affluence is created through the production and exchange of goods and services. Modern economies are competitive, but one does not often, or even usually, become prosperous by impoverishing another, or conversely one is not always poor because another is rich. In an exchange-based economy, producers want affluent rather than impoverished consumers. Consequently, when much of traditional Christian moral teaching is simplistically applied to contemporary economic issues, it is often irrelevant, if not misguided. The principal cause of poverty is no longer greed that can be easily solved by redistributing wealth, but entails a complex constellation of factors preventing individuals from participating productively within competitive markets.

The second cause prompting a Christian disdain of globalization, then, stems from insufficient contextualization, updating, and revision of traditional moral teaching on riches and material possessions in light of how modern, market-based economies work. There are certainly numerous gems from the tradition that need to be preserved, but they also need to be refined and polished if they are to provide pertinent guidance within our present circumstances. To a large extent this contextualizing, updating, and revising has not been undertaken to any significant degree by much of contemporary Christian moral teaching or ethics literature.[1] The problem is further compounded by ideological commitments, often unacknowledged, that invariably trigger an allergic reaction to anything

1. There are some notable exceptions: see, e.g., Kenman L. Wong and Scott B. Rae, *Business for the Common Good: A Christian Vision for the Marketplace* (Downers Grove, IL: InterVarsity Press, 2011); Samuel Gregg, *The Commercial Society: Foundations and Challenges in a Global Age* (Lanham, MD, and Plymouth, UK: Lexington Books, 2007); and *Economic Thinking for the Theologically Minded* (Lanham, MD, and Oxford: University Press of America, 2001).

remotely smacking of capitalism that is believed to have spawned the globalization monster.

In this book I defend globalization and in doing so address the two causes of Christian disdain noted above. My chief reasons for doing so, however, are more expansive and theological, for I am defending this purported culprit as a Christian moral theologian. But what am I defending, and why am I defending it? Globalization is an imprecise term that can mean many things, such as intercultural exchange or conflict, social and cultural homogenization, reconfiguration of political identities and loyalties, or technological integration.[2] I focus on economic globalization not only because of its popular prominence but also because of its promising means for addressing the material needs and wants of people across the globe in a more expansive and efficient manner. In this respect my thesis is quite simple: new and expanding global markets, in conjunction with an increasingly integrated global economy, are potentially best situated for addressing the material wants and needs as a necessary prerequisite for human flourishing.

Why I am defending globalization, then, is based primarily on two arguments. First, the world is part of God's good creation and as such is the source of abundant material goods that may be enjoyed by humans as God's creatures.[3] These goods, however, are not at hand but are latent and must be developed. Humans must develop this potential not only to meet their most basic needs and wants but also to more fully enjoy and share the goods of creation as part of their calling to exercise God's mandate of limited dominion and stewardship. At present, global market-based exchange offers the best means for both developing and distributing these material goods.

Second, at present, globalization offers the most realistic and promising way of exercising a preferential option for the poor. The liberalization of trade and capital investment over the past two decades has helped lift around a billion people out of dire poverty and has created a fledgling global middle class. With increased globalization these trends cannot only be sustained but also enlarged and strengthened. In short, the best way to help the poor, to love them, in part, as neighbors, is to enable them to participate more fully in new and expanding global markets.

To be clear, I am *not* contending that globalization (and its underlying capitalism) is a direct outgrowth of Christian moral thought and practice.

2. This does not imply that issues involving culture, politics, and technology are irrelevant to economic globalization as is readily apparent in the following chapters.
3. Creatures, it might be added, who bear explicitly the image and likeness of God.

More modestly, I am arguing that globalization is not inherently incompatible with some central Christian theological and moral convictions. For instance, better meeting the material wants and needs for more people is a concrete, albeit indirect, way of enacting a love of neighbor. Less modestly, I am also suggesting that the disruption resulting from new and expanding global markets can afford opportunities for the Spirit to be at work in the world in ways that have previously not been available.

Again, to be clear, I am aware that globalization is not without its problems; indeed, they are legion. I readily admit that the growth of a globally integrated economy is in need of extensive scrutiny, regulation, and reorientation. I mention some of the more pressing issues throughout the book but leave most unmentioned. Moreover, those I mention I make little effort to resolve. This is partly due to the limits of my knowledge; to paraphrase the prophet, I am neither a policy wonk nor the son of a policy wonk. More important, proposing potential solutions in any detail would distract from what I am trying to achieve in this book. My goal is to provide a conceptual understanding of globalization in and through which Christians may both critically and constructively engage this phenomenon. Globalization is admittedly deeply flawed and in need of repair; but it is nonetheless a powerful force, for both good and evil in our world, that must be reckoned with. For Christians to simply indict globally market-based exchange as, at best, a distasteful enterprise, or, at worst, an unmitigated evil is, I believe, to be both foolhardy and unfaithful if theological claims about enjoying God's good material creation and exercising a preferential option for the poor are to be taken seriously.

Finally, to be clear once again, I am *not* arguing that producing and exchanging material goods and services is synonymous with human flourishing. It is a means for achieving this objective and not an end in itself. But exchange is a vital necessity and should not be given short shrift. Humans flourish in sharing or communicating the goods of creation. Consequently, a properly ordered pursuit of producing, exchanging, and enjoying created goods can promote communicative associations in which human flourishing occurs most prominently. The instrumental necessity of economic exchange reminds us that as embodied creatures we are in want and need of many material things. But fulfilling these wants and needs through exchange is not sufficient to satisfy the longing for fellowship with others in which we flourish. Although exchange and fellowship are distinguishable, they are nevertheless inseparable; fellowship is enfeebled when exchange is impaired. To use a crude example, you cannot shop your way to happiness, but you are likely to be unhappy if you cannot easily buy or otherwise obtain what you want or need. Or as Scripture rightfully insists, we do not live by bread alone,[4] but we cannot really know this until we have more than just bread to eat. Globalization has the potential to provide this material surplus.

4. Matt. 4:4.

Acknowledgments

I need to thank many people for their help in writing this book. I am thankful that Garrett-Evangelical Theological Seminary granted me a yearlong sabbatical to undertake this project and particularly grateful to President Lallene Rector and Dean Luis Rivera for honoring my seclusion by only rarely sending e-mails to my neglected inbox. My doctoral students, Bernard Wong, Kwang-Jin Oh, William Novak, Shane Hinson, and Leonard Gaines, served ably as research assistants and helped me think through themes in this book. The librarians and staff of the United Library at Garrett-Evangelical Theological Seminary patiently and efficiently helped me find numerous books and articles for which I am most grateful. Robert Carpenter co-taught two seminars with me on globalization and Christian ethics. His practical experience gained from years of working in and with global corporations proved invaluable in helping me formulate some key concepts and ideas that are developed in this book. I very much appreciate the support of Daniel Braden and Gavin Stephens at Westminster John Knox Press not only for their editorial guidance and personal support but also for their abundant patience in waiting for a long-overdue manuscript. As always, my wife, Diana, and daughter, Erin, provided steadfast sources of strength of which they are probably unaware. While I was writing this book, Erin was married, and it was pleasure to welcome her husband, Bill, into the family—he is a brave man. My debts to Jerre and Mary Joy Stead can never be adequately repaid, and dedicating this book to them is a token of appreciation for their unending generosity, support, and friendship. Jerre's leadership roles in various global corporations were a godsend. He read the entire manuscript, making many helpful comments and criticisms, and was overly generous with his time in helping me think about globalization from the perspective of Christian ethics. I already knew that he is an excellent businessman, but in the process I discovered that he is also a good theologian. In short, Jerre and Mary Joy, thank you!

Introduction

Globalization 3.0

Globalization is not a new phenomenon.[1] As long as people living at some distance from each other have engaged in trade, a kind of global exchange has existed, because no group of human beings can be completely self-sufficient in satisfying their material wants and needs. Archaeologists have discovered Roman trade stations in India. Throughout the medieval period, Europe and Asia engaged in extensive trade, often through Muslim intermediaries. And in the early nineteenth century New England clipper ships delivered ice to Asian customers.[2] The extent of global trade and economic exchange has historically ebbed and flowed, but following Thomas Friedman's schema there are three distinct periods that encapsulate globalization.[3]

Globalization 1.0, roughly from 1492 to 1800, was driven principally by innovations in transportation and nationalism. As traveling across great distances became faster and more reliable, various European states competed and cooperated with each other in creating global markets. Globalization 2.0, roughly from 1800 to 2000, was based on further advances in transportation and, more importantly, on the development of new information and communication technologies. In addition,

1. Portions of the following are adapted from Brent Waters, "Two, or Perhaps Two-and-a-half Cheers for Globalization," *Anglican Theological Review* 92, no. 4 (Fall 2010).

2. See William J. Bernstein, *A Splendid Exchange: How Trade Shaped the World* (New York: Atlantic Monthly Press, 2008). Archaeological evidence indicates that trade between distant people began around 35,000 years ago; see Eric D. Beinhocker, *The Origin of Wealth: Evolution, Complexity, and the Radical Remaking of Economics* (Boston, MA: Harvard Business School Press, 2006), 6–11.

3. Thomas L. Friedman, *The World Is Flat: A Brief History of the Twenty-First Century, Further Updated and Expanded* (New York: Picador / Farrar, Straus and Giroux, 2007).

multinational corporations displaced nation-states as the principal players. Despite the disruptions of the Great Depression and two world wars, this second phase established globally integrated markets. According to Friedman, Globalization 3.0 begins in 2000, and its driving force "is the newfound power for *individuals* to collaborate and compete globally."[4] The convergence of the personal computer, Internet, and affordable software has rendered physical location largely irrelevant for participating in global markets as both producers and consumers. Moreover, unlike the previous periods, the principal players are increasingly ethnically diverse.

Four factors make Globalization 3.0 unique. The first factor is its *scope*. Participants in global markets now include billions of individuals, as well as companies, corporations, and financial institutions of varying size and complexity. A person in North Dakota can, with a few clicks, provide a microloan enabling an individual in Bangladesh to start a new business.[5] The relative *ease* of participation is the second factor. With a computer, tablet, or smart phone, almost anyone can enter the global marketplace. I need not leave the comfort of my home to go on an international shopping spree. The third factor is the *speed* of exchange. It is now assumed that goods and services are routinely delivered quickly to customers around the world. In the first two phases, delivering a book from London to Hong Kong was compressed from months to weeks or days. The time required is now further reduced to seconds if the text is an e-book. The fourth factor is the *fluidity* of capital, finance, and labor. Money, expertise, and workers can, at least potentially, converge anywhere in the world to produce goods and services that are sold to customers across the globe. Friedman believes the world is flat because there are fewer and fewer barriers preventing the free flow of production and consumption. Or in the words of Ian Goldin and Mike Mariathasan, "The current period of integration is revolutionary in that a larger set of changes have occurred with a pervasively wider influence than over any comparably short time in previous phases of globalization."[6]

Globalization, however, is not without its problems. Many people, for instance, are suffering the aftermath of oppressive colonial rule that was a prevalent feature of Globalization 1.0, and financial crises, widening income disparities, social unrest, widespread anxiety concerning

---

4. Ibid., 10 (emphasis original).
5. There are a number of websites that match lenders with borrowers.
6. Ian Goldin and Mike Mariathasan, *The Butterfly Defect: How Globalization Creates Systemic Risks, and What to Do about It* (Princeton, NJ, and Oxford: Princeton University Press, 2014), 10.

unemployment, and ensuing political instability are seemingly endemic to the bust-and-boom cycles of global markets. For some these challenges appear so threatening that the very future of globalization is called into question.[7] These are admittedly important issues—additional ones could be added to the list—and I address a number of them throughout the following chapters. Yet despite these concerns there are good reasons why globalization, particularly in its 3.0 manifestation, should be welcomed and supported.

Two-and-a-Half Cheers for Globalization

There are two principal reasons to welcome and support Globalization 3.0. First, economic globalization is the only realistic strategy for ameliorating poverty. Starting with the formation of the World Trade Organization (WTO) in 1995, for instance, and in conjunction with liberalized and integrative economic policies, it is estimated that nearly a billion people have escaped abject poverty, and income has risen steadily even with the recent financial crisis and economic downturn. The percentage of people living on less than $1.25 (US) a day in Brazil, for example, has been cut in half from 2.6 percent to 1.3 percent of the population while per capita Gross Domestic Product (GDP) has more than doubled from $3,431 to $7,896. More impressively, China's poverty line has fallen from 10.7 percent to 4 percent, and per capita GDP increased from $466 to $3,528. Even a desperately poor country such as Ethiopia has cut the poverty rate from 21.2 percent to 9.6 percent while increasing per capita GDP from $94 to $226.[8]

These benefits are partly the result of greater trade that creates new jobs, as well as increasing purchasing power by providing cheaper goods and services. Perhaps more important, an integrated global economy stimulates the creation of capital. This is a crucial factor in alleviating poverty, for capital is the source of investments that in turn create production, exchange, and employment.[9] In this respect, it should be emphasized that capital is not self-sustaining but must be constantly

7. See, e.g., Harold James, *The Creation and Destruction of Value: The Globalization Cycle* (Cambridge, MA, and London: Harvard University Press, 2009); Joerg Rieger, *No Rising Tide: Theology, Economics, and the Future* (Minneapolis, MN: Fortress Press, 2009); and Dani Rodrik, *The Globalization Paradox: Democracy and the Future of World Economy* (New York: Norton, 2011).

8. Statistics provided by IHS Global Insight.

9. See Hernando de Soto, *The Mystery of Capital: Why Capitalism Triumphs in the West and Fails Everywhere Else* (New York: Basic Books, 2000).

generated. Policies discouraging the creation of capital, therefore, are ultimately recipes for promoting greater poverty. As Martin Wolf has observed, the "failure of our world is not that there is too much globalization, but that there is too little."[10]

Second, economic globalization helps resist the encroachment of the "universal and homogenous state." Alexandre Kojève coined this phrase in his correspondence with Leo Strauss.[11] Kojève contends that the ordering and meaning of civil society depends on and is derived from the state. Economic exchange should, therefore, be regulated to promote political goals as opposed to political policies designed to enable the economic exchanges of private citizens. It is politicians rather than consumers that should determine what is and what is not available in the marketplace; nationalism is privileged over every other form of human association.

Strauss's retort is that when such power is concentrated in the state, tyranny is the inevitable outcome as exemplified by the rise of totalitarian regimes in the twentieth century. Some pundits claim that with the collapse of the Soviet Union and China's embrace of the free market, globalization's purported benefit of checking the encroachment of the state is now overstated. However, such an easy dismissal should be resisted, for even in a world of nearly two hundred nation-states the momentum to concentrate power in these regimes or in intergovernmental organizations is disquieting. Nationalism tends to exacerbate conflict, given contending national interests that are resolved through the threat or implementation of coercive solutions. In short, it is consumers, not politicians, who have much more at stake in preserving a peaceful world of trade and exchange.

This is not a radical libertarian proposal that envisions no constructive role for the state. There are no serious advocates of globalization that naively dismiss the state as an unqualified evil. To the contrary, capital creation, investment, production, trade, and economic exchange require the rule of law. It is not coincidental that failed states are among the most impoverished nations. The debate over globalization is not whether or not states have any role to play, but the extent of their involvement and whether that involvement serves to promote or discourage the flow of capital, finance, labor, and trade.

10. Martin Wolf, *Why Globalization Works* (New Haven, CT, and London: Yale University Press, 2004), 4.

11. See Leo Strauss, *On Tyranny* (Chicago and London: University of Chicago Press, 2000), 133–314.

This debate is both interesting and vexing because the emergence of Globalization 3.0 may be coinciding with a significant, perhaps epochal, change currently underway in political ordering: namely, the transition from the nation-state to the market-state. According to Philip Bobbitt, the nineteenth century was dominated by the state-nation. Citizens were expected to serve the interests of the state that were expressed primarily through consolidating national identities and imperial expansion. Such state-nations inevitably came into conflict with each other, and their era comes to an end in the First World War. This in turn leads to the rise of the nation-state in which the state exists to serve the interests of its citizens. The twentieth century entailed a long war, or series of wars, to establish the principle of individual freedom as the dominant political paradigm. But the victory was short-lived, for by the end of the twentieth century the market-state begins to emerge. What exactly the goals and aims of the market-state might be remains to be seen, for this transition is nascent and ill-defined.[12] If the era of the nation-state may be characterized by the centralization of power through large and cumbersome bureaucracies, then in contrast the market-state entails the dispersal of power through informal networks in and through which individuals gain access to free-flowing capital, employment, and acquisition of goods and services. Unlike the nation-state, the market-state is, or more accurately will be, populated by individuals whose interests as consumers often trump those of citizens.

If Bobbitt is correct, then this uneasy transition helps to account for the wide range of concerns and issues often associated with globalization, because at the beginning of the twenty-first century people continue to live in nation-states but within a global economy better suited for market-states. Moreover, their respective interests cannot be easily reconciled. It is in the interest of the nation-state to protect its capital, finance, manufacturing, and labor behind impenetrable borders; whereas it is in the interest of the market-state to have porous borders enabling free-flowing access. It is difficult, for example, to have much enthusiasm for the slogan "buy American" for someone residing in Pittsburgh who works for a financial institution owned by the Royal Bank of Scotland, drives a Hyundai, and has invested much of her retirement portfolio in corporations headquartered around the world.

12. See Philip Bobbitt, *The Shield of Achilles: War, Peace, and the Course of History* (New York: Knopf, 2002); and *Terror and Consent: The Wars for the Twenty-First Century* (New York: Knopf, 2008), 180–238.

The nascent transition from nation-state to market-state and its concurrent globalization is not free of potential peril. It cannot be known in advance whether privileging the emerging market-state will ultimately prove less menacing than the threat of the universal and homogenous nation-state. Some of the more prominent challenges are examined below.

Although globalization generates new employment opportunities, thereby helping ameliorate poverty and increase prosperity on a global scale, one consequence is localized short-term displacement and unemployment. For example, when manufacturing and service jobs are shifted from developed to developing regions, two things occur: new jobs are created in one locale and old jobs are lost in another, resulting in a series of subsequent dislocations. On the one hand, new employment opportunities may promote rapid urbanization, while on the other hand unemployed workers may need to migrate or immigrate to new locales in order to find new jobs. Responding to changing market demands prompt short-term disruptions for both individuals and communities. As Roger Scruton contends, "By disrupting old patterns of settlement and managed environments globalization undermines the values and expectations on which a stable way of life depends."[13]

Such disruptive shifts are not unprecedented. In 1910 33 percent of Americans were either farmers or farm laborers, while the amount declines to slightly over 1 percent in 2000.[14] Concurrently, roughly 54 percent of Americans lived in rural areas in 1910,[15] while the amount declines to slightly under 21 percent by 2000.[16] What is important to highlight in this shift is that at the end of this ninety-year period there is not a 32 percent unemployment rate comprising individuals languishing in rural communities. Rather, many people moved to cities and suburbs to find work in the industrial and service sectors. The principal difference today is the global scale and rapid pace of these shifts. Consequently, perpetual anxiety over potential unemployment may be an ongoing concern for the foreseeable future. The challenge is to determine what responsibilities the public and private sectors should have in assisting affected people to overcome these displacements, particularly in respect

---

13. Roger Scruton, *How to Think Seriously about the Planet: The Case for an Environmental Conservatism* (Oxford and New York: Oxford University Press, 2012), 21.

14. "TED: The Economics Daily," United States Department of Labor, Bureau of Labor Statistics, April 6, 2006, http://www.bls.gov/opub/ted/2006/apr/wk1/art04.htm.

15. See http://www2.census.gov/prod2/statcomp/documents/CT1970p1-11.pdf.

16. See http://www.fhwa.dot.gov/planning/census_issues/archives/metropolitan_planning /cps2k.cfm.

to learning new and marketable job skills in which they are competing not only with neighbors down the road or citizens in an adjacent state but also with individuals throughout the world.

Another challenge is that the benefits of globalization are not evenly distributed. Although a great amount of wealth has been created over the last few decades, the gap between rich and poor has grown and is continuing to grow. This wealth, however, has not been gained at the expense of the poor, because the top and bottom lines on the graph have both been rising, but the gap separating them is expanding. What the social and political ramifications of this gap might mean over an extended period of time is unknown. Whether or not it is morally significant how high the ceiling climbs so long as the floor is also rising is an open question. But to use a more familiar analogy, a rising tide does indeed lift all boats, but a growing number of modest dinghies and sloops, as well as some lifeboats and swimmers in lifejackets, alongside a few large yachts, crowd the harbor. As the recent financial crisis and recession demonstrated, the fleet remained intact, but some boats weathered the storm better than others.

Global markets require financial integration that is simultaneously efficient and vulnerable. Frequent booms and busts are therefore endemic. Free-flowing capital has facilitated investments that over the past two decades created unprecedented wealth as well as unprecedented debt. The effects in each instance are systemic. Investments in China and the tiger economies of Asia returned handsome profits to investors and pension funds, while toxic mortgages in the United States poisoned banks and investors in Europe and Japan. Easy credit fueled a rapid rise in housing prices throughout the world that in turn was highly leveraged, and when the "housing bubble" burst the incurred debt could no longer be carried. Hence, the resulting defaulted loans, underwater mortgages, tight credit, bankruptcies, and soaring unemployment.

Consequently, there is a need for greater investment transparency and financial regulation, but the unwieldy transition to a market-state makes this a daunting task, one that nation-states may be ill-equipped to address. Establishing workable agreements among nation-states, given their often conflicting interests, is no easy task as the failed meeting on climate change in Copenhagen, December 7–18, 2009, and the continual failures of the World Bank and International Monetary Fund (IMF) to adequately address the financial needs of developing nations attest. How do nation-states come to terms with free-flowing capital, labor, production, and consumers whose interests are not national or even transnational, but global? Even if agreeable international regulatory schemes could be cobbled together, they would not provide long-term stability for all sectors, given the dynamic nature of global markets. The success of globalization is predicated on the ability to rapidly shift capital, labor, and production, which in turn result in periodic dislocations at various locales around the world. When the globalized economy is efficiently generating capital, creating jobs, and producing goods and services at affordable prices, the resulting systemic stability depends on an underlying and chaotic process of frequent change and disruption.[17] Perpetual employment worries, income inequality, fluctuating housing prices, failed business ventures, and community dislocations are part of the price that must be paid to participate in the global economy.[18]

Given these anxieties, it is not surprising that nation-states try to protect their citizens. This attempt is exemplified by policies restricting trade and immigration, or bailing out failing industries. Protectionism, however, harms the citizens it purportedly tries to defend: Restricting trade results in consumers paying higher prices for inferior goods and services. Propping up failing industries often delays their eventual collapse resulting in future unemployment and the unproductive use of capital. And constraining immigration cuts off a vital source of entrepreneurs and subsequent creation of new jobs. Imagine what the price and quality of TVs would be like if Samsung and Sony were restricted from the US market; imagine if the federal government had subsidized the typewriter industry when the personal computer was introduced; and would anyone be better off without Intel, Yahoo, and Google, all cofounded by immigrants.

Protectionism is a dangerous strategy because it also promotes international tension and at times hostility. No late modern nation-state can produce all the goods and services it might need or want. Saudi Arabia, for example, can be energy independent but cannot meet its needs for agricultural and manufactured products. Moreover, as Adam Smith and David Ricardo recognized, trade always benefits both parties because of their respective comparative advantages.[19] The English trade their wool to obtain Portuguese wine because England does not have

17. See Paul Seabright, *The Company of Strangers: A Natural History of Economic Life* (Princeton, NJ, and Oxford: Princeton University Press, 2004), esp. ch. 1.

18. See Gregg Easterbrook, *Sonic Boom: Globalization at Mach Speed* (New York: Random House, 2009).

19. See Adam Smith, *An Inquiry into the Nature and Causes of the Wealth of Nations* (Indianapolis, IN: Liberty Fund, 1981), bk. 4, and Pierro Sraffa, ed., *The Works and Correspondence of David Ricardo*, vol. 1, *On the Principles of Political Economy and Taxation* (Indianapolis, IN: Liberty Fund, 2004), ch. 7.

a suitable climate for vineyards, and Portugal is not a good place to raise sheep. In this scheme it does not make sense to wage war against a trading partner, whereas when trade becomes greatly restricted, conquest may appear to be a rational strategy. Cordell Hull, Franklin Roosevelt's secretary of state, argued that high tariffs and restrictive trade policies were among the chief causes of both the world wars.[20] This is not to suggest that unfettered trade would result inevitably in world peace, but extensive trade does help to alleviate both the underlying causes and scope of international conflicts.[21]

The challenges noted above are merely a few among many accompanying the emergence of Globalization 3.0 and the transition from nation-state to market-state. Does Christian moral theology have anything to offer that might inform ethical and ecclesial leadership in this transition? Any answer to this question must first be prefaced by acknowledging that the role of the moral theologian is to neither commend nor condemn globalization in any wholesale manner. To offer a blanket endorsement or denunciation is tantamount to being for or against icebergs. The task at hand is to navigate perilous economic waters and deal with wreckage as it occurs. In what follows I sketch out four theological themes—loving global neighbors, stewardship, vocation, and renewal—that can inform how this navigation can be undertaken, and these themes are developed in more detail in subsequent chapters.

Loving Global Neighbors

Christ commands his disciples to love their neighbors.[22] There are neighbors near and far; neighbors who are friends and those who are enemies; neighbors that are known and those unknown.[23] We encounter many neighbors in economic exchanges and financial transactions, and in global markets these encounters are often anonymous and distant. Imagine, for example, that I need a new computer so I can continue to write books and articles that are read by very few people. I order the computer online. In the few minutes that it takes to complete this task, I initiate a series of global transactions. Although the lead office of the company from which I purchased the computer is located in Dallas, the server

---

20. Easterbrook, *Sonic Boom*, 7–8.
21. See Michael Mandelbaum, *The Road to Global Prosperity* (New York and London: Simon and Schuster e-book, 2014), ch. 1.
22. Matt. 22:34–40.
23. See Karl Barth, *Church Dogmatics* (Edinburgh: T. & T. Clark, 1961), III/4: 285–323.

hosting the website is in Vancouver. An office worker in Dublin reviews and processes my order. The hardware and software are manufactured in such places as Bucharest, Seoul, and Taipei. My customized computer is assembled in Shanghai, air-freighted and delivered to my door by a corporation headquartered in Memphis. Unfortunately, I can't get the thing to work, so I ring the customer service hotline and speak to a representative in Bangalore who helps me correct the problem. Although I have had no face-to-face encounters, I have nonetheless participated in an exchange involving dozens or perhaps hundreds of people across the globe.

The reader might be thinking, to invoke Tina Turner, what's love got to do with it? These anonymous and distant interactions are expressions of love because they help each other acquire needed goods and services. The reader may retort that these exchanges are motivated by self-interest that is incompatible with neighbor love. Yet love of the other can never be separated from the interests of the self. This is precisely the insight of Adam Smith's much-maligned observation that it "is not from the benevolence of the butcher, the brewer, or the baker, that we expect our dinner, but from their regard to their own interest."[24] This precept must be understood in light of his previous book, *The Theory of the Moral Sentiments*, in which he argues that there are universal needs shared by all people.[25] The baker knows that people must eat, and she satisfies her need for money by selling bread to those who are hungry. Self-interest is inescapably grounded in the necessity of cooperation. There can be no bakers without hungry customers, and no customers in the absence of bread. When Christian theology speaks of love, it does not have sentimentality in mind, for neighbor love often requires making difficult decisions entailing costly moral, social, and political consequences. It is in the interest of poor farmers in developing countries, for example, as well as consumers worldwide, to compete freely and fairly in global markets. If such free competition is taken seriously, would not a corresponding act of love, then, require governments in the United States, the European Union, and Japan to discontinue subsidizing and protecting their own farmers in order to permit fair competition? Otherwise, love is effectively voided of concrete political content.

24. Smith, *Wealth of Nations*, 26–27.
25. Adam Smith, *The Theory of Moral Sentiments* (Indianapolis, IN: Liberty Fund, 1982).

Stewardship

Stewardship is often associated with voluntary donations such as tithing and charitable contributions. This limited connotation is unfortunate, for in Christian theology stewardship embraces a much larger range of activities involving the allocation, use, and purposes of one's time, work, and financial resources. Consequently, investing within a global economy is one dimension of stewardship. As the parable of the Talents illustrates, it is the servants who double the value of the property entrusted to their care who are deemed to be good and faithful stewards.[26] There is a need, of course, to govern investing in line with the principles of honesty, justice, and other pertinent moral considerations, particularly in respect to churches and their related institutions and organizations. The issue at stake, however, is not confined to ethical principles governing denominational pension funds and institutional endowments, but also how individual Christians invest their money and how they might influence the strategies and objectives of corporations, venture capitalists, and hedge funds. If, as Martin Wolf insists, more rather than less globalization is needed to alleviate dire poverty, then investing in the most impoverished regions is a crucial moral issue. This does not denigrate the work of relief agencies, charities, and nongovernmental organizations. When people are hungry, sick, or homeless they should be fed, cared for, and provided shelter.

Yet these are emergency responses and not long-term solutions. Capital is required to develop infrastructures enabling the production of goods and services that can be purchased in global markets, which in turn creates employment. A simple example illustrates this need for capital investment. Malaria is a debilitating disease afflicting much of sub-Saharan Africa. One simple, albeit partial, remedy is providing nets under which people sleep. A charitable organization distributes thousands of free nets. Unfortunately this admittedly humane act drives several small, local companies that were struggling to produce affordable nets out of business resulting in both greater unemployment and dependency on aid. Investing in these struggling firms would have been a more productive and effective response to preventing malaria. Good stewardship of investing in a global economy ranges from simple micro lending to more ambitious ventures. This is why a growing number of neighbors in the most impoverished regions of the world are saying something to the

26. Matt. 25:14–30.

effect of send us less aid and more investment so we may join you as both competitors and partners in the global marketplace.[27]

Vocation

Stewardship leads to the third theme: vocation. It is unfortunate that many churches regard themselves to be, in effect, voluntary organizations. This implies that for the vast majority of Christians their faith and practice is something they pursue in their spare time. The work of the church is reduced to a small domain of ordained professionals who coordinate cadres of part-time volunteers. This is a highly impoverished understanding of the church, because it diminishes ministry to little more than ecclesiastically sponsored programs. Rather, in virtue of their baptism all Christians are ministers of Jesus Christ, and since there is no such thing as a part-time Christian there is also no such thing as a part-time minister. What Christians do in the workplace and marketplace, on Wall Street and Main Street, expresses and bears witness to their faith, and the ramifications of that witness are not confined to a local congregation or national denominational agency: the ramifications of Christian witness are global.

This is not to denigrate the laypersons serving as ushers and members of boards and committees. Rather, it is the acknowledgment that the church's ministry in the world is most immediately present through its people who are already there, exhibiting a love of neighbor. It is in and through the mundane activities of work and economic exchange that people are enabled to put roofs over their heads and food on their tables, and in extending these opportunities to those excluded that the church's ministry in and to the world is best performed. Consequently, the church should not be embarrassed by, much less hostile to, the requisite means of achieving these good ends: namely, the creation of capital derived through investment, exchange, and profits. If the church is to renew its *global* mission and ministry in the contemporary world, then it is incumbent to recover a vital sense of secular callings and vocations: of recovering the ministry of the baptized.

27. See, e.g., Dambisa Moyo, *Dead Aid: Why Aid Is Not Working and How There Is a Better Way for Africa* (New York: Farrar, Straus and Giroux, 2009).

Renewal

This recovery leads to the fourth and final theme: the renewal of the church's mission and ministry. Jesus Christ commands his disciples to go into the world and make disciples of all nations.[28] In every generation Christians have fulfilled this commission in a world undergoing social, political, and economic change. It is no different today. Change, and its accompanying dislocations and anxieties, is the only reliable feature of the late modern world with its globalized markets, and its inhabitants are increasingly nomadic instead of settled. Yet many churches are stuck imaginatively in a bygone era, fixated on institutional maintenance and survival. Too much time, attention, and money are spent on trying to keep the doors of failing local churches open, and propping up large and cumbersome denominational and ecumenical bureaucracies. The church continues to think in local, national, and international terms in a world that has become global, and its ministry, particularly in terms of evangelizing the world, is suffering as a result. In fixating on institutional survival, churches forsake the possibility of thriving.

Perhaps the time is ripe for some creative destruction. This is not a radical suggestion, for is this not how the Holy Spirit has always done her work? Renewal can only occur by allowing the old to pass away so the new can come into being. This means that Christians should stop thinking about the church primarily in institutional terms and more in terms of ministry within dynamic global networks. Such ministry entails a variety of forms and approaches that are able to adapt to changing circumstances, requiring in turn that they be agile, lean, experimental, impermanent, and focused on enabling the ministry of the baptized. Within such a scheme centralized institutions, structures, and bureaucracies are often a liability instead of a benefit.

Why Not Three Cheers?

To confirm the reader's suspicion, I am a proponent of economic globalization based on free trade stemming from free-flowing capital, finance, and labor. I believe it is the only practical way to alleviate poverty and promote prosperity. I am aware of the endemic problems, dislocations, and anxieties accompanying this transition from nation-state to market-state. I also acknowledge that even if globalization should fulfill its promise and resolve all its problems in a just manner, that as

28. Matt. 28:16–20.

a Christian I can only give it two-and-a-half cheers. Why? To answer this question, I turn briefly to F. D. Maurice. Late in his career Maurice delivered a series of lectures at Cambridge University that were later published under the title of *Social Morality*.[29] He argues that a longing for universal fellowship is a healthy desire. Human beings are social creatures that seek the company of others. This is exemplified on a small scale in such associations as families, and in nations on a larger scale. Together, these private associations and civil communities constitute what Maurice calls a "universal society." What is important to stress in this scheme is that a universal society is constituted by a rich variety of how private associations and civil communities are organized. True universality does not destroy particularity.

Maurice is aware that the longing for universal fellowship can be easily corrupted, the most obvious example being a quest for universal empire. Empire is based on the assertion of dominion as embodied in the pretensions of the imperial leader, resulting in tyranny and subsequent loss of freedom. Through its conquests, empire destroys the particularity of private associations and civil communities; the many become one by negating their respective identities, customs, and traditions, because empires require autonomous individuals who in their isolation can be easily dominated. In contrast, Maurice lifts up the kingdom of God as the ideal expression of the universal society, because the kingdom binds together without negating the particularity of its members; the many compose the one. The church embodies, albeit imperfectly, this kingdom, for at Pentecost the church becomes a universal society; the many voices bear witness to a common Lord.

Although Maurice's historical analysis is often inaccurate, and his arguments at times eccentric, he nonetheless offers some helpful imagery for understanding our present circumstances. His critique of universal empire is applicable to the more egregious encroachments of the universal and homogenous state which globalization tempers. State-controlled economies do not empower the livelihood of citizens or protect their freedom. Maurice, however, would be quick to remind that a universal and homogenous market is no panacea. The voracious consumption of goods and services can also create estranged and isolated individuals who are every bit as susceptible to domination and manipulation. Consumerism alone cannot provide an adequate moral foundation for private associations and civil communities as bastions of freedom.

---

29. F. D. Maurice, *Social Morality* (London: Macmillan and Co., 1869).

Taking Maurice's lead, Christians should lift up the ideal of the universal and pluriform church as an alternative model. Drawing on Paul, the church is composed of a variety of gifts: a body consisting of parts drawn from every race and nation. The church is a universal fellowship embracing the particularity of its members. Such a model helps resist the homogenizing impulse of the state that is predicated on coercion and the homogenizing tendencies of the market based on consumption. In contrast, the form of church's social life is *koinōnia*, which can be variously translated as "community," "communion," or "communicate." In the words of Oliver O'Donovan: "To 'communicate' is to hold some thing as common, to make it a common possession, to treat it as 'ours,' rather than 'yours' or 'mine.' The partners to a communication form a community, a 'we' in relation to the object in which they participate."[30] Equality and freedom are established and preserved by communicating the goods of creation with one another. Communication is therefore not synonymous with either conferral or exchange but orders a pluriform pursuit of shared goods.

Communication not only enables Christians to resist the universality and homogeneity of either the state or the market but also informs how the church, as a universal society, pursues its ministry in and to the world. The church may serve as a reminder that the bonds of fellowship cannot be reduced to those that are solely political or economic; that not all human associations are merely relationships of power or exchange; that people do not live entirely in and for the state or the market.

In the remainder of this book I explain in greater detail why Christians can give economic globalization two-and-a-half cheers but not three. My thesis is simple: if humans are to flourish, then economic exchange is a necessary but not sufficient condition. Part 1 focuses on the question of necessity. Late moderns often fail to recognize the extent to which they are sustained by the countless, daily, mundane exchanges that are transacted in the marketplace. If it were not for the efforts of Adam Smith's prosaic butcher, brewer, baker, and their customers, daily life would consist of little more than the dreary and arduous search for food and shelter in order to survive. Markets are efficient tools for both sustaining and improving the quality of human life, and globalization has greatly expanded the number of people enjoying its benefits. Globalization is

---

30. Oliver O'Donovan, *The Ways of Judgment: The Bampton Lectures, 2003* (Grand Rapids, MI, and Cambridge, UK: Eerdmans, 2005), 242.

admittedly not without its problems as exemplified by the anxieties and issues noted above. These problems should not be ignored or glossed over as some champions of globalization tend to do but neither are they fatal as some critics presume. In short, global markets are good mechanisms for assisting the necessity of economic exchange for the greatest number of people.

In part 2 I argue that although economic exchange is necessary, it is not a sufficient condition for human flourishing. Exchange is a means of obtaining a greater good and not an end in its own right. If exchange serves as an ill-fitted end, the result is an endless and meaningless cycle of production and consumption. If humans are to flourish, they must aspire to be something more than being producers and consumers. What purpose should economic exchange serve? The short answer is communicating the goods of creation. The concept of communication, or koinonia, sketched out above, is developed in greater detail and then applied to the issues of political ordering, stewardship, freedom, and justice.

As a Christian, I feel no great compulsion to be either an ardent defender or critic of globalization. All our efforts of political, social, and moral ordering are plagued by disordered desires; yet these tasks must nonetheless be undertaken in obedience to Jesus Christ, resulting in acts that are cautious and subject to amendment as needed over time in response to changing circumstances. Hence my two-and-a-half cheers for globalization represents my theological convictions that it is, at present, the best possible option in an imperfect world.

Part 1

Sustaining Human Life

Why Exchange Is Necessary . . .

Chapter One

Christian Moral Theology and Economics

Christian moral theology has never been entirely comfortable with the topic of riches and possessions. This discomfort is extended to economics, given its association with the creation and distribution of wealth. This discomfort ranges from a reticent distaste of economic exchange as a necessary but crude activity to an evil and destructive practice requiring virulent opposition. This discomfort in turn influences a spectrum of moral assessments of globalization, and more broadly the related issues of capitalism and affluence.

Indeed a popular narrative is promulgated within certain influential Protestant and Catholic circles that the rich have always obtained and maintained their wealth by exploiting the poor. The affluence of the powerful comes at the expense of the weak. Globalization is simply the latest chapter in this sad saga. This story line claims a clear lineage originating in Scripture and descending on through the Christian moral tradition to the present day. It is an admittedly simple and thereby compelling story. It is also a simplistic and thereby misleading story.

In the remainder of this chapter I summarize some of the more prominent features of this narrative and identify some counterthemes it overlooks in its biblical and theological pedigree. I also argue that this story requires extensive revising because its authors and narrators have largely failed to adequately contextualize the topic.

Camels and Needles

In this narrative of the wealthy perennially exploiting the poor, the parable of the rich young man in Mark 10:17–31[1] encapsulates its principal

1. See also Matt. 19:16–30 and Luke 18:18–30.

themes. A rich young man asks Jesus what he must do to have eternal life. The young man has scrupulously obeyed God's commandments, but Jesus informs him that he lacks one thing—he must sell everything he has, give the proceeds to the poor, and follow him. The lad is unwilling to do this, and Jesus remarks, "It is easier for a camel to go through the eye of a needle than for someone who is rich to enter the kingdom of God."[2]

Three salient precepts may be derived from this parable. First, wealth is an impediment to faith. It is extremely difficult, if not effectively impossible, for a rich person to enter the kingdom of God. Second, distributing one's wealth to the poor is a prerequisite for following Jesus, and by implication, accumulating wealth is incompatible with being a follower of Jesus. Third, the poor are the most deserving recipients of the redistribution of wealth. There were other civic and religious institutions, for instance, that would have benefitted from such largesse, but Jesus does not mention them.

Jesus' teaching and ministry as recorded in the Gospels reinforce these tenets. In the parable of the rich man and Lazarus, for example, it is the rich man who suffers the torment of hell.[3] In another parable a rich farmer who worries about how best to store his abundant harvest is dismissed as a fool,[4] for a person's life has nothing to do with one's possessions. Most pointedly, Jesus foretells a destiny of misery for the rich and well-fed.[5] When Zacchaeus promises fourfold restitution to those he has cheated and to give half of what he owns to the poor, Jesus commends it as a salvific act.[6] Moreover, Jesus insists that his disciples, following his own example, leave their sources of livelihood, such as fishing or tax collecting,[7] and forbids them to worry about how they will eat or be clothed, but to simply sell their possessions and give the proceeds to the poor.[8] And they are worthy recipients of such benefaction: Jesus keeps company with the poor and destitute, blessing them in his teaching[9] and condemning those who ignore them.[10]

---

2. Mark 10:25.
3. Luke 16:19–31.
4. Luke 12:13–21.
5. Luke 6:24–25.
6. Luke 19:1–10.
7. Mark 1:14–20; 2:13–14.
8. Luke 12:22–34.
9. Matt. 5:1–10 and Luke 6:20–23.
10. Matt. 25:31–46.

Early converts in Jerusalem pooled their financial and material resources and redistributed them according to individual needs.[11] The fledgling church is admonished not to favor its rich members or in any way demean those who are poor and to clothe and feed those who are in need.[12] More pointedly, Christians are advised to be content with the food and clothing they have, and those wishing to be rich fall into all sorts of temptations and wander away from the faith. "For the love of money is a root of all kinds of evil."[13] Moreover, there is an extensive and complementary prophetic literature denouncing the unjust treatment of the poor, and proclaiming the hope of God's deliverance and justice.[14]

Much of the early patristic literature reiterates these biblical themes. For example, the *Didache* echoes biblical teaching on almsgiving. Tertullian, in his *Apology*, simply assumes that the early church in Jerusalem is the ideal model of Christian community, mentioning a fund for the poor to which church members made voluntary contributions,[15] and Cyprian insisted that wealthy Christians support poorer members of the church.[16] Later writers, however, developed more elaborate assessments of wealth. John Chrysostom chastised well-fed and clothed Christians who ignored or were indifferent to the hungry and homeless,[17] and he urged the rich to donate the income earned from investments to the poor.[18] Moreover, if everyone followed the lead of the early church in Jerusalem, poverty would be eliminated.[19]

According to Ambrose, private property—and the wealth it generates—is unnatural. Humans are by nature social and interdependent creatures, "created to help each other."[20] Almsgiving was paying a debt incurred by seizing public property and making it private. As bishop of Milan, his influential preaching prompted generous benefaction to restore, at least

11. Acts 2:42–47; 4:32–37.

12. Jas. 2; 1 Cor. 11:17–22.

13. 1 Tim. 6:10; see also vss. 6–9.

14. See, e.g., Isa. 10:1–4; 28:17; 59; 61:1–3; Jer. 5:26–31; Amos 2:7; 5:11–24; 8:4–6.

15. See Helen Rhee, *Loving the Poor, Saving the Rich: Wealth, Poverty, and Early Christian Formation* (Grand Rapids, MI: Baker, 2012), 107–8.

16. Cyprian, *On the Lord's Prayer*, in Alexander Roberts and James Donaldson, eds., *Ante-Nicene Fathers*, vol. 5 (Peabody, MA: Hendrickson, 1994), 447–57.

17. *Homilies on the First Letter to the Corinthians*, as cited in Daniel K. Finn, *Christian Economic Ethics: History and Implications* (Minneapolis, MN: Fortress Press, 2013), 80–81.

18. *Homilies on the Gospel of Matthew*, in Finn, *Christian Economic Ethics*, 91.

19. *The Dispersion of Property*, in Finn, *Christian Economic Ethics*, 92–93.

20. Peter Brown, *Through the Eye of a Needle: Wealth, the Fall of Rome, and the Making of Christianity in the West, 350–550 AD* (Princeton, NJ, and Oxford: Princeton University Press, 2012), 133. Ambrose, *Duties of the Clergy*, vol. 1, bk. 32.

in part, this broken social harmony between rich and poor. Although wealth is tainted by these social divisions, generous giving eases the stigma; redistribution is effectively restitution to the poor who have been harmed by the rich. With proper spiritual guidance, wealth can be used to achieve good purposes. Basil the Great went even further, insisting that one's food, clothing, and money belongs to those in need.[21]

The anonymous Pelagian author of *On Riches* offered a more critical assessment of wealth.[22] Following Pelagius, wealth was grounded in the will, and was therefore the "product of avarice, which was the *wish* to be rich."[23] Since wealth stems from the desire to want more, it is therefore intrinsically evil. Consequently, the vice of avarice is the root desire for wealth, and avarice can never be satiated. In this drive to satisfy what cannot be satisfied, crimes are inevitably committed. Private property corrupts that which is naturally common into a brutal zero-sum game of acquisition. In this competition, the wealth of the few can only be gained by impoverishing the many: In Peter Brown's words, "Whether they were aware of it or not, the rich had actively created the poor. For the rich had won the remorseless tug-of-war for limited resources, which took place to the benefit of the rich. Every time someone overstepped the divinely ordained line of mere sufficiency by becoming rich, others were pulled down into poverty."[24] This treatise stripped the rich of any excuse for being wealthy. Wealth can never be used in a good or right way because its accumulation always entails injustice. The only way to eliminate poverty is to eliminate private wealth.

John Cassian presumably echoed these premises in lifting up Egyptian monastic life as the ideal model because it preserved the original simplicity of the early Jerusalem church. One could enter a monastery following a compulsory disposal of one's personal possessions. Monks were utterly dependent on the abbot for the basic necessities of food and clothing. This total disposing of material goods generated an absolute equality among the monks, because they were equally dependent on the abbot. Moreover, monks were required to support themselves through physical labor, an act challenging the basic economic premise of the late Roman Empire:

---

21. *I Will Pull Down My Barns*, in Finn, *Christian Economic Ethics*, 88–90.

22. *On Riches*, in B. R. Rees, *Pelagius: Life and Letters* (Woodbridge, UK, and Rochester, NY: Boydell, 1991).

23. Brown, *Through the Eye of a Needle*, 311 (emphasis original).

24. Ibid., 315.

In Cassian's opinion, the monk was the exact opposite of the leisured rentier. He was the only productive member of society. He depended on himself to feed himself. Everyone else was like a beggar, living on the *agape*—the handouts—of others. Landowners collecting rents; emperors collecting taxes; compared with monks, they were all parasites, expecting to be fed by others.[25]

In short, the rich pursue a life of plunder.

Subsequent generations of theologians refined many of these biblical patristic and monastic themes. Francis of Assisi taught that a life of itinerancy and poverty was required in order to emulate Jesus. The orders he founded renounced owning private possessions other than the bare necessity of clothing, and their livelihood depended on alms. In later medieval thought, an impoverished life was often portrayed as idealized norm. The "widespread poverty, vagrancy, and underemployment of the late medieval period was legitimated by the church's ideology of poverty."[26] Economic exchange was, at best, a vulgar necessity, requiring extensive regulation.

Thomas Aquinas expended considerable time and attention in detailing what kinds of economic and financial exchanges were permissible. Exchange is a natural activity that should benefit both buyer and seller.[27] Following the Golden Rule, no one should sell a thing for more than it is worth, or buy a thing for less than it is worth. Selling a thing for more than it is worth is deceit, which is a sin, and presumably an honest consumer will pay the seller more if the object in question is underpriced. The price is based on the quality of the thing being sold, and if the price is not just, then the relationship between buyer and seller is one of injustice. Consequently, the wicked inclination to sell as high as possible and buy as low as possible must be resisted for the sake of justice. Trade is also a natural activity, enabling the existence of households and communities,[28] but the only real value of merchants is to "move goods from places of plenty to places of scarcity."[29] Traders may add a modest increase to the

25. Ibid., 417.

26. Carter Lindberg, "Luther on Poverty," in Timothy J. Wengert, ed., *Harvesting Martin Luther's Reflections on Theology, Ethics, and the Church* (Grand Rapids, MI, and Cambridge, UK: Eerdmans, 2004), Kindle edition, ch. 7.

27. See *Summa theologiae*, 2-2, q.77, a.1 (Kindle e-book, The Complete American Edition, translated by the Fathers of the English Dominican Province).

28. Ibid., a.4.

29. Odd Langholm, *Economics in the Medieval Schools: Wealth, Exchange, Money and Usury according to the Paris Theological Tradition 1200–1350* (Leiden and New York: Brill, 1992), 220.

price of the goods they sell as compensation for their time and labor. If trading is conducted to maximize profit, however, it becomes a vice and is therefore sinful and unjust.

Thomas also contends that usury[30] is always wrong because it involves selling something that does not really exist which is an unjust act.[31] All objects have their proper use, and if sold for something other than its rightful purpose the resulting profit is unjust because it involves double payment. Money was invented for the purpose of enabling exchange, and can therefore only be properly consumed. Money used to make more money, in short, is an unnatural act. Moreover, usury is wrong and unjust because it exploits the neighbor in need whom we are commanded to love and assist rather than exploit. More explicitly, "Money cannot be sold for a greater sum than the amount lent, which has to be paid back: nor should the loan be made with a demand or expectation of aught else but of a feeling of benevolence which cannot be priced at a pecuniary value, and which can be the basis of a spontaneous loan."[32] To require interest is tantamount to obliging the borrower to loan the lender money at some future date.

During Martin Luther's career, trade increased dramatically. Concurrently, large banks and other commercial firms were created to facilitate the capital and financing required by these new ventures. Luther had grave misgivings about this enterprise. In his treatise *Trade and Usury*,[33] he asserts that since merchants believe they have the right to sell their goods for as much as possible, how can trade ever be moral?[34] He assumes that maximizing profit can only be achieved at the expense of consumers, exhibiting a disregard for the needs of neighbors in satisfying the greed of merchants. Such exchange is contrary to both natural law and Christian love, effectively rendering trade to "nothing but robbing and stealing the property of others."[35] Consequently, he argues that merchants should be guided by the maxim that they sell their goods at prices that are right and fair. These prices should be determined by the time and effort expended in producing a product in comparison

30. For Thomas, "usury" and "lending" are virtually synonymous.
31. *Summa theologiae*, 2-2, q.78, a.1.
32. Ibid., a.2.
33. Martin Luther, *Trade and Usury*, in Walther I. Brandt, ed., *Luther's Works*, vol. 45 (Philadelphia, PA: Fortress Press, 1962).
34. Luther also insists that foreign trade was making Germany poor; see ibid., 246–47.
35. Ibid., 248.

with similar work performed, and any collusion by merchants to fix prices should be prohibited.[36]

In addition, buying and selling should be on a cash only basis. Lending is perilous and best avoided, for a loan always runs the risk of becoming a gift that is not returned. Lenders accepting this risk, therefore, should not be able to turn to the state to collect unpaid debt on their behalf. More important, "You cannot make money with just money."[37] Charging as high an interest rate as possible, then, is clearly illicit because it fails to display a love of neighbor. In a truly Christian society, commercial banking would not be necessary, and he advocated strict regulation of commerce and banking by the civil authorities, a proposal that fell largely on deaf ears.

If neighbors are truly in need, then they should be provided what is required rather than exploiting the need into an opportunity to enrich the lender or merchant. Consequently, Luther endorsed the creation of common or community chests.[38] Civil authorities should confiscate monastic holdings, and after making provision to care for inmates for the remainder of their lives, use the remaining endowments (in conjunction with subsequent gifts, offerings, and a modest tax) to make "gifts and loans" out of "Christian love to all the needy of the land, be they nobles or commoners."[39] In addition, the property could be converted to schools and housing. Luther justified this seizure and use on the basis that it better reflected the intent of original donors to help the poor rather than enriching the church.

Some Anabaptists attempted a radical recovery of the early church in Jerusalem by establishing communities in which all things were held in common.[40] Through a recovery of biblical teaching stressing the equality believers shared in Christ, a genuinely Christian society could be established. Many Anabaptist teachings were appropriated by disgruntled peasants in reactions to heavy taxation, laws restricting land ownership, and restrictions on trade and labor mobility that kept them impoverished, prompting the Peasants' War. Among the demands promulgated in the

---

36. Luther also suggests that wise and honest men should be appointed to review prices; see ibid., 249–50.

37. Ibid., 299.

38. See Martin Luther, *Ordinance of a Common Chest*, in Walther I. Brandt, ed., *Luther's Works*, vol. 45 (Philadelphia, PA: Fortress Press, 1962). I am indebted to Anna Johnson bringing this text to my attention.

39. Ibid., 172. The chest was administered by local trustees selected on an annual basis (182–84), and disbursements included assisting children of poor parents, orphans, widows, the homeless, ill, and elderly, and maintaining schools and hospitals (187–91).

40. See James M. Stayer, *The German Peasants' War and Anabaptist Community of Goods* (Montreal and Kingston: McGill-Queens University Press, 1994), pt. 2.

Twelve Articles of 1525 was abolishing serfdom; unrestricted fishing and hunting; common ownership of forests, meadows, and fields; reducing rents, leases, and taxes on land farmed by peasants; and abolishing inheritance taxes. The principal justification for these demands was that current laws and practices were contrary to Scripture and Christian teaching, because they effectively suppressed the love, peace, and unity taught by Christ. Liberating the peasants from their oppression was both God's judgment and will, and the peasants often identified themselves with the Israelites suffering Egyptian oppression.[41] Indeed, some of the more prominent leaders of the revolt envisioned the establishment of a total Christian state and society that would be ruled by the gospel rather than greed.[42] Although Luther was initially sympathetic with many of the peasants' demands,[43] he later vehemently denounced them as doing the "Devil's work."[44]

Denouncing capitalism's unjust and avaricious acquisition of wealth as the principal cause of poverty became particularly acute in the nineteenth and twentieth centuries. In the United States, the social gospel was a loose movement that demanded fundamental political, social, and economic changes and called for policies designed to promote the redistribution of wealth; these changes and policies would benefit the poor, primarily through greater regulation of markets, and increase the power of labor unions.[45] Such leaders included Robert T. Ely, an economist and founder of the Christian Social Union, and Washington Gladden, a leading Congregational pastor and member of the Progressive Movement who promoted the total unionization of the workforce. The most prominent and articulate leader of the social gospel movement, however, was Walter Rauschenbusch, a Baptist minister and theologian who taught at Rochester Theological Seminary. Drawing on the prophetic tradition of the Old Testament, the social teachings of Jesus, and early Christian practices stressing equality and sharing of possessions, he simultaneously decried the unjust economic conditions of the poor while advocating a

41. See Peter Blickle, *The Revolution of 1525: The German Peasants' War from a New Perspective* (Baltimore, MD, and London: Johns Hopkins University Press, 1981), ch. 1.

42. Ibid., ch. 8.

43. Martin Luther, *Temporal Authority*, in Walther I. Brandt, ed., *Luther's Works*, vol. 45 (Philadelphia, PA: Fortress Press, 1962).

44. Martin Luther, *Against the Robbing and Murdering Hordes of Peasants*, in Robert C. Schultz, ed., *Luther's Works*, vol. 46 (Philadelphia, PA: Fortress Press, 1967).

45. See Robert T. Handy, ed., *The Social Gospel in America, 1870–1920: Gladden, Ely, Rauschenbusch* (New York: Oxford University Press, 1966), and Ronald C. White and C. Howard Hopkins, eds., *The Social Gospel: Religion and Reform in Changing America* (Philadelphia, PA: Temple University Press, 1976).

series of political reforms promoting more widespread democracy and social justice.[46] Private property, inequality, and individualism were the chief causes in creating the present crisis, and must be displaced with social solidarity and common ownership of property. In short, a Christian social order would be one recovering and establishing "communistic ownership and management of the fundamental means of production."[47] Later Protestant voices reiterated these themes, stressing socialistic or highly regulated economies, redistributive schemes, or radical reformulations of economics based on overtly theological principles emphasizing material abundance that should be shared rather than creating artificial scarcity.[48]

Modern Catholic social teaching is also used to corroborate a consistent Christian suspicion, if not repudiation of capitalism. Donal Dorr, for instance, contends that the dominant and consistent thread throughout this literature is that the rich and powerful are blinded to realities of the present world. Consequently, Christians are required to be in solidarity with the poor as the "privileged instruments of God in sharing in the saving work of Jesus."[49] According to Dorr, Leo XII "committed the Catholic Church officially to a rejection of a central thesis of the liberal capitalism of the Western world, namely, that labor is a commodity to be bought at market prices determined by the law of supply and demand rather than the human needs of the worker."[50] This fundamental commitment to labor rights, and the poor more broadly, is solidified in subsequent papal encyclicals and is accompanied by more pointed criticisms of capitalist principles. Pius XI coined the phrase "social justice" in rejecting the concentration of wealth and power and rejecting free competition as "a myth and an ideology."[51] The pope advocated some form of free

---

46. See Walter Rauschenbusch, *Christianity and the Social Crisis* (Louisville, KY: Westminster/John Knox Press, 1991), and *A Theology for the Social Gospel* (Louisville, KY: Westminster John Knox Press, 1997).

47. Rauschenbusch, *Christianity and the Social Crisis*, 388.

48. See, e.g., Emil Brunner, *The Divine Imperative: A Study in Christian Ethics* (London: Lutterworth Press, 1937), chs. 23–25; Reinhold Niebuhr, *Moral Man and Immoral Society: A Study in Ethics and Politics* (Louisville, KY, and London: Westminster John Knox Press, 2001); Paul Tillich, *The Socialist Decision* (New York: Harper and Row, 1977); M. Douglas Meeks, *God the Economist: The Doctrine of God and Political Economy* (Minneapolis, MN: Fortress Press, 1989); Ronald J. Sider, *Rich Christians in an Age of Hunger: Moving from Affluence to Generosity* (Dallas, TX: Word, 1997); D. Stephen Long, *Divine Economy: Theology and the Market* (Abingdon, UK, and New York: Routledge, 2000); and Daniel M. Bell Jr., *The Economy of Desire: Christianity and Capitalism in a Postmodern World* (Grand Rapids, MI: Baker, 2012).

49. Donal Dorr, *Option for the Poor and for the Earth: Catholic Social Teaching* (Maryknoll, NY: Orbis, 2012), 4.

50. Ibid., 19.

51. Ibid., 49–52.

enterprise as a middle course between socialism and capitalism, a system that presumably neither exploits labor nor generates exorbitant wealth. John XXIII urged the nations of the world to work together to promote the common good particularly in respect to the poor, envisioning a kind of economic growth that is more favorable to the poor.[52] Pope Francis through both his words and deeds reiterates this concern for the poor and has expressed grave misgivings of market competition.[53] This corpus of papal social teaching inspired related literature on such topics as the need for labor, property, and tax reform,[54] condemning capitalism as systemic social and political oppression,[55] and condemning markets more broadly as a principal source for deforming the desires of late moderns in general and Christians in particular.[56]

Given the principal precepts of the preceding narrative, globalization, with its dynamic and highly competitive markets, is ostensibly incompatible with Christian moral teaching. But is the tradition as univocal in its disapproval of riches and possessions as the narrative insinuates?

Counterthemes

One of the principal problems with the preceding narrative is that it overlooks or ignores some prevalent counterbiblical and historical themes. To return to Jesus' teaching on camels and needles, for instance, he also offers the admonition that "for God all things are possible"; even the rich enter God's kingdom.[57] Moreover, in his parable of the talents,[58] he commends the two servants who doubled the money entrusted to them while condemning the one who did nothing but protect the funds in his care. In the parable of the shrewd manager,[59] Jesus does not endorse the

52. Ibid., ch. 5. According to Dorr, John XXIII was naive in believing that economic growth was a better option for the poor than redistributing wealth, since growth allegedly creates more poverty, although Dorr does explain why this is so.

53. See "Faith, Hope—and How Much Change? Pope Francis's First Year," *The Economist* (March 8, 2014); cf. Andrew Ferguson, "Speed Reading the Pope," *The Weekly Standard* (December 23, 2013).

54. See, e.g., John A. Ryan, *Economic Justice: Selections from Distributive Justice and a Living Wage* (Louisville, KY: Westminster John Knox Press, 1996).

55. See, e.g., Gustavo Gutiérrez, *A Theology of Liberation: History, Politics, and Salvation* (Maryknoll, NY: Orbis, 1988).

56. See, e.g., William T. Cavanaugh, *Being Consumed: Economics and Christian Desire* (Grand Rapids, MI, and Cambridge, UK: Eerdmans, 2008).

57. Mark 10:27.

58. Matt. 25:14–30; see also Luke 19:12–27.

59. Luke 16:1–14.

manager's creative accounting, but applauds his cunning use of wealth and property. Although the point of the story is to remind his followers that they cannot serve two masters—God and money—Jesus does not denounce wealth per se, but only its false role as a master to be served. Jesus does not disparage the necessity of gainful employment, and his parable of the vineyard workers is hardly a ringing endorsement of late modern notions of fair labor practices.[60] As noted above, in separating the sheep from the goats, God's judgment falls on those who fail to meet the needs of the poor and indigent, but it does not specify how these needs should be best met.

Most of the New Testament is mute on economic exchange and the accumulation of wealth, and Paul not only insists that people should work so they do not become a burden on others but also criticizes idleness, going so far to assert that "Anyone unwilling to work should not eat."[61] In practice, the vast majority of early congregations did not follow the example of the church in Jerusalem, and many depended on the patronage of affluent households.[62] Paul spent considerable time among his Gentile churches taking up a collection for the destitute church in Jerusalem,[63] because its initial pooling of possessions produced a community that came to own virtually nothing in common. Finally it should be stressed that in Revelation it is not commerce, trade, or wealth that is identified as the source of the approaching evil that will engulf the world but the growing political power and idolatrous pretensions of the imperial state to claim and seize property as its own.

The appeal to prophetic denunciation of wealth largely ignores prominent countervailing themes throughout the Old Testament. Work, for example, is highly valued; indeed the world itself is seen as a work of God, and commerce, so long as it is conducted honestly, is praised as a means of providing material blessings. Laziness "makes a man poor," while diligence "brings wealth,"[64] as the "blessing of the LORD."[65] Moreover, the prophetic denunciations are not so much directed at wealth and commerce per se but more toward the crushing taxation of monarchal or imperial regimes. In addition, poverty is not assigned any particular

---

60. Matt. 20:1–16.
61. 2 Thess. 3:10.
62. See James D. G. Dunn, "The Household Rules in the New Testament," in Stephen C. Barton, ed., *The Family in Theological Perspective* (Edinburgh: T. & T. Clark, 1996); see also Rhee, *Loving the Poor, Saving the Rich*, 37–38.
63. See, e.g., 1 Cor. 16:1–4.
64. Prov. 10:4 NIV.
65. Prov. 10:22.

virtue or value, and one "shall look in vain for direct praise of the poor or of poverty in Jewish literature," and within rabbinic teaching there was often a "high estimation of riches" and "contempt for poverty."[66]

Among the patristic writers, Clement of Alexandria points out that the rich young man in Jesus' parable[67] is not commanded to relinquish his possessions but his love of wealth in order to be saved.[68] Poverty in itself is not a sign of righteousness. Some individuals, for instance, may give away all their material possessions but continue to own their souls, leading to spiritual conceit and pride. Crushing poverty rather than wealth is a more likely cause of a broken spirit. Clement also asks a practical question: if all Christians renounce their wealth, how can they help the poor? There is a just and unjust use of wealth, and the just use of wealth should be welcomed because it can benefit one's neighbors. Clement likens such benefaction to a splendid trade and divine business.

Augustine does not contend that Christians are required to sell all their possessions in order to enter God's kingdom. They should instead see their wealth as a divine gift, providentially entrusted to their care, inspiring in turn a generous giving of alms to the poor. In addition, monks admitted to his monastery were not required to surrender their possessions, and there was no uniform dress code to mask social distinctions or class differences. Augustine is largely indifferent to wealth per se, believing that it was not money that made a person good or evil, but whether a person used money for good or evil purposes. Pride, not riches, was the enemy; a humble rich man could use his wealth to do good.

Although the medieval scholastics maintained a prior emphasis on almsgiving and prohibitions against usury, there was a growing, albeit cautious, recognition that markets played a needed role in determining the price of goods, services, and labor in ways that were not incompatible with Christian theological convictions. A grudging respect for trade and commerce was acknowledged as a way of moving goods from locales of plenty to those of want. Additionally, some scholars, particularly Franciscans, began to identify the need for financing commercial ventures that helped meet basic human needs in a more efficient manner, concocting ways for circumventing usury restrictions that anticipated modern

66. Martin Hengel, *Property and Riches in the Early Church: Aspects of a Social History of Early Christianity* (Philadelphia, PA: Fortress Press, 1974), 17, 22.

67. Matt. 19:16–23.

68. Clement of Alexandria, *Who Is the Rich Man That Shall Be Saved?*, in Alexander Roberts and James Donaldson, eds., *Ante-Nicene Fathers*, vol. 2 (Peabody, MA: Hendrickson, 1994). In order to be perfect, the young man is admonished to sell his possessions; see Rhee, *Loving the Poor, Saving the Rich*, 77–88.

banking and capital creation.[69] These conceptual innovations, in part, helped to promote and justify increased trade, commerce, and banking throughout late medieval and early Renaissance Europe, especially in the Italian city-states.[70] Moreover, although Luther was highly skeptical of banking, commerce, and trade, he recognized that poverty was not a virtue to be emulated but a problem to be solved through both charity and financial ventures as witnessed by the establishment and management of the community chest.[71]

Although John Calvin shared many common convictions with Luther, such as the centrality of Scripture, he was more accommodating to changing economic circumstances and practices.[72] Calvin believed that God intended humans to use creation to meet their material wants and needs—hence the need to work. The resulting unequal distribution of owning property and the fruits of one's labor, however, were not consequences of sinful exploitation but the workings of an inscrutable divine providence. This did not mean that Calvin encouraged indifference toward the poor or was unaware of the temptations that often accompanied wealth. He admonished the rich to help those in need and counseled rich Christians to live frugal and unpretentious lives. Since wealth was distributed through God's providence, the rich were stewards rather than owners of the wealth that God had entrusted to their care and good use. In this respect, the poor were best helped not by pooling common possessions as the early Christians in Jerusalem had done but through the provision of employment that paid a sufficient wage. This need for employment prompted Calvin's permissive teaching on charging interest on loans. He argued that the biblical prohibition against usury reflected an agricultural economy in which interest was used to crush the livelihood of poor farmers. But employment in an increasingly urban context was derived primarily through trade and commercial activities, requiring in

69. See Langholm, *Economics in the Medieval Schools;* see also Stephen J. Grabil, ed., *Sourcebook in Late-Scholastic Monetary Theory* (Lanham, MD, and Plymouth, UK: Lexington Books, 2007).

70. Robert S. Lopez, *The Commercial Revolution of the Middle Ages, 950–1350* (Englewood Cliffs, NJ: Prentice-Hall, 1971); Quentin Van Doosselaere, *Commercial Agreements and Social Dynamics in Medieval Genoa* (Cambridge, UK, and New York: Cambridge University Press, 2009); and Lisa Jardine, *Worldly Goods: A New History of the Renaissance* (New York and London: Norton, 1996).

71. A similar scheme was established in Geneva. See Jeannine E. Olson, *Calvin and Social Welfare: Deacons and the Bourse française* (Cranbury, NJ, and London: Associated University Presses, 1989).

72. See Finn, *Christian Economic Ethics*, ch. 10.

turn investment, and sufficient capital could only be generated through borrowing and lending.[73] Calvinism was deeply influential in shaping the economic thought and practices of many subsequent Protestants, as well as capitalist principles more broadly.[74]

The criticism of competition and market-based exchange was not as univocal as often portrayed. Many modern papal encyclicals, for instance, affirmed private property while decrying the "errors" of socialism and communism.[75] More recently, John Paul II's condemnation of Marxist influence on some strands of Catholic theology, particularly liberation theology, and emphasis on liberty and the power of the human spirit suggests a qualified endorsement of entrepreneurism and capitalism when "rightly understood."[76] These positive emphases have prompted a number of writers to pen accounts of market-based economies as being compatible with Catholic social teaching,[77] and additionally some Protestants have offered a defense of capitalism as being an outgrowth of biblical and doctrinal teaching.[78]

These biblical, historical, and theological counterthemes do not invalidate the narrative outlined in the preceding section. But they do demonstrate that it is an incomplete and superficial account. Contemporary globalization is not the latest chapter in the saga of the rich enriching themselves at the expense of the poor because no such clear and straightforward story line exists within the Christian moral theological tradition. The story is much more complex and opaque. But if this is the case,

73. For a comprehensive overview of Calvin's social and economic thought, see André Biéler, *Calvin's Economic and Social Thought* (Geneva, Switzerland: WCC Communications, 2005).

74. See, e.g., Max Weber, *The Protestant Ethic and the Spirit of Capitalism* (London and Boston, MA: Unwin, 1985); and Stephen Innes, *Creating the Commonwealth: The Economic Culture of Puritan New England* (New York and London: Norton, 1995).

75. See, e.g., Richard L. Camp, *The Papal Ideology of Social Reform: A Study in Historical Development* (Leiden: Brill, 1969), esp. ch. 3.

76. See Michael Novak, *The Catholic Ethic and the Spirit of Capitalism* (New York: Free Press, 1993), esp. pt. 2.

77. See, e.g., Michael Novak, *The Spirit of Democratic Capitalism* (Lanham, NY: Madison Books, 1991); Robert Sirico, *Defending the Free Market: The Moral Case for a Free Economy* (Washington, DC: Regnery, 2012); and Maciej Zieba, *Papal Economics: The Catholic Church on Democratic Capitalism, from* Rerum Novarum *to* Caritas in Veritate (Wilmington, DE: ISI Books, 2013).

78. See, e.g., John Schneider, *Godly Materialism: Rethinking Money and Possessions* (Downers Grove, IL: InterVarsity Press, 1994); John R. Schneider, *The Good of Affluence: Seeking God in a Culture of Wealth* (Grand Rapids, MI, and Cambridge, UK: Eerdmans, 2002); and Brian Griffiths, *The Creation of Wealth: A Christian's Case for Capitalism* (Downers Grove, IL: InterVarsity Press, 1984).

where does it leave us in understanding and assessing the emerging globally integrated economy?

Context Matters

What is missing in what I have characterized as the "camel and needle"
narrative is an adequate appreciation of changing social and political
contexts. The "camel and needle" narrative assumes that certain key
biblical texts are clear and unequivocal, and subsequent theological and
moral emendations preserve and fortify their clarity. Such an assumption,
however, effectively dismisses shifting intellectual, social, and political
contexts as effectively irrelevant in revising subsequent moral assessments
other than the extent to which they must be dismissed, opposed,
or embraced in order to preserve the purity of the initial message.
Consequently, the narrative simply proclaims as obvious and unassailable
facts that wealth has been and always will be an impediment to faith; that
redistribution of wealth has always been and will continue to be needed;
that the rich always have and continue to make themselves wealthy at
the expense of the poor. Globalization undoubtedly perpetuates these
trajectories, and should therefore be opposed.

Yet the above counterthemes demonstrate that the initial message and
subsequent emendations were never as pure as their proponents assume.
Indeed, I suppose these counterthemes could be used to cobble together
a counternarrative that contends that wealth per se has never been and
never will be an automatic impediment to faith; that charity is what the
poor have always needed and continue to need; that the rich are made rich
and the poor are made poor through God's inscrutable providence. But
such a narrative would be equally unsatisfactory because it also ignores or
dismisses changing intellectual, social, and political circumstances over
time. A satisfactory Christian understanding and assessment of globalization does not entail any narrative drawn from selective biblical and historical proof texts, because such a story already knows the answers before
any questions have been asked.

Good answers come from good questions. If the Bible and history are
to assist Christians in asking the right questions about globalization, then
they must undertake the difficult task of contextualizing these sources.
The work of many contemporary ethicists and moral theologians
routinely incorporates biblical and historical scholarship that pursues
this task. Why, then, has there been little perceived need to contextualize
moral assessments of globalization and economics more broadly? I

have a colleague, Charles Cosgrove, who teaches New Testament. He propounds what I call the Cosgrove dictum: the need and urgency for contextualization is proportional to the urgency of prior ideological commitments.[79] On the one hand, if prior commitments seem to contradict the "clear" meaning of biblical or theological texts, a great deal of contextualization is undertaken to demonstrate that the meaning is not so clear as first assumed, particularly in light of the contemporary setting. On the other hand, if there is seemingly little tension between prior commitments and the "clear" meaning of biblical and theological texts, the need to contextualize is greatly diminished and the textual relevancy is presumed rather than demonstrated.

For example, a great deal of contextualization in respect to sexual ethics has been undertaken, indicating that the apparently absolute prohibitions against fornication, adultery, divorce, and homosexuality are not necessarily applicable in light of contemporary values and mores.[80] The point is to neither commend nor challenge the veracity of these efforts, but to identify one issue where a strong need for contextualization has been recognized and pursued. For many critics of globalization, however, a perceived need to contextualize is often not admitted or muted. Consequently, the "clear" meanings of biblical and theological texts are asserted in ways that would warm the heart of any literalist.

This lack of contextualization can lead to some peculiar and at times perilous criticisms of globalization. The teachings of the New Testament reproving wealth and property, for instance, were made in the context of an economy based predominantly on the natural fecundity of the earth. Wealth was derived from such things as precious metals, timber, and most importantly food. When wealth is based on the land the resulting economy is a zero-sum game, for the amount of land is limited: the easiest way to increase one's wealth is to acquire someone else's land. This could be accomplished by conquest or seizing land as payment of debt or taxes, at times also resulting in the enslavement of debtors who provided a source of cheap labor for extracting wealth from the land. Consequently, the criticisms of wealth recognized the injustice of a system in which the wealthy obtained their riches by seizing the property of others, and maintaining them through enslaved labor. Redistributing wealth and prohibiting usury were ways of protecting the weaker players in a zero-sum economy, and

79. See also Charles Cosgrove, *Appealing to Scripture in Moral Debate: Five Hermeneutical Rules* (Grand Rapids, MI: Eerdmans, 2002).

80. See, e.g., James B. Nelson, *Embodiment: An Approach to Sexuality and Christian Theology* (Minneapolis, MN: Augsburg, 1978).

selling one's possessions was also a way of decreasing one's vulnerability since the rich cannot seize from you what you do not possess.

Late modern economy, however, is not a zero-sum game, for wealth is derived primarily through the production of goods and services, and through subsequent trading and commercial transactions. Productivity is not a tangible thing like land and is therefore not as limited. Increased productivity thereby increases wealth. The wealthy do not become rich because they somehow seize productivity from someone else, but in creating greater opportunities for economic exchange. Through increased productivity, commerce, and employment, both rich and poor ideally benefit even though an expanding income gap often results.[81] Moreover, productivity and the consumption of goods and services are predicated on available capital, finance, labor, and credit. To simply apply the "clear" biblical and historical teachings of redistributing wealth, prohibiting interest loans, and liberating oneself from possessions would probably, as I argue in the remaining chapters of part 1, harm rather than help the poor, particularly in lesser developed countries.

Contextualizing the entire sweep of the "camel and needle" narrative, as well as the counterthemes, is beyond the scope of this inquiry. But an early pivotal moment serves to disclose a crucial contextual setting in the initial development of Christian moral, social, and political thought on economics. This moment involves the rise of Christianity during the late Roman Empire, presaging the transition from late antiquity to medieval Europe.[82] For Rome, "wealth was land turned by labor into food, which in the case of the rich, was turned into sufficient money to be turned into privilege and power."[83] The sprawling estates of aristocratic families were dedicated to feeding an expansive empire. Brown estimates that 60 percent of Roman wealth was accumulated at the annual harvest, which in turn required the labor of 80 percent of the population. This system created large income discrepancies. In addition to slaves, labor was provided by tenant farmers who routinely lost up to 67 percent of their income to rents and taxes. Brown estimates that around 10 percent of the population was prosperous, while the remaining 90 percent were relatively poor;[84] a gap that also reinforced traditional social divisions.[85]

81. See "The Onrushing Wave: The Future of Jobs," *The Economist* (January 18, 2014).
82. The following description draws heavily, though not exclusively, on Peter Brown's insightful analysis *Through the Eye of a Needle*.
83. Brown, *Through the Eye of a Needle*, 3.
84. See ibid., 8–13.
85. See Rhee, *Loving the Poor, Saving the Rich*, 19–27.

Policies implemented by Constantine, in conjunction with concurrent events, initiated some crucial changes in this system. The new emperor flooded the market with gold coinage that provided an alternative to land as a sign of wealth. He did this in part to create new wealth among his Christian supporters who were primarily urban merchants and tradesmen and who tended to be modestly affluent but not rich by Roman standards. The first Christian emperor needed to counterbalance the power of aristocratic families that were almost entirely pagan. The creation of this new wealth created a "degree of social stratification that was unprecedented even by Roman standards."[86] Constantine also granted certain social privileges to the church because of its reputation of caring for the poor. In addition, a series of disastrous invasions and civil wars was fomenting civil unrest, forcing aristocratic landowners to forge better relationships with tenant farmers in order to maintain agricultural production.

These changes also prompted a gradual transformation in the purpose and object of public benefaction. For pagan Romans, "civic generosity" was both a "duty and delight."[87] The rich were expected to be generous, especially to the cities in which they dwelled. They built grand structures and paid for lavish public events, and cities reciprocated by bestowing honors on their benefactors. In short, such giving reflected a love for one's city. But with Constantine, the emperor and empire began to compete for this affection and its accompanying benefaction. It was an attempt to shift loyalty from the particularity of one's city to the universality of the one empire.

The church took this shift a step further. Giving to the city should be replaced by giving to the poor. As the empire became increasingly Christian, its citizens should create a society worthy of their faith. This emphasis challenged the pagan notion of reciprocal benefaction. Generosity should not be a means of procuring honor and recognition, but a selfless act motivated by a loving concern for the poor. This emphasis on the plight of the poor also tended to stigmatize the wealthy, transforming poverty into an issue of justice rather than misfortune. The poor came to see themselves increasingly as victims of oppression. They were "much more like the plebs of Rome, as they saw themselves—vulnerable persons compared with the rich but by no means beggars. They belonged to the traditional core of society, not to its margins. They were persons with rights for which they might cry out."[88]

86. Brown, *Through the Eye of a Needle*, 15.
87. Ibid., 62.
88. Ibid., 80.

Christian bishops were the most public and vocal advocates of the poor. Ambrose's stinging indictment of the rich was also an invitation to give generously to the church, whose care for the poor was correcting the injustice of their impoverishment. Although he was motivated by theological and moral convictions, his action as a bishop also helped solidify social and political alliances initiated earlier by Constantine. Ambrose was the first aristocrat to become a bishop. He used his wealth to endow the church in Milan, reflecting but also reorienting the pagan practice of reciprocal benefaction. His family, however, was not old wealth, for his father had allied himself with Constantine's new regime. His actions should not be seen as a series of cynical machinations, for the church in Milan met a real need: "In a society where the elites and the subelites were more than usually fragmented and set in competition with each other, a church provided a space where groups of different backgrounds could come together."[89] In the basilica the unnatural and unjust divisions created by wealth and private property were inoperative. In this respect, Ambrose showed little interest in the doctrine of the fall. The world was in decline, but it was possible to reverse this momentum and pursue some recovery of its original harmony. This recovery, led by the church, would ripple through a society deeply divided between rich and poor.

In contrast, Augustine did not see the world as divided between rich and poor, but was better characterized as relationships between patrons and friends. Patronage made it possible for him to initially ignore issues of personal wealth and poverty. "Augustine had grown up in a social world where what you owned was less important than who you knew."[90] Social mobility, not the division between rich and poor, was his principal concern. Throughout his career he preached very little about poverty, other than almsgiving. His social thought focused on small groups of friends and other public associations. Society was held together by mutual affection, and was therefore fragile. This premise provided the basis for the rudimentary outlines of his ecclesiological and social teaching. For Augustine, not all Christians were called to live a life of perfection in which the surrendering of one's possessions was a prerequisite. Such a presumption was grounded in heretical Pelagian teaching that was both unscriptural and impractical. Society was not a monastery writ large. Rather, monastic life prefigured the New Jerusalem on a small scale, and such an eschatological inkling fortified the love that Christians share in the City of God. But this is not the case in the earthly city. For Augustine,

89. Ibid., 124.
90. Ibid., 154.

in "normal human society" private property is essential. "After Adam's fall, private property guaranteed and protected by a strong state was the best humans could hope for. Only a regime of private property validated by imperial law could fend off the worst effects of pride, avarice, and violence that had come to be so deeply rooted in the human condition." In comparison to monastic life, "Normal society arose from the clash of fallen human wills. It belonged to a doomed present. The union of hearts and minds in a monastery, by contrast, was a glimpse of the future."[91] Although the mundane acts of putting bread on the table and a roof over one's head distracted one's time and attention from more important spiritual concerns as well as being plagued by such evils as poverty and slavery, these activities were not to be despised. Mediocre Christians play an important role in God's providential governance of the world.[92]

This tension between perfection and mediocrity remained largely unresolved, particularly as the church tried to embrace both. In doing so, the church effectively became a marketplace of both spiritual and economic exchange. Through their generosity, the rich "were not condemned to be forever camels. By giving (to the saints and to the poor) they might bypass the terrible, cramped eye of the needle. They were allowed by God to use their earthly treasure so as to purchase heaven through giving it to the poor."[93] In transferring wealth, particularly property, monastics were free to pursue a simple life, imitating the poverty of Jesus and ancestors in the faith. This transfer also took place within an empire in decline, ravaged by civil wars and ensuing civil unrest. As political power shifted to local jurisdictions and away from an imperial universality, there was a corresponding economic shift from aristocratic estates to monasteries that were underwritten by the stability of a universal church.[94] As Ambrosiaster observed, an orderly society required strong imperial rule that should be mirrored by an ecclesial polity that increasingly was forced to fill the political void.[95]

The church's attempt to provide some kind of universal cohesion was amplified as the western Roman Empire rapidly disintegrated into a series

91. Ibid., 180; see also Augustine of Hippo, *City of God*, esp. bk. 19.
92. See R. A. Markus, *The End of Ancient Christianity* (Cambridge, MA, and New York: Cambridge University Press, 1990), ch. 4.
93. Brown, *Through the Eye of a Needle*, 235.
94. An interesting subtext to this shift is how virginity and celibacy advocated by certain parties in the church threatened the pagan aristocracy that was based on marriage and family. See Brown, ibid., chs. 17–18; see also Brent Waters, *The Family in Christian Social and Political Thought* (Oxford: Oxford University Press, 2007), 1–23.
95. See Ambrosiaster, *Quaestio*, 115.59.

smaller kingdoms and principalities. As the church obtained more and more property, its landholdings inevitably became centers of commercial activity, and the church effectively became the largest employer, because the surviving estates had become fortifications dedicated to protecting its dwindling labor force in times of civil unrest or invasion. Consequently, priests and bishops were often pressed into political roles in the absence of stable governments. An elderly Augustine worried that the distinction between civic and ecclesiastical leaders was becoming blurred, and by the late sixth century the church had displaced the Senate as the protector of Rome. The church was not accountable to any other political authority in how it managed its growing wealth, purportedly for the sake of the poor and therefore indirectly to the broader civil society. With the death of the western empire, the basic structures of medieval society were created and subsequently refined and codified.

This brief historical excursus demonstrates that Christian thought and practice has over time adapted to changing economic, social, and political circumstances. With the collapse of the western Roman Empire, civic benefaction was replaced with charity for the poor, the church supplanted aristocratic households as the principal landowner and source of wealth, and the universal empire was displaced by the universal church. These changes, however, were not easily made and often proved contentious. For example, there was a tension between the pursuit for spiritual perfection, in which possessions were regarded as an impediment, and the necessity of attending to material well-being, a tension that endures to the present day. Similar patterns of adaptation would continue throughout church's history: the medieval debates over regulating property, finance, work, and commercial activities; the development of the so-called Protestant work ethic; modern industrialization and division of labor. To what extent these adaptions were faithful or unfaithful to the gospel was and continues to be debated. Consequently, any claim of invariable Christian moral teaching on economics is simplistic and misleading, and hence the need to reassess and revise moral teaching in light of new contextual challenges. Globalization is a new context forcing such reassessment and revision, and I initiate this process in the following chapters by examining some basic late modern economic concepts.

Chapter Two

Markets, Competition, and Cooperation

The previous chapter provided a historical overview of the uneasy relationship between economics and Christian moral theology. Some critics draw upon selected strands of this history to condemn contemporary globalization. In brief, they claim that Christian moral teaching unequivocally denounces wealth because it is obtained at the expense of the poor. Globalization with its emphasis on free-flowing capital, trade, finance, and labor is simply the latest chapter in this sad legacy of the rich exploiting and further impoverishing the poor. I argued, however, that there are counterthemes that challenge the sweeping character of this critical narrative. The relationship between economics and Christian moral theology is much more complex than these critics admit, requiring a great deal of contextualizing.

I also argued that contemporary globalization forces another, perhaps pivotal context. This chapter initiates an exploration into this prospect by examining the integral relationship among markets, competition, and cooperation. A plea for patience is in order. In almost all of the following paragraphs the reader will probably mutter something to the effect that well, it's a bit more complex than that. And it is, for the relationship among markets, competition, and cooperation is more multifaceted than I describe. But at this juncture I am striving for a descriptive simplicity of some crucial concepts and assumptions underlying globalization, and I address accompanying layers of complexity in subsequent chapters.

Markets

Exchange is a fundamental and ubiquitous feature of human life. Something so basic as a conversation involves exchange: you talk and I listen, and then I talk and you listen. More profoundly love is not one-sided but involves a give and take whose symmetry may change over time. At its most basic level an exchange means that what is mine becomes yours, and what is yours becomes mine. Exchange is a vital and ingrained component of human life, a quality captured rather nicely in Johannes Althusius's observation that God "did not give all things to one person, but some to one and some to others, so that you have need for my gifts, and I for yours."[1] Humans, then, are not only inherently dependent but also drawn to one another. Again as Althusius insists, "man by nature is a gregarious animal born for cultivating society with other men, not by nature living alone as wild beasts do, nor wandering about as birds."[2] Exchange both discloses and enables this necessity to interact.

Trade is an obvious form of exchange. I have something you want and you have something I want, so we swap. In this exchange both of our respective wants are met. A market is an efficient mechanism to facilitate exchange. If I have things that other people want, it is a cumbersome waste of time to wander about searching for individuals who want the things I have and who in turn have things I want that we can trade. A market provides a place that helps solve this problem by bringing traders into close proximity. Bartering in a confined marketplace, however, is still an inefficient expenditure of time, for I still need to wander about in search of potential trading partners. The invention of money helps to solve this problem as a convenient means of assisting exchange.[3] As a vendor I sell things to people who want them, and I in turn enter the marketplace with my money to purchase things I want from other sellers. In this respect, a market matches supply with demand. If I quickly sell the things I bring to the marketplace, then I realize that many people want them, and I will bring more the next time. Conversely, if I sell few of my things, then I will bring fewer next time in response to diminished demand.

There were two influential insights in the late eighteenth and early nineteenth centuries that greatly expanded and improved the efficacy of markets. The first is Adam Smith's concept of the division or specialization

1. Johannes Althusius, *Politica*, trans. Frederick S. Carney (Indianapolis, IN: Liberty Fund, 1995), 23.

2. Ibid., 22.

3. See Adam Smith, *An Inquiry into the Nature and Causes of the Wealth of Nations* (Indianapolis, IN: Liberty Fund, 1981), bk. 1, ch. 4; see also Niall Ferguson, *The Ascent of Money: A Financial History of the World* (New York: Penguin, 2008).

of labor.[4] Self-sufficiency is not a good strategy for satisfying one's basic needs for food, shelter, and clothing. I will spend virtually all my time undertaking various agricultural, cooking, carpentry, and stitching tasks, many of which will be done poorly. If, however, I am particularly skilled at making clothes, I should spend my time making and selling garments and then use my money to purchase the products or skills of other specialists such as farmers, bakers, and carpenters. Such specialization has two principal benefits: (1) it creates greater productivity through a more efficient use of time and labor, satisfying the wants of consumers in a more timely and sustained manner; (2) if there is sufficient demand, then more producers will enter a market to satisfy these wants, in turn lowering the price of the wanted item.[5] A market efficiently matches supply with demand, which simultaneously increases the purchasing power of consumers while generating greater national wealth.

David Ricardo offered the second influential insight. Building on Smith, his basic contention is that if individuals cannot be self-sufficient, then the same is true of nations.[6] Since natural resources and agreeable climates are not evenly dispersed across the globe, no nation can affordably meet all the needs and wants of its people. In England, for example, it is cheap to produce wool but inordinately expensive to produce port wine, whereas in Portugal the opposite is true. Trade can be used to rectify these natural deficiencies. Again, following Smith, nations should follow a strategy of specialized labor or production; a nation should produce primarily wanted things it can assemble inexpensively. In Ricardo's words, "It is quite as important to the happiness of mankind, that our enjoyments should be increased by the better distribution of labour, by each country producing those commodities for which by its situation, its climate, and its other natural or artificial advantages, it is adapted, and by their exchanging them for the commodities of other countries. . . ."[7] Trade ideally provides a comparative advantage to trading partners: it is to the advantage of England to produce an abundance of wool and Portugal an abundance of port so they may trade their respective surpluses. According to Ricardo, such trade lowers the price of port in England and the price of wool in Portugal, which in turn effectively increases the productivity of labor in both countries.

---

4. See Smith, *Wealth of Nations*, bk. 1, chs. 1–3.

5. This is why Smith was, in part, adamantly opposed to the "mercantile system"; see ibid., bk. 4, chs. 1–2.

6. See David Ricardo, *On the Principles of Political Economy and Taxation* (Indianapolis, IN: Liberty Fund, 2004), esp. ch. 7.

7. Ibid., 132.

Smith and Ricardo's insights have been challenged, hotly debated, and refined by subsequent generations of economists, political philosophers, politicians, and policy wonks.[8] Nonetheless, the general concept of specialized production and labor and the general concept of comparative advantage are two forces driving global markets. A few of the more prominent implications of these concepts are summarized below.

Global markets promote *increased production of goods and services*. As national trading barriers become less restrictive new markets are opened. Consequently, increased demand is met through imports and exports. For example, Saudi Arabia exports oil and imports manufactured goods. The increased production of goods and services prompted by globalization, however, incorporates a broader range of activities than merely importing and exporting between countries—the situation is more intricate than producing excess wool and port in two given locations. A car company headquartered in Japan builds manufacturing plants in the United States, or an American electronics firm manufactures and assembles a product line in China. In addition, communication technologies enable the exchange of services involving little movement of physical objects or personnel. A business located in England may contract the accounting services of a firm in India, and an Indian corporation may use a British consultancy. Moreover, corporations use an expansive network of suppliers and distributors scattered around the world to meet the growing demands of global customers.

Global markets promote *lower prices of goods and services*. The increased demand accompanying enlarged markets creates economies of scale that lower the cost of production that is passed on to consumers through lower prices. In tandem, larger markets also stimulate cost-saving technological innovations. Greater demand stimulated by global markets may also lead to fluctuating or higher prices for certain items, especially commodities. Petroleum, for instance, is a relatively scarce commodity due to expanding industrialization around the world. The cost of extraction increases as the supply of easily extractable petroleum declines, and is further compounded by periodic regional instability, environmental policies discouraging or prohibiting exploration and drilling, and price fixing. Higher prices, however, may also prompt technological innovation and capital investment that increases the supply of scarce items leading to

8. See, e.g., Jagdish Bhagwati, *In Defense of Globalization* (Oxford and New York: Oxford University Press, 2007); Martin Wolf, *Why Globalization Works* (New Haven, CT, and London: Yale University Press, 2004); and Joseph E. Stiglitz, *Making Globalization Work* (New York and London: Norton, 2007).

lower prices. Fracking, for instance, has significantly lowered the price of natural gas in North America.

Global markets promote *employment.* Satisfying the needs and wants of consumers within new and expanding markets requires a larger workforce with applicable skills. New jobs are created by existing firms expanding into new markets or by startups attempting to take advantage of new opportunities. American and European electronic firms, for instance, manufacture and sell products in China, and Chinese startups have also entered the Chinese and global markets. This expansion has a derivative effect on employment prompted by the need for additional supplies, distribution, sales and advertising, as well as accounting, consulting, and legal services. Even with the financial crisis of 2008 global employment has steadily increased since 2000.[9]

Global markets promote *capital investment.* Taking advantage of new and expanding markets requires the investment of capital to obtain the requisite equipment, resources, personnel, and the like. These investments are provided through a variety of channels such as banks, venture capital and private equity firms, pension and sovereign wealth funds, and direct governmental grants or purchase of shares. Capital, however, is not limited to financial investment, but includes equipment, property, time, and expertise. Since businesses require a skilled workforce and supportive civil society in order to succeed, then providing adequate schools, infrastructure, housing, and health care is also a form of capital investment. In this respect the work of charitable or nongovernmental organizations (NGOs) may also be regarded as a kind of capital investment or what is often referred to as social capital. Investing capital in global markets also blurs national borders and nationalities. Investors in private equity firms, for example, are located around the world, and the investments of these firms are similarly scattered.

Global markets promote the *creation of wealth.* Meeting the increased demand generated by new and expanding markets results in a return on invested capital, which is distributed through such channels as profits for investors, wages paid to employees, and payments to suppliers and distributors. This income is expended on the consumption of goods and services, which in turn increases demand prompting further capital investment and greater productivity. In the absence of wealth, the economic exchange required to sustain civil society is greatly diminished. Over the last

9. See International Labour Organization, *Global Employment Trends 2014* (Geneva: International Labour Office, 2014), http://www.ilo.org/wcmsp5/groups/public/---dgreports/---dcomm/---publ/documents/publication/wcms_233953.pdf.

two decades, a nascent global middle class has been created in developing economies adopting liberalized trading and investment policies.[10]

Global markets create *regulatory challenges*. A well-ordered, efficient, and justly governed market requires the rule of law. Contracts must be enforced, property must be protected from unwarranted seizure, consumers protected from fraud, working conditions need to be monitored for safety, and policing is needed to prevent crime. In the absence of law, exchange is displaced by aggression, seizure, and intimidation. The purpose of government is to exercise the rule of law in ways that enable the flourishing of civil society. Moreover, in pursuing this purpose the state must have the ability to coerce. In this respect, the just exercise of coercion by the state is a good to be valued.[11] No serious proponent of a market-based economy argues that there is no need for the state. Rather, the debate is over the extent to which regulation is needed or required. One end of this spectrum contends that regulation should be confined to such activities as the military, policing, judicial bodies, and, perhaps, oversight of the production and distribution of potentially hazardous materials. The other end asserts that the state should regulate extensively in order not only to protect citizens from potential harm but to achieve other social and political goals. Ideological commitments, cultural traditions, and various interests often dictate where policies fall along this spectrum. For example, one country may value its tradition of individual freedom and entrepreneurship expressed through low taxes and minimal regulation with little concern for the resulting income inequality. Another country values its tradition of social solidarity and equity as exemplified through extensive regulation and high taxes designed to redistribute income. As I argue in the following section, however, the competition promoted by global markets creates a number of regulatory issues and challenges.

Competition

The preceding description of global markets is admittedly untroubled, even idyllic. New and expanding markets spur production of goods and services that lowers prices, and promotes greater employment, investment, and wealth. Create free markets around the world and all will be

10. See "Two Billion More Bourgeois: The Middle Class in Emerging Markets," *The Economist* (February 12, 2009); for an example of the effects on a country that has largely failed to successfully implement liberalized trading and investment policies, see "The Tragedy of Argentina: A Century of Decline," *The Economist* (February 15, 2014).

11. See Daniel K. Finn, *Christian Economic Ethics: History and Implications* (Minneapolis, MN: Fortress Press, 2013).

well—not quite. Globalization is not without its warts and blemishes. As also suggested, there are regulatory challenges that need to be addressed in response to a number of pressing issues. As will be seen throughout the following chapters, there is little consensus on how best to address these concerns, and some appear insoluble. But this is to anticipate. In this section I examine competition as a principal force stimulating the productivity of global markets while also contributing to some of its most troubling issues. Global markets, in short, both enlarge the number of competitors and intensify their competition.

Before turning our attention to global markets, however, a few general comments about competition are in order. Humans evidently enjoy competing as demonstrated by their behavior in politics, workplace, sports, and even in the home. There are a variety of evolutionary, sociological, psychological, economic, and philosophical explanations why this is the case, and my point is not to explain why humans compete but merely to indicate that they do. Competition inevitably produces winners and losers. One candidate wins an election while others lose; some employees are promoted while others are not; one team beats the other in a game; a daughter has her way at the expense of disgruntled siblings. Efforts to concoct competitive situations that forbid winning and losing often prove futile. I once ran into a doctoral student who was bringing his daughter home from a soccer match. I asked her if she played in a league that didn't keep score. "Yeah," she replied, "but we won 8 to 1." The adage it's not if you win or lose but how you play the game is certainly true, but winning is nevertheless more enjoyable than losing.

Competition not only describes, in part, human behavior, but it also promotes the good of civil society over time. Competition enables more efficient exchange for satisfying needs and wants. This is particularly the case in global markets predicated on the specialization of labor, and the comparative advantages of trade. Marketplace competition also produces winners and losers. At the beginning of the twentieth century, for instance, carriage manufacturers and blacksmiths lost out to cars and service stations. Even among the class of winners there are losers—when was the last time you drove a Studebaker to Flying A? As markets open and expand around the world, so too does the scope of competition—GM does not compete solely with Ford but with European and Asian brands across the globe. These global markets also intensify competition in which market share can be quickly gained or lost: in 2006 Nokia and Sony-Ericsson dominated the global mobile phone market, only to be replaced seven years later by Samsung and Apple.

The preceding anecdotes illustrate the intense and dynamic character of competitive forces in meeting a greater range of wants and needs on a global scale. Over time this competition has benefitted civil society by providing cheaper goods and services, creating new jobs, and generating unprecedented wealth and affluence, which in turn have helped to lift over a billion people out of abject poverty. These benefits, however, have not come smoothly or evenly; producers, employees, and communities continue to suffer short-term or permanent losses. It is important to keep this tension in mind when assessing economic globalization. Ardent proponents tend to champion the long-term benefits while ignoring or discounting the short-term detriments. Conversely, zealous critics tend to fixate on short-term damages while overlooking the long-term benefits. Both perspectives are myopic, resulting in distorted assessments of the pressing issues accompanying globalization that, as I argue in subsequent chapters, cannot be solved by either free markets or state interventions alone. The issue is not how to either unleash or domesticate globalization, but how to direct competitive global markets toward serving the long-term good of civil society while mitigating the short-term suffering experienced by some individuals and communities in the process. But again, this is to anticipate, and we must first turn our attention to a more narrow understanding of competition.

Competition, Productivity, and Innovation

New and expanding markets generate greater demand for goods and services. Producers compete with one another to satisfy this demand. In order to capture a larger market share, a producer must usually offer a desired product at either a lower price or superior quality than those of competitors. When one producer dominates a market there is no incentive to increase productivity or innovate. Some readers may remember the days when *the* telephone company offered customers two styles and three colors of a telephone that they could not own but only rent. With the breakup of telephony monopolies, consumers can now purchase a wide variety of landline, mobile, and Internet communication products offered by competing producers at more affordable prices and better quality. Although competition benefits civil society, there is no guarantee that all competing producers will succeed. Many startups fail (recall the fervid days of the dot-com bubble), and some established firms may be forced to reinvent themselves or go out of business—IBM no longer manufactures personal computers, and RCA is a memory. Innovation may also greatly diminish or eliminate entire sectors. With the advent of digital technologies, demand for typewriters and photographic film has virtually disappeared, and the Internet is starting to take market share away from telephone and cable companies. This competitive pressure to increase productivity and innovate is a boon for consumers, but it is accompanied by greater risks for employees and investors.

Competition and Pricing

The benefit of lower prices for civil society has already been noted, but a bit more needs to be said. Lower prices increase the purchasing power of consumers, thereby increasing the compass of their disposable income. If I can pay less for this I can use my excess money to buy more of that, stash it under my mattress, or make a charitable contribution. Lower prices provide individuals with a wider range of options for how they will expend their income. Global markets intensify this proclivity by expanding both the number of potential consumers and competing producers. Once a critical demand for a product is established, more competitors enter the market. This is why, in part, a new product is expensive when first introduced but the price falls rapidly when competing brands enter the market. When the first HD televisions were introduced they were expensive and only a few brands were available. They are now relatively inexpensive, and consumers may select models from a widening range of brands. As already noted, increased productivity and innovation is one way to lower prices. Another way of lowering production costs is to decrease the cost of labor, and a global labor market makes this an attractive option.

Competition and Employment

Meeting the increased demand generated by new and expanding markets requires the creation of new jobs. The creation of jobs over time, however, is neither smooth nor linear. Over the past two decades, globalization has put more people to work, but this has also entailed displacement and loss of jobs. One reason for this "chaotic progress" is that the same global markets that spur the competitive production of goods and services also generate a larger and more competitive labor market. In many sectors workers compete for jobs on a global scale, and the wages paid are dictated by the needed skills that individuals bring with them to the job market. Consequently, workers are affected disproportionately in light of the skills needed by the production of goods and services. Wages paid to employees are not necessarily determined by the value of the work or service performed. For example, I value the weekly collection of my rubbish and the software programs on my computer, and on reflection I probably value the rubbish collection more highly given the unseemly consequences of uncollected garbage. So why is the software designer paid a higher salary than the garbage collector? Because of the demand for their respective skills. Tossing trash in a truck requires few skills that can be learned quickly,[12] whereas designing software requires many skills that cannot be quickly learned or acquired.[13] Consequently, there are potentially many competitors for the job of trash collector and few for software designers. One hundred people competing for ten trash collecting jobs is going to drive wages lower, while ninety software designers competing for one hundred jobs will push them higher. Wages paid to individuals with similarly specialized skills may also be paid differently in response to consumer demand. I assume, for instance, that members of a medical school faculty are paid higher salaries than their colleagues in the theology faculty. Almost everyone needs a doctor, while, alas, few people require the services of a theologian.

There are a variety of ways that producers of goods and services may take advantage of the global labor market. One way is to locate production where there is a surplus of workers that can be employed at lower wages, a strategy that is particularly cost effective in respect to work requiring few skills. If factory workers can be hired for $5 an hour in locale A as opposed to $10 an hour in locale B, then there is a strong incentive to build a factory in A rather than B.[14] Alternatively, the amount of labor available, and thereby cheaper labor, can be increased through lenient immigration policies or visiting-worker programs. Communication technologies can also be employed to tap remote locations, such as the legendary call centers in India. It should not be assumed that the supply and demand pressures of the global labor market are confined to low-skill jobs. Basic accounting, legal, and medical imaging analyses services can be easily outsourced through the Internet, and many of the visas requested by American high-tech companies are for mid-range jobs that effectively

12. Given the increased use of mechanical collection, physical strength is becoming less of a requirement for employment.

13. In addition, many individuals lack the intellectual proclivities to acquire and master the requisite skills.

14. However, lower labor costs alone do not determine this decision. There are offsetting costs to consider, such as initial capital investment, social and political stability, tax rates, and existing infrastructure.

keep labor and production costs relatively low.[15] In addition, anticipated technological innovations are putting jobs at risk that were once assumed to be invulnerable.[16]

A global labor market creates highly dynamic, if not chaotic conditions in which new jobs are being created while old ones are lost in the process. This dynamism is prompted by the ability to relocate or outsource production and/or relaxed migration restrictions. In both instances the supply of labor is greater than demand, placing a downward pressure on wages that are presumably offset by lower prices of goods and services. In competing for jobs, there is a constant flux of temporary winners and losers. For example, to lower the price of clothing, companies often relocate their factories to locales with lower labor costs. The tag "Made in America" gave way to "Made in China," which is now giving way to "Made in" such countries as Vietnam, Sri Lanka, and Jordan. In each instance former garment workers will need to learn new and applicable skills that enable them to compete in global labor markets. Over time the dynamic nature of global marketplace competition is able to create new jobs for displaced workers. Anticipated technological advances, however, may challenge this assumption. Digital technologies may revolutionize manufacturing. 3D printing, for instance, will enable the production of goods in various locales that are closer to consumers, thereby undercutting the competitive advantage of lower labor costs that developing countries currently enjoy.[17] In addition, individuals are not only competing with each other for jobs, but also with machines. Many manufacturing jobs have already been lost to robots, and with advances in computerization and artificial intelligence (AI) jobs in such areas as word processing, technical writing, retail, and accounting are now at risk.[18]

Within a highly dynamic global labor market, one crucial issue is to devise ways to ensure that workers do not remain unemployed and unproductive for extended periods of time. Ardent proponents of globalization assure us that the market itself will take care of this problem, for it always stimulates creative individuals to create unforeseen opportunities: Who could have predicted in 1900 that millions of people would

15. See Charlotte Allen, "Silicon Chasm: The Class Divide on America's Cutting Edge," *The Weekly Standard* (December 2, 2013).

16. See Erik Brynjolfsson and Andrew McAfee, *The Second Machine Age: Work, Progress, and Prosperity in a Time of Brilliant Technologies* (New York and London: Norton, 2014).

17. See "The Third Industrial Revolution: The Digitisation of Manufacturing Will Transform the Way Goods Are Made—and Change the Politics of Jobs Too," *The Economist* (April 21, 2012).

18. See "The Onrushing Wave: The Future of Jobs," *The Economist* (January 18, 2014).

today be employed in various IT firms; so who knows how people will be employed in the coming decades? Fair enough, but how can the market alone prepare people with appropriate skills for jobs that cannot even be envisioned? Conversely, fervent critics of globalization point to these pressures on the global labor market to justify extensive intervention and regulation by the state but fail to recognize that it is the competitive dynamism of the market that creates jobs in the first place. This dynamism in turn depends on available capital.

Competition and Capital Investment

Meeting increased demand for goods and services requires the investment of capital. Money, equipment, time, and expertise must be invested to produce a particular product. Since producers compete with one another to capture market share, so too do their respective investors. New and expanding global markets enlarge both the potential supply of capital and settings where it may be invested. Let us imagine that there is a high demand for a new widget in locale A. For a variety of reasons, however, it is expensive to produce the widget in locale A, but cheap in locale B. In order to maximize the return on invested capital, production is located in locale B. In addition, sufficient capital may not be available, so additional sources are tapped in locales C and D. Expanding both the sources and locales of capital investment ideally produces a wide range of benefits. Consumers in locale A obtain widgets at lower prices and jobs are created in marketing, sales, distribution, and maintenance. Employment is created in locale B where the widgets are manufactured, and investors in locales A, C, and D enjoy a return on their invested capital. Global markets, however, intensify competition among investors to maximize return on their invested capital, thereby creating more potential winners and losers. Investors may not enjoy much if any return on their capital if a producer loses market share to a producer of better widgets or if a new gadget eliminates the demand for widgets. Competition to maximize return on capital invested by various private and public sources may also prompt risky and imprudent ventures as witnessed by the financial crisis of 2008.[19] Competition among locales where capital is invested is also intensified. Locale B may lose out to locale E if the latter offers a more profitable setting, such as minimal worker and environmental protections.

---

19. See, e.g., Gillian Tett, *Fool's Gold: How the Bold Dream of a Small Tribe at J. P. Morgan Was Corrupted by Wall Street Greed and Unleashed a Catastrophe* (New York: Free Press, 2009).

Critics of globalization argue that the drive to maximize profits inevitably promotes a race to the bottom among competing locales.[20]

Competition and Wealth Creation

If competitive markets are operating as intended, then increased productivity, lower prices, employment, and return on capital investment should result in greater total wealth over time. And this is what has occurred over the past two decades in which unprecedented wealth has been created despite periodic financial crises and recessions. It is estimated that the total global wealth of households increased from slightly over $100 trillion in 2000 to slightly under $250 trillion in 2013, and this trend line encompassed every continent.[21] Since competitive markets create periodic winners and losers among producers, workers, and investors it would also be expected that the distribution of income and wealth among individuals would be uneven, and again this has been the case, for the gap between rich and poor has widened since 2000. Whether or not this gap matters is contentious, but two general observations on wealth and income should be noted. First, although there are winners and losers in any competitive market, winners do not become wealthy at the expense of the losers. Wealth and income are generated by productivity and return on capital investment, not by seizing the wealth and capital of competitors. The goal of a widget producer is to capture as much market share as possible, and this is best achieved by producing a widget that is more attractive to consumers in terms of price and quality. Second, income and wealth must be assessed in terms of purchasing power that varies widely across the world. What is important is not how much one makes but how much one keeps or can spend. For example, if the cost of living in locale Y is twice as much as that in locale Z, financially I would be better off accepting a job offer in locale Z at 60 percent of what I could make in locale Y. Or alternatively, if I am forced to take a 5 percent pay cut but the prices of the goods and services I purchase decline by 10 percent, then I have more disposable income to either spend or save, thereby increasing my wealth. What the widening income gap does not

20. See, e.g., Joseph E. Stiglitz, *Globalization and Its Discontents* (New York: Norton, 2002).
21. See *Global Wealth Databook 2013* (Credit Suisse Research Institute, 2013), section 2. The Credit Suisse Research Institute identifies global economic trends for corporate and individual clients.

readily disclose is the varying purchasing power in the space between a steeply rising ceiling and gradually rising floor.

Competition and Regulation

Given the dynamic nature of competitive global markets, it is not surprising that nation-states try to safeguard their respective interests. Enjoying the benefits of globalization, however, entails a number of difficult challenges, for it is not clear what these interests are and how they are best defended. In the remainder of this section I note briefly a few of the more pressing regulatory issues that are revisited throughout the following chapters.[22]

Traditionally nation-states have protected their interests and those of their citizens by establishing solid borders, both literally and figuratively, that can be regulated and policed. Competitive global markets make these borders more porous and difficult to maintain, because they create pressures to eliminate jurisdictional barriers preventing the flow of production, labor, and capital. Although *protectionism* might appear to be an attractive option for bolstering these borders, it is a counterproductive strategy. Policies may be adopted, for instance, to protect the producers, workers, and capital of a particular nation-state through a combination of such things as high tariffs, restrictions on labor migration and outsourcing, and regulating the inflow and outflow of capital. Such practices may protect producers and their employees from the ill effects of global competition while keeping foreign capital out and domestic capital closer to home. But these goals are achieved at the cost of higher prices, greater unemployment, and the stagnation or diminishment of wealth. Moreover, greater global poverty would be one consequence if many nation-states were to adopt protectionist policies, because the comparative trade advantages of poorer nations would not be enjoyed. One challenge of globalization is how governments may best protect the interests of their citizens as both consumers and competitors at a time when national borders are becoming more like membranes rather than walls.

Another challenge is the issue of *income inequality* and widening wealth gap. There are a number of reasons why a nation-state might want to make income and wealth less unequal. Rightly or wrongly, there is a widely held perception that this disparity is unfair, injurious, or undesirable

---

22. For a more comprehensive overview of regulatory issues and challenges, see Ian Goldin and Mike Mariathasan, *The Butterfly Defect: How Globalization Creates Systemic Risks, and What to Do about It* (Princeton, NJ, and Oxford: Princeton University Press, 2014).

and could lead to social unrest and political instability. One popular solution that is often proffered is to use taxes to redistribute income and wealth. This is probably not an effective and sustainable policy. Increasing the tax rates on corporations and affluent individuals does not necessarily increase revenue that can be redistributed. Higher taxes may also provide an incentive to shelter rather than invest wealth in ventures that would increase productivity and create new jobs, thereby diminishing potential revenue to be redistributed. Additionally, wealthy individuals and corporations may choose to relocate to nations with more favorable personal and corporate tax rates, further diminishing tax revenue to be distributed. Moreover, there is scant evidence that such redistributive schemes actually increase the employment opportunities, income, or wealth of the purported beneficiaries, because the gap is not solely the result of how financial resources are obtained but is also created by a much wider range of social circumstances and conditions.[23] However, some redistribution is both necessary and desirable to prevent civil society from degenerating into a chaotic collection of competing interests on a highly uneven playing field. Consequently, one challenge posed by globalization is how governments can encourage less coercive means for investing in the social capital of civil society; and this is a crucial issue, because market competition exists alongside and is dependent on the cooperation that stems from and sustains civil society.

Cooperation

The previous section may give the impression that global markets are domains of strife and unremitting conflict. This is simply not true, for competition is only one aspect of what is entailed in economic exchange, and fixating on it in isolation from other factors creates an incomplete perception. Trust, for example, is an essential prerequisite of exchange.[24] In the absence of trust, exchange becomes a tortuous enterprise fraught with anxiety, for there is always the fear of being cheated. Yet humans engage in countless exchanges on a daily basis without much thought, much less worry. The fact that fraud is relatively rare and offends our

23. See Jerry Z. Muller, "Capitalism and Inequality: What the Right and the Left Get Wrong," *Foreign Affairs* (March/April, 2013). One example of such a condition is the tendency of people to marry individuals with similar incomes so that in circumstances where two-income families are routine the income gap will enlarge over time.

24. See Paul Seabright, *The Company of Strangers: A Natural History of Economic Life* (Princeton, NJ, and Oxford: Princeton University Press, 2004); see also Francis Fukuyama, *Trust: The Social Virtues and the Creation of Prosperity* (New York: Free Press, 1995).

moral sensibilities when committed is a compliment to the prevailing trust that has been violated. Moreover, daily exchanges occur primarily among strangers, and this unique capacity to trust others beyond spheres of kinship is foundational to civil society.

Why do humans largely trust one another? It is not because they have angelic natures; we are fallen creatures. It is also not due entirely to a fear of being punished for violating trust, although it is one, rather effective, motivation. It is due primarily to necessity: if humans are to flourish beyond the level of subsistence, then they must cooperate. Such cooperation grows out of a basic trust that is neither naive nor cynical, but fittingly guarded. This necessity is reflected in Adam Smith's principle of specialized labor. When I choose to make widgets and you to make gadgets that we can exchange, we are implicitly agreeing to cooperate in satisfying each other's wants and needs. These cooperative choices are replicated in various associations constituting civil society, particularly in respect to the production and exchange of goods and services.

Yet how can cooperation exist alongside competition in civil society, since they are apparently antithetical? Because they are not antithetical but intricately related; cooperation and competition are not antonyms but more akin to two sides of the same coin. A simplistic example may illustrate. If I want to play baseball, then I need other players to form a team. My team in turn needs other teams in order to play the game, and all the teams need umpires to enforce the rules of the game. Without each of these elements the game of baseball cannot be played, and cooperation and competition is interwoven in each element. I need to cooperate with my fellow players, but I also compete with them for starting positions. Competing teams need each other in order to play the game, and they cooperate by following the rules. Umpires enable this mix of competition and cooperation by enforcing rules fairly rather than arbitrarily and by not favoring one team over the other.

Similarly, if civil society is to flourish, it requires both cooperation and competition. Civil society comprises various associations such as households, civic organizations, schools, small businesses, corporations, financial firms, and the like. These associations implicitly cooperate with each other through the specialization of producing goods and services. I don't go to the bank to buy my groceries, and I don't go to the supermarket to do my banking.[25] Competition is pursued both

---

25. In the spirit of full disclosure, I actually do a lot of my banking while in the supermarket because a branch is conveniently located in the same building, but my grocer is not my banker. There is, however, a cooperative and mutually beneficial relationship between the bank and grocery store.

within and among these associations, particularly those producing goods and services. Employees within a firm compete with each other for promotions or jobs at other firms, and businesses compete for market share. When this competition is properly ordered, individuals, households, and other associations benefit through lower prices, greater employment, and investment opportunities. Consequently, civil society as a whole is enriched and strengthened through orderly competition. When competition is ordered badly, individuals, households, and other associations suffer the ill effects of higher prices, unemployment, and limited investment opportunities, thereby weakening civil society. Members of civil society are not served well by the likes of monopolies, cartels, or cronies. Properly ordered markets, therefore, enable people to live and work together, to compete and cooperate, because their principal interactions entail exchanges governed by shared basic rules.

Who is in a position to enable the ordering of this competition? In this respect, the state may be likened to an umpire. Umpires are not players but are responsible for ensuring that the game is played by its rules. Likewise, the state is not a competitor but regulates competition in ways that promote the flourishing of civil society. Consequently, the state enforces these rules—laws and policies—fairly and consistently, amending or repealing them in response to changing needs through appropriate legislative channels. Civil society is weakened when the state intrudes or regulates in an arbitrary manner, changes the rules through executive fiat, determines in advance who shall be winners and losers, or becomes a competitor.

This analogy is obviously too simplistic to capture fully the competitive and cooperative nature of civil society and its proper relationship with the state. Much of part 2 is devoted to further explicating how the state may order competition and cooperation in ways that promote the flourishing of civil society, particularly in light of new and expanding global markets. The purpose of the preceding exercise was simply to highlight the necessary relationship between competition and cooperation. This necessity also reveals an interdependency that many late moderns, on both the left and right, often ignore: namely, that individuals need each other in order to exchange goods and services that meet their respective wants and needs. So-called autonomous individuals who are oblivious to each other do not inhabit markets. Again, a few simple examples will illustrate.

Sellers Need Buyers

I cannot be a producer if there is no one to buy my product. No matter how good a widget I might make, if no one wants it I have nothing to sell. There is a tacit cooperation among producers to specialize in producing needed or wanted goods and services, and markets help to both identify demand and facilitate the mutual need between sellers and buyers. Conversely, *buyers need sellers*. If I want or need a gadget that I am unable to make and no one else makes it, my want or need is unsatisfied. Individuals cannot survive, much less flourish, if they cannot obtain needed or wanted goods and services. Again, markets enable the necessary exchange underpinning civil society exemplified in acts of buying and selling, as well as exerting a useful tension between the seller's interest to sell at the highest price possible and the buyer's interest to purchase at the lowest price possible. Maintaining this tension through competitive markets ultimately strengthens the cooperative bonds of civil society, by simultaneously enabling producers to sell at a profit and consumers to purchase goods and services at lower prices. If one or the other pole collapses, then civil society suffers either from a deficit of goods and services or from higher prices.

Employers Need Employees

If I am producing widgets that are in high demand, I cannot do all the work myself, and I need to hire other people to help me. The production of goods and services requires cooperation between producers and workers. Conversely, *employees need employers*. If there is no one to hire me, I cannot exchange because there is nothing I can produce or consume to any great extent. Through their work, employees help to produce items that are exchanged through selling and buying. In addition, the wages paid to employees broaden the range of goods and services that are exchanged. Markets again exert a useful tension between the producer's interest of paying low wages in order to maximize profit and the employee's interest in being paid high wages to maximize his or her purchasing power. Maintaining this tension through a competitive labor market ultimately strengthens the cooperative bonds of civil society by simultaneously allowing employers to lower the cost of production while also providing employment. If one or the other pole of this tension collapses, then civil society suffers either from the unavailability of goods and services or from unemployment.

Lenders Need Borrowers

After purchasing some goods and services that I want, I discover that I have some money left over. I wish to lend this money to someone that is able to produce a new widget, and I expect some return on my investment. But if there is no one willing or able to borrow my money, then I cannot lend it and my excess cash sits idly under my mattress, and, more broadly, the members of civil society are deprived of a widget. Conversely, *borrowers need lenders*. If I am willing or able to produce a new widget but lack the necessary capital, I must borrow the requisite funds. But if no one will lend me their money I cannot produce the widget, and members of civil society will again be deprived of a needed or wanted item. Credit drives, in part, exchange. Credit often needs to be extended in order to create the necessary capital for a new or existing venture. Markets help to match the supply and demand for credit, while exerting a useful tension between the lender's interest to maximize return and the borrower's interest to secure funding as cheaply as possible. Maintaining this tension through a competitive credit market ultimately strengthens the cooperative bonds of civil society by simultaneously enabling a return on lending while making borrowing affordable. If either pole collapses, then civil society suffers the effects of stagnant or decreased productivity and employment.

Civil Society and the State

The state exists to protect its citizens and promote the interests of the private associations that make up civil society. As noted in the previous section, the dynamism of new and expanding markets makes these tasks daunting. These tasks are made more difficult because the roles of protecting citizens and promoting the interests of civil society are often in conflict. On the one hand, globalization benefits civil society through increased productivity, lower prices, new employment opportunities, and creation of capital. On the other hand, individuals may be harmed by diminished wages, unemployment, and unavailable access to credit and creation of capital. The competitive market forces that produce overall affluence and wealth in the long run also impoverish some individuals, at least in the short term. The principal challenge of the state is to simultaneously enable civil society to benefit from the dynamism of competitive global markets while alleviating the harm inflicted by certain segments of the population it governs. In short, how does the state harness creative market forces while softening the impact of the destruction that accompanies them? How can the state provide social stability within global markets that appear to be inherently destabilizing? As I argue in the next chapter, the modern nation-state may not be up to this challenge.

Chapter Three

Creative Destruction, the Market-State, and the Holy Spirit

The previous chapter examined the complex relationship among markets, competition, and cooperation. Globalization has amplified the macrobenefits of this relationship over time, while exacerbating liabilities at the micro level for some people. In aggregate, new and expanding global markets have increased employment, purchasing power, affluence, and wealth across the world over the past two decades. At the same time, many individuals and communities suffered unemployment, displacement, decreased purchasing power, and diminished standards of living. Seemingly the long-term benefits for civil society afforded by competitive markets cannot, at least for the time being, be separated from accompanying short-term uncertainties and anxieties. Moreover, the dynamism generated by new and expanding global markets intensifies both of these tendencies. As Gregg Easterbrook has observed, it should be anticipated that "in the near future, most of the world will attain the free-market advantages long enjoyed in the West, especially ample goods of rising quality and declining real-currency price."[1] Yet these advantages will be invariably accompanied by "job instability, economic insecurity, a sense of turmoil, the unfocused fear that even when things seem good a hammer is about to fall."[2]

The dynamism of global markets produces an overarching systemic stability derived from underlying turbulence. From a global perspective, economic exchange—the production and consumption of goods and services—is relatively stable and secure. Granted this stability is

1. Gregg Easterbrook, *Sonic Boom: Globalization at Mach Speed* (New York: Random House, 2009), xiv.
2. Ibid., xii.

periodically disrupted by natural catastrophes, civil unrest, or political acts such as war and embargoes, but global markets have proven remarkably resilient in adapting to changing circumstances while efficiently matching supply with demand. A simultaneous and ongoing process of creation and destruction, however, achieves this relative stability: new jobs are created while old ones are destroyed; new ventures succeed while old corporations go bankrupt. Moreover, virtually no corner of the world is immune from what occurs elsewhere—real estate markets in China and Mexico can positively or adversely affect retirement portfolios in Europe and North America. The anxieties and uncertainties stemming from dynamic global markets cannot be removed, at least for the foreseeable future. Globalization is a package deal. Enjoying its benefits requires enduring its anxiety, for they are inescapably intertwined. The creativity generated by global markets is predicated on a destructive capability. The ensuing "risk cannot be removed because it is endemic to globalization. It is a process to be managed, not a problem to be solved."[3]

Creative Destruction

Joseph Schumpeter coined the phrase "creative destruction" to characterize the dynamic quality of markets, and capitalism in general. The "essential point" of capitalism is that it is an "evolutionary process" that cannot be easily controlled or regulated.[4] Indeed, such attempts only serve to stymie or even negate the destructive competition that in turn drives creativity. "Capitalism, then, is by nature a form or method of economic change and not only never is but never can be stationary."[5] This change is based on the development of new consumer goods, methods of production, transportation, and industrial organization. These innovations require the constant creation and destruction of products and the firms producing them. Genuine capitalism is unlike mercantile schemes designed to "curtail production in order to extort profits," and contrary to mainline classical economic theory the goal of "equilibrium in perfect competition" is not only difficult to sustain but also counterproductive.[6] Rather, production is increased to maximize

3. Ian Goldin and Mike Mariathasan, *The Butterfly Defect: How Globalization Creates Systemic Risks, and What to Do about It* (Princeton, NJ, and Oxford: Princeton University Press, 2014), xiii.

4. See Joseph A. Schumpeter, *Capitalism, Socialism and Democracy* (New York and London: Harper Perennial, 2008), 82.

5. Ibid., 83.

6. Ibid., 79–80.

profit, and equilibrium is not an objective that can be achieved through various policies and regulations but is a consequence of the creative destruction resulting from competition. For Schumpeter, much of the criticism of capitalism is misplaced, because the "problem that is usually being visualized is how capitalism administers existing structures, whereas the relevant problem is how it creates and destroys them."[7] Consequently, it is the entrepreneur rather than established enterprises or the state that drives economic growth.

Two salient observations are gleaned from Schumpeter's portrayal of capitalism as an evolutionary process of creative destruction. First, it should not be surprising that globalization is driven by rapid and wide-ranging innovation. With new and expanding global markets there are strong incentives for entrepreneurs to compete with each other in developing new products and more efficient modes of producing them. Over the last few decades this has been especially prevalent in the IT and communication sectors. Many individuals and firms have made fortunes in creating the cornucopia of electronic gadgets that now clutter the workplace and household, and many unsuccessful competitors have also been destroyed in the process.

Second, it should not be surprising that globalization causes income inequality, and a widening gap between rich and poor. The entrepreneurs who are the first to develop new or innovative products will initially corner the market, thereby maximizing the return on investment in the absence of competition. Schumpeter admits that successful innovations effectively entail monopolistic practices.[8] For example, Microsoft provided 97 percent of operating systems worldwide in 2000. Yet over time competitors entered the market leveling the distribution of income. By 2012 Microsoft's market share had fallen to 20 percent, primarily as a result of such innovations as smart phones and tablets.[9]

It may be objected that Schumpeter's emphasis on the entrepreneur is misplaced, since global markets are dominated by large private and public organizations. Admittedly most of the major players in global markets are large organizations such as publicly traded and state-owned corporations, and private equity and pension funds, but those that have flourished have often acted in entrepreneurial ways, taking to heart the

7. Ibid., 84.
8. Ibid., ch. 8.
9. Tim Worstall, "Microsoft's Market Share Drops from 97% to 20% in Just over a Decade," *Forbes* (December 13, 2012), http://www.forbes.com/sites/timworstall/2012/12/13/microsofts-market-share-drops-from-97-to-20-in-just-over-a-decade/#6c83a4b8763f.

adage "change or die." It is telephones and tablets, not desktop computers, that made Apple successful. In addition, many of the new jobs created over the past two decades on a global scale can be described as self-employment opportunities made possible with the advent of the Internet, microlending, and peer-to-peer investing. Counterintuitively, globalization may help the little guy or gal compete more effectively by creating strategic niches.[10]

Given Schumpeter's exuberant description of capitalism as a vibrant evolutionary process, it is surprising, even shocking, that in answer to his question, "Can capitalism survive?" his terse reply is "No, I don't think it can." Capitalism promotes an entrepreneurial creativity that will lead to its own destruction. The competitive drive to innovate simultaneously lowers the cost of production and return on investment. Rapid technological development, for example, means that entrepreneurs cannot dominate the markets for particular goods and services for an extended period of time, thereby diminishing both their profit and incentive to innovate. Eventually consumer desire will be effectively satiated, resulting in a stable equilibrium between supply and demand. Over time, incomes will be leveled and the gap separating rich and poor narrowed. Capitalism will then atrophy because entrepreneurs will have nothing to do, and socialism will effectively be achieved. With its process of creative destruction, capitalism is its own gravedigger.[11]

Schumpeter's prediction of capitalism's ultimate demise is not as straightforward as first meets the eye. He wrote in an ironic style in which his anticipated eulogy of capitalism is actually its defense. According to Jerry Muller, Schumpeter adopted this strategy because the mid-twentieth-century academic milieu in which he wrote was dominated by leftist ideology.[12] Any overt defense of capitalism would be dismissed out-of-hand, so he had to somehow bait his fellow intellectuals, particularly young economists who could still be influenced—hence, his "strategy of ostensible concurrence." "As an ironic work, its overt contention is the opposite of its intended message. The explicit thesis of *Capitalism, Socialism, and Democracy* is that capitalism will be superseded as Marx predicted, but not for the reasons he had predicted it."[13] If socialism

10. See Thomas L. Friedman, *The World Is Flat: A Brief History of the Twenty-first Century, Further Updated and Expanded* (New York: Picador / Farrar, Straus and Giroux, 2007); and Easterbrook, *Sonic Boom.*

11. Schumpeter, *Capitalism, Socialism and Democracy,* 61.

12. See Jerry Z. Muller, *The Mind and the Market: Capitalism in Modern European Thought* (New York: Anchor Books, 2003), ch. 11.

13. Ibid., 307.

displaces capitalism, it will be due not to capitalism's failure but to its success.

If Schumpeter is correct, then, ironically, the most ardent socialist should be the biggest cheerleader of global capitalism since it will hasten the eschaton of economic equilibrium no longer driven by unsatisfied desire—help entrepreneurs put themselves out of business. But one suspects that Schumpeter has his tongue firmly in his cheek when he suggests that desire can be satiated. Entrepreneurs are presumably adept at creating new desires; and should that fail, then they can always appeal to old-fashioned avarice. A future socialist golden age is permanently on hold.

Schumpeter's ironic thesis also creates a thorny political dilemma, particularly in respect to contemporary globalization. On the one hand, if a regime wants to promote the aggregate material well-being of its citizens, then it must participate in global markets to take advantage of its creative production of goods and services. But this also necessitates subjecting its citizens to unremitting anxiety and uncertainty in the wake of the markets' destructive forces. On the other hand, a regime may choose to defend its citizens from such anxiety and uncertainty by restricting participation through various protectionist policies. But the cost of such protection is the diminished aggregate material well-being of its citizens. Moreover, finding some kind of reasonable trade-off is problematic, given the contending interests at stake as well as the dynamism of global markets and the constantly shifting political issues it generates. More troubling, the nation-state, at least as traditionally conceived, may not be well suited to ameliorate, much less resolve, this dilemma.

Market-State

Why is the nation-state ill-equipped to deal with the dilemma posed by globalization as indicated above? The principal purpose of the nation-state is to protect and promote the interests and well-being of its citizens. Accomplishing this task has usually entailed securing physical borders from attack, unlawful entrance and exiting, and laws, policies, and institutions dedicated to regulating the production and consumption of goods and services that in turn provide employment and taxes. Within a globalized context, however, this protective and promotional purpose is rendered problematic if not contradictory. Adopting policies enabling free trade, foreign investment, and labor migration provides many citizens with a wider variety of affordable items, generating greater aggregate purchasing power and affluence, but at a cost to some individuals of unemployment or underemployment.[14] In the United States, for example, affordable clothing and furniture are now largely imported, displacing many garment and furniture workers. Conversely, adopting policies that restrict trade, foreign investment, and immigration may protect various economic sectors and preserve jobs, but at the cost of greater production and labor costs that are passed on to consumers through higher prices, thereby diminishing aggregate purchasing power and affluence. To return to the United States, if the so-called big three automobile companies and their employees had been protected by preventing the importation or domestic manufacturing of foreign competitors, imagine what the ensuing cost, selection, and quality of cars might now be. It would appear that in responding to new and emerging global markets, no nation-state can pursue its protective *and* promotional purposes without harming the interests and well-being of at least some its citizens.

Is there a better option that late modern governments might adopt? Philip Bobbitt insists there is, namely, by evolving from nation-states to market-states. Before examining what the market-state is and why it is better equipped to deal with the simultaneously creative and destructive economic forces driving global markets, some historical context is needed. According to Bobbitt, the emerging market-state is the latest stage in a six-part series of modern epochal moments.[15] The sixteenth century was dominated by the "Princely State" that was dedicated to establishing the power of regional dynastic leaders. In the following century the "Kingly State" solidified dynastic legitimacy and was in turn replaced in the eighteenth century by the "Territorial Nation" that enriched countries and aristocracies through state management of monopolies and colonial acquisitions.[16]

It is the last three transitions in this schema that are most pertinent. The "State Nation" of the nineteenth century consolidated national identity through further imperial expansion and domination. Government

14. There are other factors such as technological innovation, environmental regulations, and tax rates that also contribute to unemployment and underemployment. In addition, importing goods and services creates employment and investment opportunities. See Michael Mandelbaum, *The Road to Global Prosperity* (New York and London: Simon and Schuster, 2014), ch. 2.

15. The following schema using century designations represents a rough correspondence.

16. See Philip Bobbitt, *Terror and Consent: The Wars for the Twenty-First Century* (New York: Knopf, 2008), 189–93; for a more detailed account of these transitions, see Philip Bobbitt, *The Shield of Achilles: War, Peace, and the Course of History* (New York: Knopf, 2002), chs. 7–8.

organized the activities of the people it governed to serve the interests of the state. In the twentieth century this priority was reversed in the "Nation State" in which the state exists to promote national interests and welfare of citizens. The primacy of the Nation State was established through the "Long War" (1914–1990) in which liberal democracy established its preeminence over the competing ideologies of fascism, National Socialism, and communism. Liberal democrats had little time to celebrate their victory, however, for almost as soon as the first brick fell from the Berlin Wall the nascent "Market State" was born.[17]

What exactly is the market-state and how does it differ from the nation-state? According to Bobbitt, the purpose of the market-state is to "maximize the opportunity of its citizens."[18] The market-state is oriented toward promoting opportunities for individual citizens rather than their collective welfare. The principal factors driving the emergence of the market-state include the "globalization of markets," mobility of capital, inability of nations to control their currencies and economies, rapid transnational economic growth, the "universalization of culture," and advances in communication and information technologies. Each of these forces simultaneously erodes the authority of the nation-state while increasing the necessity of its market-state replacement.[19] Consequently, the "basis for the state's legitimacy" shifts, in part, "away from assuring mass welfare and towards maximizing individual opportunity."[20] One result is that the "market state is classless and indifferent to race, ethnicity, and gender, but it is also heedless of the values of reverence, self-sacrifice, loyalty, and family."[21]

Since the market-state is oriented toward maximizing the choices of individuals rather than the welfare of groups, its citizens tend to conceive themselves as consumers rather than producers. Since consumption drives exchange, citizens of the market-state are oriented toward consuming goods and services. Consequently, they tend to prize individual autonomy over productive solidarity and identity. This reorientation transforms prevailing perceptions and tasks of political governance, particularly when the transition from nation-state to market-state is seen in light of increasing globalization. The dynamism of new and expanding global markets and the concomitant emergence of the market-state require not

17. See Bobbitt, *Terror and Consent*, 194–98; see also Bobbitt, *The Shield of Achilles*, chs. 2–4, 8–9.

18. Bobbitt, *Terror and Consent*, 191.

19. See ibid., 86–87; Bobbitt, *The Shield of Achilles*, 228–35.

20. Bobbitt, *Terror and Consent*, 87.

21. Ibid., 90.

only a diminishment of national interests but also "that we think in terms of global relations rather than international relations."[22] This change in thinking further weakens the "collectivist values represented by the nation-state" by turning "attention to the benefit of individuals."[23] The respective tasks of the nation-state and market-state, then, are not easily reconciled. The interests of the nation-state are to be culturally insular, limit competition, and promote international accord through a series of highly structured and controlled governmental institutions. In contrast, the interests of the market-state are to be culturally permeable, promote competition, and pursue mutual interests through temporary alliances of private initiatives, corporations, NGOs, and restricted governmental involvement. The "nation-state is process-oriented, churning out impartial rules and regulations to promote desired behavior, the market-state pursues its objectives by incentive structures and sometimes draconian penalties, not so much to assure that the right thing is done as to prevent the social instability that threatens material well-being."[24] In this respect, Margaret Thatcher and Ronald Reagan may be seen as among the last leaders of the nation-state, whereas Tony Blair and George W. Bush are among the first market-state leaders.[25]

The transition from nation-state to market-state will not be smooth, and will likely be accompanied by ferocious forms of confrontational politics, perhaps including violent reactions from both the left and right. This is reflected in the increasing fragmentation of various religious, cultural, and ethnic groups in which the state is coming to be seen as a nemesis rather than a guardian in terms of their respective interests. Although this trend is troubling it is not unexpected or necessarily toxic, for the nascent market-state will initially take on a wide variety of forms of governance. Together, these forms of governance will be proficient at establishing and maintaining various markets. Markets alone, however, are not equipped to assure political representation of religious, cultural, or ethnic groups, and the market-state will eventually need to develop or enable ways to address this deficiency should it be judged to be a liability. Arguably, the withering of religious, cultural, and ethnic identities come to be seen as an advantage in furthering the interests of consumers.

According to Bobbitt there are presently three viable options for governing the emerging market-state. One option is what is characterized

22. Bobbitt, *The Shield of Achilles*, 338.
23. Ibid., 469.
24. Ibid., 229.
25. Ibid., 222.

as the *mercantile state*. Its overriding objective is to dominate selected global markets through a combination of selective protectionist and liberal trade policies designed to enrich its citizens "at the expense of its trading partners."[26] Typically a mercantile state has a literate and ethnically homogenous population that is maintained through highly restrictive immigration policies and promotes saving over consumption, since goods and services are produced primarily for export rather than domestic markets. The principal strength of the mercantile state is its provision of social stability achieved principally by protecting jobs and promoting the welfare of citizens through the extensive accumulation of personal financial resources supplemented by a minimal public safety net. Its primary weakness is that its self-dealing trading practices create suspicion, resentment, and hostility among other nations, and it is doubtful if it can sustain sufficient economic growth over time. Japan is an example of a mercantile state.

A second option is the *managerial state*. A managerial state "seeks power through its hegemony within a regional economic zone."[27] This power is asserted through a series of formal treaties and alliances with other nations in a geographic region. As the most astutely managed partner, whose economic strength is typically obtained through the production of exported goods and services, it tends to dominate these alliances. The managerial state uses its alliances to amplify its political and economic clout within both regional and global markets. Conversely these formal alliances also impose a weakness by constraining policy options, particularly monetary and financial policies that may over time adversely affect its citizens, while also inhibiting quick responses to unfolding geopolitical events. Germany, given its prominent role in the European Union, is an example of a managerial state.

A third option is the *entrepreneurial state*. It is simultaneously committed to creating opportunities for its citizens to take advantage of dynamic global markets, while also mitigating competitive ill effects by enabling public and private cooperative efforts. The entrepreneurial state tends to promote free trade and is politically decentralized, ethnically, culturally, and religiously diverse and depends on immigration (or outsourcing) to provide cheap labor. Employment and the production of goods and services are geared principally for domestic markets in conjunction with marketing, distribution, and consumption of imports. The principal strength of this option is an agility to adapt to and take advantage of

26. Ibid., 284.
27. Ibid., 283.

opportunities afforded by the dynamism of global markets that ideally serve the interests of most of its citizens most of the time. Its weakness is that the interests of some of its citizens are harmed almost all of the time.

Bobbitt admits that each of these options for governing the emerging market-state have inherent "pitfalls," and one "is not more moral or necessarily more benign than another."[28] He nonetheless favors the entrepreneurial option, particularly as the one that should be pursued by the United States, and in many respects is its only feasible choice. The United States lacks ethnic and cultural homogeneity as well as the shared values of thrift and saving, which are presumably prerequisites for the mercantile state. Additionally, the attendant isolationist stance would exacerbate rather than help contain geopolitical tensions. Moreover, the requirement of greater centralized control over production of targeted goods and services runs counter to its political customs and traditions. The managerial state is also unrealistic because American political and economic interests would not be served by a strong regional alliance given the constraints it would impose on economic and geopolitical policies; "creating a second EU" makes little sense.[29] Furthermore, globalization may render geographic proximity increasingly irrelevant, being displaced by transient alliances of common interests not dictated by shared locale. Bobbitt suggests, for instance, that the United States might be better served if it "were part of a 'virtual' region, composed of the United Kingdom, Singapore, India, the Philippines, and Canada."[30]

Most important, the entrepreneurial option best incorporates the American traditions and values of limited government, private initiative, and cooperative associations. These are strengths that should be used in governing the emerging market-state. In many respects an entrepreneurial governance of the market-state embraces the creative destruction of global markets as an opportunity to promote the aggregate material well-being of its citizens, but an opportunity admittedly fraught with uncertainty, risk, and anxiety. Such governance is, to say the least, challenging, because the "very nature of the entrepreneurial state . . . will not make either leading or following easy."[31]

Bobbitt is certain that the latest round of globalization is necessitating changes in how nations are governed. The question is not whether the nation-state will be supplanted by the market-state, but how quickly

28. Ibid.
29. Ibid., 287.
30. Ibid.
31. Ibid., 288.

or slowly this transition takes place. But there are two important caveats. First, how exactly the emerging market-state will eventually come to be governed is unknown. Bobbitt's three models are highly speculative. Which option will eventually become dominant cannot be predicted, and unanticipated models may emerge. Nonetheless, these models disclose that the nation-state is probably entering a new era of historical change in reaction to the creative destruction accompanying the dynamism of new and expanding global markets. This change in turn exacerbates the tension between the state's purpose to both protect its interests (the emphasis of the mercantile and managerial options) while also maximizing the economic opportunities of individual citizens (the emphasis of the entrepreneurial option).

The second caveat is that although the market-state is already emerging, the nation-state is not about to disappear anytime soon. In Bobbitt's words, "At the beginning of the twenty-first century, we still live in nation states and their legitimizing mission—to better our material well-being—still defines the contemporary state. Yet this mission is becoming harder to fulfill, and publics know this. Few contemporary national groups . . . seek their fulfillment in a relationship" between themselves and "the nation state."[32] For the foreseeable future governments will attempt to act in ways intending to protect the welfare of the nations they govern, only to discover that these purportedly protective measures impede the economic interests and opportunities of their citizens. This is particularly true in the case of providing security in a world where increasingly asymmetrical wars are waged between states and nongovernmental groups, or nation-states attempt to assert their interests against other nation-states without recourse to armed conflict.[33] At the time of this writing, for example, the United States and European Union are attempting to respond to Russia's incursion into Ukraine. To date, the American and European states have been unable or unwilling to undertake any military action, but have undertaken putative economic sanctions. Yet given global financial integration, any measures taken against Russia will also undoubtedly punish the economic interests of some of its own citizens. The coercive power of the state becomes less effective as global markets penetrate national boundaries and blur national interests. Although globalization may lessen the prospect of international war, the emerging market-state is no guarantee that such warfare will be rendered obsolete. Although Germany was Britain's largest trade partner in 1914, their respective

32. Bobbitt, *Terror and Consent*, 195–96.
33. See ibid., pt. 1.

economic interests did not prevent them from waging a devastating war against each other for four long years.[34] More sobering, Bobbitt suggests that another epochal war may be required to establish the dominance of the market-state as was the case in the previous transition from state-nation to nation-state.[35]

The purpose of examining Bobbitt's account of the emerging market-state is neither to challenge nor to endorse the veracity of his predictions. Rather, it is to simply note that globalization is prompting changes in how nation-states relate to one another and how they are governed. Given the dynamism of new and expanding global markets, it is reasonable to assume that something like a market-state is beginning to emerge, and it is also reasonable to assume that the transition from nation-state to market-state will be a troubled and uncertain one. I have used Bobbitt to help set economic and political contexts in order to probe what is, for the purpose of this chapter, the more important question: how should Christians in general, and Christian moral theology in particular, respond to the creative destruction of global markets and the accompanying rise of the market-state?

Work of the Holy Spirit

In this section I assume that globalization, at least in the foreseeable future, will continue to expand. The extent of this growth will ebb and flow in response to unforeseen financial and political events, but the overall expansion of global markets, complete with their dynamic creativity and destruction, is now a set trajectory. Or at least I hope my assumption is true. A collapse or constriction of global markets would, I fear, represent either isolationist or xenophobic reactions to calamitous political events or the resurgence of ideologies espousing totalitarian planning and control.[36] And it would be the poor who would suffer the most in each of these instances. This is why, in part, any sweeping denunciation and attempt to dismantle global markets as I argued in chapter 1 is both unrealistic and incompatible with Christian moral teaching professing to help the poor. This is not to deny that there a host of political and ethical issues that should be addressed, but a wholesale

---

34. In 1910, for example, Norman Angell argued that the benefits of trade trumped the benefits of coercive aggression, thereby virtually assuring that war would never again be waged between major nations; see *The Great Illusion: A Study of the Relation of Military Power to National Advantage* (New York and London: G. P. Putnam's Sons, 1910).

35. See Bobbitt, *The Shield of Achilles*, xxvii.

36. See Goldin and Mariathasan, *The Butterfly Defect*, 4.

opposition to globalization is based on a puzzling reactionary fear of the future toward which God is purportedly pulling creation and its creatures. Are Christian theologians and moralists really prepared to insist that God cannot possibly be at work within new and expanding global markets? Consequently, the assumed prospect of more expansive global markets should not be grudgingly accepted as a given but guardedly welcomed by Christians as a potential opportunity to serve the world in loving obedience to their Lord. In the following two chapters I argue that the creative destruction generated by global markets offers the best possible means of creating sufficient affluence that is needed, in part, to alleviate poverty on a global scale.

I also assume that something like Bobbitt's entrepreneurial market-state is best equipped to attain the extensive affluence that is needed to combat poverty. Its emphases on limited and decentralized government, private initiative, and cooperative associations afford it certain advantages in using the dynamism of global markets in comparison to the mercantile and managerial options. If, as assumed, globalization follows its expansive trajectory, then the requisite homogeneity of the mercantile state and regional constraints of the managerial state become liabilities for using the creative dynamics and coping with the destructive forces of global markets. Moreover, prolonged attempts at defending perceived mercantile and managerial interests may over time serve to diminish the scope of affluence and perpetuate poverty on a global scale. Again, this does not suggest that the emerging entrepreneurial market-state is free from a host of pressing moral and political issues that need to be addressed, particularly in respect to how increased affluence is best used to promote the alleviation of poverty. An entrepreneurial governance of the market-state, however, represents the most realistic and effective option for tackling these issues in ways that Christians can, to a great extent, support.

In the remainder of this chapter, I argue why Christians may offer their support by drawing upon certain theological and moral strands noted in chapter 1. This support for the emerging entrepreneurial market-state, however, is not exclusive, normative, or unqualified. Theological and moral arguments could also be made in favor of the mercantile and managerial options, but since entrepreneurial governance purportedly affords certain advantages, its preferred status is, in part, pragmatic. However, I am also not arguing that the entrepreneurial model is preferred because it is an outgrowth originating in Christian theological and moral thought. Rather, I am contending that it is not incompatible with core theological and moral convictions so long as entrepreneurial governance promotes the lawful and just creation of affluence, and in ways that help alleviate poverty. In short, the emerging market-state is simply the best possible option at this particular time in God's unfolding providential care of the world.

Throughout its history Christianity has been remarkably adept in adapting to a variety of both favorable and unfavorable political circumstances. The church has pursued its mission and ministry within empires, kingdoms, totalitarian regimes, and nation-states governed in accordance with a range of ideologies. It has endured and at times thrived under conditions of persecution, toleration, indifference, and established or de facto privilege. The church has also pursued its mission and ministry within a variety of economic systems. It has endured and at times prospered within agrarian, mercantile, socialist, communist, and capitalist economies. In each of these instances, Christians have offered both counsel and resistance. To what extent the counsel has been wise and the resistance warranted is subject to debate, but the point is that Christian political and economic thought has developed out of a long tradition of responding to changing circumstances, and hopefully it has learned from both its achievements and failures. The advent of an incipient market-state in reaction to the creative and destructive dynamism of global markets is not out of character with the church's experience of the world that it loves and serves in obedience to Christ.

This adaptability is not merely due to expediency. Rather, it originates in Scripture and is refined in subsequent theological deliberation and exposition. Jeremiah, for instance, counsels the exiles to "seek the peace and prosperity" of Babylon, for "if it prospers, you too will prosper." They should therefore construct "houses and settle down; plant gardens," and have families.[37] The prophet urges his people to live their lives where they are presently and not pine for where they might prefer to be. In 1 Timothy, Christians are enjoined to pray "for kings and all those in authority" in order that they might "live peaceful and quiet lives."[38] More broadly, Saint Paul teaches that all earthly governments derive their authority from God.[39] The governing authorities should be shown due respect, but their authority is limited. Government is authorized by God to legislate and regulate, to protect and tax, but only to a limited extent. Christians are thereby required to pray *for* their political leaders, but not *to* them. Consequently, Christians can never give their total loyalty to any

37. See Jer. 29:4–7 NIV.
38. See 1 Tim. 2:1–2 NIV.
39. See Rom. 13:1–7.

particular regime, for such fidelity is reserved for God alone. This is why governments and their leaders are simultaneously upheld and resisted; why some Christians have been magistrates and others martyrs.

This adaptability, and the ensuing tensions between affirmation and resistance, is captured in Augustine's account of the two cities demarcating Christian faith and practice.[40] The City of God and City of Man do not exist as parallel and antithetical realms nor as overlapping and contrasting spheres. Rather, in this time between the Word's incarnation and Christ's Parousia the heavenly city is embedded within its earthly counterpart. Their relationship is not necessarily one of perpetual antagonism or harmony. Since God authorizes both cities, albeit for different purposes, it is not surprising that they share a common desire for peace and concord. Given their differing purposes and loves, the means used to achieve this goal are often in tension: the heavenly city looks to mercy and grace while the earthly city turns to coercion and punishment. These divergent means, however, do not invalidate their respective acts; mercy does not negate the need for punishment or vice versa. Augustine both appeals to Rome to use its coercive power against the Donatists, while also pleading for clemency of prisoners awaiting execution; he praises Rome for keeping brigands and invaders at bay, while also condemning the empire as a counterfeit commonwealth because it loved glory more than justice. In this present time, before the end of time, the two cities are comingled, and attempts in the meantime to identify their respective citizens are a fruitless waste of time. The City of Man will eventually be supplanted by the City of God, but its final establishment will be entirely a matter of divine timing and prerogative.

Nevertheless, citizens of the heavenly city are never entirely at ease during their sojourn in the earthly city, for it is not their true home. This is why Augustine likens the Christian life to one of pilgrimage.[41] Since Christians anticipate their eventual home of eternal fellowship with God, they are restless in the meantime. They are pilgrims residing temporarily but not permanently in the City of Man. A pilgrim, however, is not synonymous with a nomad who wanders constantly and aimlessly.[42] As transients, pilgrims are free to reside at various locales for varying periods

---

40. See Augustine, *Concerning the City of God against the Pagans*, trans. Henry Bettenson (London and New York: Penguin, 1972).

41. Ibid., bk. 15.

42. For a more detailed description of the differences between pilgrims and nomads (particularly late modern nomads), see Brent Waters, *Christian Moral Theology in the Emerging Technoculture: From Posthuman Back to Human* (Farnham, UK, and Burlington, VT: Ashgate, 2014), pt. 2.

of time. They are not unlike Jeremiah's exiles and are well advised to build houses, have families, and engage in commerce wherever they might happen to be for a time. If the earthly city is not a permanent home, then one particular place is not necessarily worse than another.

In addition, since the earthly city is a provisional institution whose limited authority has been given by God, its governance and methods of exchange are also not permanent and are subject to change over time. Unlike many of his contemporaries, Augustine was not particularly distraught by the fall of Rome, the purportedly eternal city.[43] Rome had played a useful role for a time, but in God's providential ordering of creation, empires, as well as other political and economic systems, come and go. There is within Augustine and the tradition of moral theology he inspired a remarkable indifference toward forms of political governance. Christian political and economic thought does not (or should not) begin with a normative a priori form of political governance or system of economic exchange. This indifference, however, does not imply a slavish or resigned acceptance of any political and economic systems that happen to be presently dominant. Rather, such forms are assessed in light of core scriptural and theological convictions and within the strictures of particular histories, traditions, and cultures.[44] The emerging market-state, then, should not necessarily prompt a reactionary defense of the nation-state it is presumably displacing, particularly if it proves more adept at creating global affluence in ways that are better equipped at alleviating poverty. Yet neither can there be an unqualified endorsement of the emerging market-state, for if over time superior political and economic systems for creating affluence and relieving poverty should emerge, there would be no compelling reason to defend the market-state.

So far my argument for the emerging entrepreneurial market-state has been muted, somewhat along the lines that it may not be any worse than other alternatives. That is not a foundation for a ringing endorsement, but neither is it a basis for any sweeping denunciation. My diffidence is warranted not only by indifference toward particular political and economic systems but also by a core theological conviction that God, through the Holy Spirit, is at work in the world creating something new. The advent of something new is bound to engender uncertainty, even anxiety, but the church has diminished its mission and ministry to the world when it has

---

43. See Theodor E. Mommsen, "St. Augustine and the Christian Idea of Progress: The Background of the City of God," *Journal of the History of Ideas*, 12:3 (June 1951): 346–74.

44. See Oliver O'Donovan, *The Desire of the Nations: Rediscovering the Roots of Political Theology* (Cambridge, UK: Cambridge University Press, 1996), esp. chs. 1, 4, and 7.

confused this new work as a threat to be resisted because it has become too closely tied to particular political structures and economic ideologies. Consequently, instead of assuming that globalization is an entirely destructive force that should be repelled, might it be better to ask, does the emerging market-state as a response to global markets with their creative destruction offer opportunities for the work of the Holy Spirit that were previously not available?

Before answering this question, a few words are in order to indicate what I mean by the "work of the Holy Spirit." In the Bible, the Holy Spirit is portrayed as being analogous with the "mind,"[45] "truth,"[46] and "power"[47] of God, and is called an "advocate"[48] and "helper."[49] The work of the Spirit is to help people stand firm in the faith and be sanctified by God's truth.[50] This work is seen most prominently in gifts given by the Spirit, such as wisdom, knowledge, healing, prophecy, discernment, speaking in tongues and their interpretation,[51] and the three great gifts of faith, hope, and, most important, love.[52] There are, then, different kinds of gifts, but they are given by the same Spirit through which "God works . . . them in all men."[53] Although no formal doctrine of the Trinity is propounded in Scripture, subsequent generations of theologians based their doctrinal formulations of the triune God on biblical teaching. It is important that the Holy Spirit is the third person of the triune God and is as equally divine as the other two persons. The work of the Holy Spirit is not the work of one-third of God, but the fullness of God. The work and gifts of the Spirit are also fully and completely the work and gifts of the Father and the Son.

Three pertinent observations are in order regarding the work of the Holy Spirit. First, the work of the Spirit bears witness to and supports a *unity in diversity*. To reiterate Paul's teaching, there are many gifts but one Spirit. This unity in the Spirit, however, does not negate difference; catholicity is not achieved at the expense of particularity. Following F. D. Maurice,[54] genuinely universal faith and practice does not necessarily

45. Rom. 8:27 and 1 Cor. 2:10–16.
46. John 14:17.
47. Luke 1:35 and Acts 1:8.
48. John 14–16.
49. Heb. 13:6.
50. 2 Thess. 2:13 and 1 Pet. 1:2.
51. 1 Cor. 12:7–11.
52. 1 Cor. 13.
53. 1 Cor. 12:4–6 NIV.
54. See under "Why Not Three Cheers?" in the introduction to this volume.

require the destruction of distinct customs and dialects, and in many respects strengthens such particularity in resisting the homogenizing tendencies of empires and the universal and homogenous state more broadly. This unity in diversity as a work of the Spirit is exhibited prominently at Pentecost in which the many bear witness to the One.[55]

Second, the Holy Spirit *cannot be controlled*. The Spirit blows where it will,[56] steadfastly refusing any attempts at being domesticated, manipulated, or conjured. The Spirit is not at the beck and call of anyone. If the Spirit could be invoked to do our bidding, it would be prevented from accomplishing one of its principal works: namely, to be bringing in the new.[57] As sinners, humans tend to resist something genuinely new because of fear and a myopic imagination. Even late moderns, despite their rhetoric praising creativity and novelty, often prove to be unimaginative and unadventurous. To borrow from Henry Ford: "If I had asked people what they wanted, they would have said faster horses." The work of the Spirit is to remind us that change is possible and can be welcomed, and that the future is often not what we expect or anticipate, or even what we might prefer.

Third, the work of the Holy Spirit is not confined to the ecstatic or unusual but is also *prevalent in the mundane*. It is through the commonplace activities of everyday life that the great spiritual gifts of faith, hope, and love are most formative and operative. In our being honest, courteous, kind, helpful, caring, reliable, trustful, and the like, the Spirit is at work in making us faithful, hopeful, and loving people. This is not to be confused with sentimental or calculative behavior, but the mundane ways that people relate to families, friends, and strangers in a civil manner. There is nothing more mundane than economic exchange. As I have argued repeatedly, marketplace exchange is the requisite activity that sustains civil society and the lives of the people who constitute it. Are we to believe that the same life-giving Spirit is somehow entirely absent from such a ubiquitous human activity? This does not suggest that globalization is a work of the Spirit, but it does acknowledge that the Spirit is or can be at work in global markets.

If, however, a process of creative destruction drives global markets, how can I as a Christian assert that the Holy Spirit is at work? Nowhere in Scripture or doctrine is the Spirit portrayed as a destroyer. True, but the work of the Spirit in bringing in the new nonetheless entails some

55. Acts 2:1–12.
56. John 3:5–8.
57. See, e.g., 2 Cor. 5:17 and Rev. 21:5.

destruction of the old. If the Spirit is at work in liberating captives, freeing the enslaved, enabling the disenfranchised, ending oppression, and the like, then the destruction of culpable regimes and outmoded institutions is necessary: necessary, because old wineskins cannot contain new wine.[58] Creative destruction is not the work of the Holy Spirit, but can we not say that the destructive and creative forces generated by global markets afford new opportunities for the Spirit to be at work?

Given the Spirit's freedom to accomplish its work in new and unforeseen ways, it would be foolish to predict what these opportunities might be in any detail. Some general and suggestive inklings, however, might be hazarded in a provisional manner, and I conclude this chapter by exploring one possible opportunity. Dynamic global markets and their concomitant market-states offer the opportunity to craft new forms of human association that transcend previous geographical, national, political, and cultural constraints. Advances in transportation, communication, and information technologies are rendering geographical proximity increasingly extraneous in pursuing commerce and economic exchange. These exchanges in turn promote a broader range of interaction and association among individuals of diverse nationalities, cultures, and ethnicities who share the pursuit of improving their material well-being by using their respective comparative advantages of competitive global markets. New forms of political governance are also required in response to these emerging patterns of association. And again to reiterate, this opportunity to explore new forms of human association is not without its risks, some of which I address in part 2.

The church, which is also a work of the Holy Spirit (despite regrettable appearances to the contrary on occasion), intimates what this opportunity might entail. The church is not a territorial religion. The church exists wherever two or three are gathered in Christ's name.[59] There are admittedly locales dedicated for worship, but ultimately anyplace will do to gather the church. Christianity is a global religion. The church's members are drawn from every race and nation. At its best, the church has incorporated distinct cultural traditions in proclaiming and practicing its common faith, and this diversity is further augmented by the variety of spiritual gifts given to its members. Within the church racial, class, and sexual identities and stereotypes that create divisions and prejudice are displaced by a shared faith—in Christ there is "neither

58. See Matt. 9:17 and Luke 5:37–39.
59. See Matt. 18:20.

Jew nor Greek, slave nor free, male nor female."[60] In short, the church provides a suggestive model for how pilgrims might live in a world in which they are not entirely at home.

Admittedly the ideal church I described in the preceding paragraph does not and has never existed. There is substantial historical and socio-logical evidence to demonstrate its many failures to be a pilgrim church. Nevertheless, the church is a treasure in an earthen vessel, and the ideal it contains is worth pondering and striving after. Globalization may offer an opportunity to the church to learn something new about living a pilgrim life, and this learning in turn might prove suggestive to others navigating the promising and perilous terrain of dynamic global markets. In this respect, the church as an association based on communication (koinonia) rather than exchange may also indicate ways for reorienting markets toward enabling the flourishing of communities and associations as opposed to isolated individuals pursuing an endless cycle of production and consumption. But this is to anticipate chapter 7, and I must first make the case why creating greater affluence is, at present, the preferable way for ameliorating poverty on a global scale.

60. Gal. 3:28 NIV.

Chapter Four

The Good of Affluence

Affluence is a good that should be pursued. For a book that is pur-portedly about economic globalization and *Christian* ethics, this may appear to be an incongruent assertion. As noted in chapter 1, the Bible contains some harsh condemnations of wealth that are frequently reiterated by subsequent generations of moral theologians up to the present day. But as was also noted, these denunciations were met with countervailing biblical, moral, and theological arguments. In short, the economic contexts for creating wealth have changed over time requiring a more nuanced assessment of how prosperity is created and used. Particularly in light of contemporary globalization, the growing affluence of individuals and societies around the world may offer a promising opportunity to address the problem of poverty in an efficacious *and* Christian manner.

In this chapter I describe what affluence is and what it is not. I subse-quently argue why affluence is a good and why it is good to be affluent. In making this argument I offer a number of pragmatic reasons, and, more important, a number of theological and moral reasons why affluence is a good that should be pursued. The reader should keep in mind that this chapter is also written to provide a platform for addressing the scourge of poverty that is best combated through the creation of greater affluence. I address this topic in the following chapter.

What Affluence Is and Is Not

Affluence designates a surplus over what is required in satisfying basic needs and wants; it implies an abundant flow, supply, or profusion. In this respect, some individuals or communities have an abundance of talent, goodwill, tolerance, or kindness. To be affluent also confers more discretion in how a surplus is used or applied. If, for example, I have an abundance of spare time I have greater freedom in how I spend it. Affluence is also relative and contextual. In a variety of ways I am more and less affluent in comparison to other people, and that status shifts in differing contexts. To return to the example of free time, as an academic I have greater discretion in how I allot my time in comparison to a surgeon but less so than a retiree.

Although affluence has these broader connotations, I am restricting the following discussion to an abundance or profusion of money, property, and capital since this book is about *economic* globalization. Affluence, then, refers to surplus money, property, and capital over what is required in satisfying basic material needs and wants. Having a surfeit of capital and financial resources both sustains *and* enriches the lives of individuals and communities. If I do not need to expend all my money on providing shelter, sustenance, health care, and clothing, I have the discretion to use what is leftover in ways I judge will benefit me or others. I can buy a book, attend a concert, invest, or make a charitable contribution out of my abundance. Such economic affluence is again relative and contextual. I assume I am more affluent than some academics and less so than others, and I can enjoy greater affluence by living in Hampton rather than in Evanston given their respective costs of living.

Although "affluence" and "wealth" are often used synonymously, this is not necessarily the case, at least in ways that I am using the term. Rather, I am referring to a social setting in which having surplus economic resources at one's disposal is regarded as a norm, or an achievable goal, whereas wealth refers to an order of magnitude of surplus resources that few attain. Affluence and wealth, then, are related but not identical—the rich are affluent, but the affluent are not necessarily rich. Globalization creates a new social context for assessing the moral status of affluence. When surplus economic resources become a given or attainable norm, a wholesale condemnation of the resulting affluence is effectively made extraneous unless one is prepared to argue that widespread involuntary poverty is an inherently superior way of life. Judging by the way that many critics of globalization, and more broadly capitalism, actually live their lives, poverty is not really an option that is pursued with much enthusiasm. This is why simply parroting prominent moral and theological teachings condemning wealth seems quaintly out of touch with contemporary economic circumstances. The bulk of this teaching was formulated in contexts in which poverty was the given norm that very few escaped, and widespread affluence was simply unattainable. Increasingly the challenge for Christian moral theology is how should economic exchange be ordered in a world in which affluence, rather that poverty, is becoming ascendant?[1]

Before examining some of the particular moral challenges posed by this shift in social context, a bit more needs to be said about what affluence is. Perhaps the best way to proceed is to briefly indicate what it is not or how it should not be construed.

Affluence is not a virtue, but neither is it a vice. Although affluence is a good, it can be pursued in either virtuous or vicious ways. Affluence may be attained or enjoyed in prudent, temperate, just, and honest ways, and it may also be attained and used in foolish, inordinate, unjust, and deceitful ways. An affluent person is neither inherently a saint nor a scoundrel. But as was noted in chapter 2, economic exchange, and its resulting affluence, is predicated on trust that is best promoted through the practice of key personal and civic virtues. Consequently, although affluence is not a virtue in its own right, its properly ordered pursuit and enjoyment may help promote a virtuous life.[2]

Affluence is not necessarily due to desert. Admittedly affluence may be a reward for hard work, thrift, and initiative, and individuals have a right to enjoy the fruits of their labor. A person, however, may become affluent, even wealthy, through good luck such as winning a lottery or being the beneficiary of a bequest. The point is that affluence can be attained in a variety of ways, and the means do not always dictate the ways that the ensuing abundance is used. For example, after decades of frugal self-denial an individual may choose to spend his nest egg in a self-indulgent and frivolous manner, whereas the lucky gambler may use her winnings in a prudent or philanthropic way.

Affluence is not a reward for moral conduct. In respect to economic exchange, honesty is certainly the best policy. Any resulting affluence, however, is not a direct consequence of honest behavior. Rather, honesty, as well as the other virtues, may indirectly support the attainment and proper enjoyment that affluence brings. No one is or should be paid for telling the truth or performing any of the virtues, for doing so would have

---

1. See John R. Schneider, *The Good of Affluence: Seeking God in a Culture of Wealth* (Grand Rapids, MI, and Cambridge, UK: Eerdmans, 2002), ch. 1.

2. For accessible and insightful accounts of the virtues, see Josef Pieper, *The Four Cardinal Virtues* (Notre Dame, IN: University of Notre Dame Press, 1966), and Gilbert C. Meilaender, *The Theory and Practice of Virtue* (Notre Dame, IN: University of Notre Dame Press, 1984); see also Rebecca Konyndyk DeYoung, *Glittering Vices: A New Look at the Seven Deadly Sins and Their Remedies* (Grand Rapids, MI: Brazos, 2009).

a corrupting influence on the practice of the virtues and the resulting formation of character. Should people only tell the truth if they are paid? On certain occasions, taking a moral stand may lead to impoverishment rather than affluence. Affluence, then, does not automatically bestow moral superiority, and poverty does not necessarily confer moral defect. Despite the strength of moral conviction and conduct, some people can never escape poverty due to social and political circumstances preventing them from doing so. Conversely, neither does poverty entail a morally superior status nor should it be presumed that the affluent are the beneficiaries of ill-gotten gain. The relationship between the affluent and impoverished is not in all instances one of victims and oppressors.

Affluence is not a reward to the spiritually deserving. Contrary to proponents of the so-called prosperity gospel, faithful followers of Jesus Christ are not, to use a crude analogy, guaranteed a lucrative payout or dividend. Discipleship is not akin to an investment in which one is entitled to a return on spiritual capital. God may indeed bestow material blessings on some individuals, but such bestowal is entrusted to the care of recipients entailing certain rigorous expectations regarding its faithful stewardship.[3] Moreover, faithfully following Christ may at times require suffering and involuntary impoverishment, or God may call some into vocations requiring voluntary poverty. The way of Jesus Christ is certainly one of blessing and beatitude, but it is also the way of the cross. Consequently, affluence is a good, but it is a penultimate and not an ultimate good.

Affluence is not a fig leaf for avarice. To assert that affluence is a good that should be pursued is not a rhetorical sleight of hand to justify an extreme desire to possess an inordinate amount of money, property, or possessions. To the contrary, affluence serves as a check against avarice, for affluence is not an end itself but a proximate good that enables the pursuit of other goods. One does not (or should not) aspire to become affluent for its own sake. Rather, affluence is sought to better enable the meeting of material needs and wants, and expending, investing, or donating excess financial resources or capital helps others do the same. Market-based exchange is the most efficient method for pursuing, distributing, and increasing aggregate affluence among groups of people of varying scale, and people who are restricted or prevented from participating in markets are disadvantaged in pursuing the proximate good of affluence. This is why, as argued in the following chapter, enabling widespread participation in expanding global markets is needed to ameliorate poverty on

3. See, e.g., Matt. 25:14–30.

a global scale. Granted, the avaricious may take advantage of these new and expanding global markets, but that does not invalidate the necessity of enabling a more extensive pursuit of affluence in order to combat poverty.

Now that I have briefly indicated what affluence is not, some further elaboration may be added to what affluence is. Affluence designates a surplus of money, capital, and property beyond what is required in satisfying material needs and wants. There is a difference between a need and a want. Traditionally, the dividing line has been drawn to designate basic material goods that are required to sustain life at minimal levels over time, such as the necessities of shelter, sustenance, and health care.[4] Wants are desires that can be satisfied through goods and services beyond or in addition to the satisfaction of basic necessities that individuals believe will improve or enhance the quality of their lives. I need a house, for example, but I want a mansion. Again traditionally, the satisfaction of meeting basic necessities over subjective wants has been given moral priority, and rightfully so. Particularly in the largely zero-sum economies of antiquity and medieval Europe that were based on severe scarcity, consuming or hoarding more than what one needed was to deprive others from obtaining material goods that were needed to sustain their lives at minimal levels. The harsh biblical, theological, and moral denunciations of property, wealth, and consumption are explicable within these economic contexts, for the relatively few were affluent at the direct expense of the poor.

There is, however, no fixed or universal list of needs and wants. The dividing line is imprecise because it varies in accordance to specific contexts and functions, and change over time. The needs and wants of particular locales are not identical. The need for shelter on a tropical island differs from that of a locale on a far northern latitude, and people on the island may want air conditioning while people in the far north may want centralized heating. Function also helps to determine what is needed and what is wanted. Scholars need different tools to accomplish their work as opposed to physicians. I do not need a stethoscope, and I presume that my doctor would have little, if any, use for my library. Moreover, the standards used to determine what constitutes the satisfaction of basic needs or necessities change, often radically, over time. What was regarded as minimally acceptable housing in early seventeenth-century London is presumably different in the twenty-first century. And unlike my seventeenth-century counterparts I need a computer, as well as my

---

4. Nonmaterial necessities such as rest and affection could be added to this list.

library, to accomplish my work, and my doctor needs more sophisticated diagnostic instruments in addition to his stethoscope.[5]

Although there is a difference between wants and needs, however they may vary and change over time, how both are satisfied in a late modern global economy differs markedly from their ancient and medieval predecessors. In brief, affluence is no longer the result of zero-sum acquisition. Excess economic resources are not attained, consumed, and invested by seizing scarce property at the expense of others. Rather, in the words of John Schneider, the "truth is that in modern market economies the main way that people acquire wealth is not by taking it away from someone else, but by taking part in its *creation*."[6] The biblical, theological, and moral denunciations of property, wealth, and consumption surveyed in chapter 1, then, need to be reevaluated in light of a different economic context: namely, that of new and emerging global markets. It is satisfying wants through the expenditure and investment of excess economic resources that drives the commerce, the production and consumption of goods and services, which enlarges the scope of those creating capital and wealth. The pursuit of affluence enables others, especially the poor, to better meet their basic material needs, and in turn their wants, thereby generating greater aggregate affluence. To uncritically and simplistically adopt the dictates of refraining from commerce, consumption, and investment, because the pursuit of affluence is immoral or evil is to consign the poor to what is effectively their lot in life.

But this is to anticipate the principal arguments in the next chapter. It may suffice at this juncture to claim that the pursuit of affluence within new and expanding global markets promotes a broader range of economic exchange that generates greater commerce, production, consumption, and employment that are the most effective means of combating poverty. Or in other words, if one is serious about ameliorating poverty around the world, then there is a presumptive moral imperative to create affluent societies given the opportunities, privileges, and comforts they afford. And, as I argue throughout the remaining chapters, a globalized economy also has attendant responsibilities, particularly for the affluent, that cannot be ignored. Before moving on, however, I must first pause to describe why affluence is good.

---

5. The stethoscope was not actually invented until the nineteenth century. Prior to that the physician placed his ear on a patient (auscultation) to listen for telltale sounds.

6. Schneider, *The Good of Affluence*, 32 (emphasis original).

Why Affluence Is Good, and Why It Is Good to Be Affluent

In this section I undertake two tasks. The first is to describe why affluence is a good. My reasons may be characterized as largely pragmatic, in that the pursuit of affluence is a practical means of enabling a wide range of people to pursue a greater number of mutually beneficial goods. The second task is to make a normative case for why it is good to be affluent, particularly for Christians. My principal thesis is that humans may appropriately use and enjoy the material goods of God's creation, and that a properly ordered pursuit of affluence enables this use and enjoyment so that its pursuit is not incompatible with being a disciple of Jesus Christ. This is the more difficult task given the highly critical assessment of affluence that has traditionally dominated Christian theological and moral thought. In making my case I draw from the counter biblical, theological, and moral themes surveyed in chapter 1, and in doing so also initiate a reassessment of this negative evaluation of affluence in light of the contemporary global economy.

There are many reasons why affluence is a good that should be pursued, but I will concentrate on six. These reasons are presented in an admittedly simple, unproblematic, and ideal manner, but they serve as a basis for more complex arguments that are developed throughout the remaining chapters.

First, affluence is good because *abundance is generally better than scarcity*. Having insufficient material and economic resources to meet such basic needs as shelter, sustenance, and health care is the most apparent indication of involuntary poverty. One's life is dire if none of these basic needs can be met, and only slightly less miserable if one must choose among either having a roof over one's head, eating, or treating an ailment. A person may also be anxious if she is utterly and constantly dependent on the benevolence of others in providing the resources for meeting her most basic needs. Such misery and anxiety is greatly relieved when one has sufficient resources to meet these needs, and further improved if there are excess resources enabling one to obtain a more comfortable house, eat more nutritious meals, and treat an ailment that is bothersome but not life threatening. It is even better if a person has more abundant resources to satisfy certain wants that he believes will enrich the quality of his life. The pursuit of affluence creates an abundance of material and economic resources that help individuals and communities overcome the debilitating and impoverishing constraints of scarcity.

Second, affluence is good because it *promotes responsibility*. Work is the most prominent way for obtaining the requisite economic resources to satisfy a person's material needs and wants. Such work may entail physical labor—for example, building a hut for oneself—but more routinely it involves a job in which one is paid a wage or salary. When properly ordered, employment may promote such values as diligence, honesty, reliability, attention to detail, teamwork, and learning and successfully performing new skills—qualities, it should be noted, that benefit employees, employers, and customers. Such behavior is often rewarded with increased wages or salaries. As workers gain more discretionary income, they may also choose to further improve their lives by expending or investing their excess money in prudent rather than reckless ways. In this respect, the prospect of greater affluence afforded by good work that is amply rewarded may encourage greater responsibility in both the workplace and household.

Third, affluence is good because it *provides a more secure basis from which individuals may pursue other goods.* This security was adumbrated in the first reason on how affluence enables the meeting of wants in addition to needs. If individuals spend almost all their waking hours meeting their basic needs, the goods they may pursue are highly restricted since they lack sufficient abundance to satisfy more expansive wants. Affluence affords greater opportunities to enjoy such goods as literature, art, music, leisure, participate in volunteer activities, or simply spend more time with friends and family. In this respect, affluence is good because it can enrich the lives of individuals, families, communities, and societies beyond levels of mere subsistence.

Fourth, affluence is good because it *enables generosity*. It is easier to be generous when one has abundant rather than scarce economic resources. Forsaking shelter, sustenance, or health care in order to give a gift or make a donation, for instance, is more a sacrificial than generous act. Affluent societies simply produce greater amounts of charitable contributions and gifts to various organizations and worthy causes. Moreover, such giving is not an exchange or investment. Benefactors transfer money, property, or other forms of capital to another person or organization without the expectation of a reciprocal act. Donors may enjoy being publicly recognized or honored for their largesse, but they do not receive a financial or monetary return on their donated capital. Such benefaction presumably supports worthwhile activities that benefit civil society, so that generosity is a good that is fostered by greater or more widespread affluence. In this respect, the affluence generated by new and expanding global markets has the potential to increase the scope and amount of generous benefaction.[7]

Fifth, affluence is a good because its *pursuit is predicated on and promotes trust*. As discussed in chapter 2, economic exchange is largely based on trust. In countless daily exchanges it is routinely taken for granted by the parties in an exchange that they will not be cheated or defrauded. And it is exchange, and thereby trust, that makes possible the pursuit of affluence on a wide basis. If there were no presumed trust among strangers, then exchange would be confined to tight niches of dependable confidants. But trust is not synonymous with naivety. Certain safeguards, often in the form of contracts or other legally binding agreements, are established to ensure compliance by the parties of an exchange, especially in regard to large transactions, banking, and international trade; trust is not negated by verification. To assert something to the effect that contracts are for people who do not trust each other goes too far. If there is no modicum of presumptive trust that the parties to an exchange are at least motivated by their respective self-interests in keeping promises, then why would either "sign" the contract in the first place? Trust, however, exerts its greatest influence within communities or societies whose members share common values and familiar practices, and there is much variability across cultures to whom trust is extended and how it shapes practices of economic exchange.[8] This admittedly poses a daunting challenge: namely, one of formulating procedures that instill trust across a range of differing cultures in ways that do not unduly disadvantage certain participants in competitive global markets. Presumably a world characterized by basic trust, however minimal, is preferable to one of wide-ranging mistrust, and globalization as a means for creating greater and more expansive affluence has the potential to assist this effort.

Sixth, affluence is a good because it helps to *sustain and strengthen civil society*. Again, as discussed in chapter 2, competition within new and expanding global markets generates greater aggregate affluence among a wider range of people over time. As was also noted, this competition, counterintuitively, strengthens the cooperative bonds of civil society.

---

7. It may appear that this paragraph contradicts Jesus' teaching on the poor widow placing two small copper coins into the temple treasure chest in which he commends her for giving all that she has in contrast to the rich who only gave a portion of their wealth (Mark 12:41–43). What Jesus is praising, however, is her sacrifice that he finds more commendable in this instance than the generous offerings of the wealthy that incur no hardship. But there is no direct condemnation of the wealthy for not giving all that they have.

8. See Francis Fukuyama, *Trust: The Social Virtues and the Creation of Prosperity* (New York and London: Free Press, 1995).

Affluent societies are afforded more opportunities to form voluntary private and public associations that promote the common good, or at least certain pervasively shared goods. It is telling in this regard that the most stable societies are affluent, whereas the most destabilized societies are universally impoverished, and there is a strong correlation between levels of respective participation in global markets. In short, the more a nation competes in global markets the more affluent it tends to become, and the less a nation competes in global markets the less affluent or even more impoverished it tends to become; and the vitality of their respective civil societies prosper or suffer accordingly.

It may be objected that the preceding reasons are insufficient or unconvincing for making a case that affluence is a good that should be pursued. At best, all I have demonstrated is that affluence may bestow some residual benefits both for oneself and others. Moreover, a critic might contend that the bestowal of these benefits, particularly on a global scale, is far more complex and problematic than I portray, and this criticism is again correct. But I have already admitted on a number of occasions in previous chapters that globalization is not without its many problems, so I beg my critic to grant, for the sake of argument, that the benefits of affluence can be pursued, attained, and enjoyed on a global scale. Should my critic grant my request, however, she will be quick to remind me that I have still not made a normative case for *why* affluence is a good and why it is good to be affluent, especially for Christians given the seemingly clear biblical, theological, and moral teachings against commerce, riches, and wealth. Her admonition leads me to my second task of making such a case. What follows is neither a systematic nor comprehensive account of why, particularly for Christians, affluence is a good and why it is good to be affluent, but a few suggestive biblical, theological, and moral themes that are further developed throughout the remainder of the book.

A properly ordered pursuit, use, and enjoyment of affluence help Christians to take delight in the material abundance of God's good creation. In the opening chapter of Genesis, God declares on six occasions that what God has created is "good," and adds a resounding "very good" at the end for good measure. Moreover, God declares that the created world is a good place for humans to live, work, and flourish. The world God created is material and physical, and the human creatures inhabiting the world are also physically embodied. Consequently, the material well-being of humans is not an extraneous consideration but indispensable to what it means to be a creature created, we are told, in the image and likeness of God.[9]

9. Gen. 1:27.

Schneider insists that the "goodness of the creation . . . is unthinkable apart from its materiality," because it is as "essential" to being a good creation "as the physical body is to a fully human identity."[10] The proper response to this materiality is *delight*; taking pleasure in and enjoying the superfluity of creation that not only sustains the physical well-being of humans but also enables their flourishing. The opening chapter of Genesis "makes clear that not all excess and extravagance is wantonness," and taking delight in creation's lavish materiality is an "expression of God's glory, of human dignity, and of the goodness of life in this world." More baldly, Schneider asserts that it is the "condition of affluence alone that makes full delight possible."[11]

In taking delight, creation and its physical abundance is received as a *blessing*. Humans are fortunate that God has placed them in a world well suited to satisfying their material needs and wants. The first creation story recorded in Genesis may be read as an extended benediction. It is important to note, however, that God's blessing is most prominently pronounced on the seventh day, the day God rests.[12] The superfluity of creation both enables and requires a Sabbath, and with it *leisure*.[13] Leisure is not, as late moderns often assume, spare time to kill or do with as one chooses. Rather, as Josef Pieper maintains, "leisure is a receptive attitude of mind, a contemplative attitude, and it is not only the occasion but also the capacity for steeping oneself in the whole of creation."[14] To leisurely engage the whole of creation is to also take delight in its material abundance. Consequently, affluence may be regarded as a means enabling one to take delight in the blessing of abundance that makes leisure possible, as well as its attendant capacity to steep oneself in the whole of creation. If one's time and energy is used exclusively or predominantly in meeting basic material needs, there is little or no time for leisure.

Yet if leisure is a requisite condition for taking delight in the material abundance of creation, why is this blessing frequently unavailable or withheld? Or in more stark terms, why throughout human history have the vast majority of people been subjected to abject poverty, experiencing

10. Schneider, *The Good of Affluence*, 57.

11. Ibid., 61.

12. See Genesis 2:2–3.

13. For a more detailed account of how Sabbath and leisure are related, see Brent Waters, *Christian Moral Theology in the Emerging Technoculture: From Posthuman Back to Human* (Farnham, UK, and Burlington, VT: Ashgate. 2014), pt. 3.

14. Josef Pieper, *Leisure: The Basis of Culture; Including "The Philosophical Act"* (San Francisco, CA: Ignatius Press, 2009), 46–47.

creation as a place of scarcity and unremitting toil rather than abundance and leisure? This does not appear to be a very good creation. It is important to emphasize, however, that in contrast to other ancient creation stories, Genesis does not explain the origin of human misery as being the will of the creator, and therefore endemic to creation. Rather, the "burdensomeness of life" is a consequence of the fall in which the ordering of human life in a good creation becomes deeply distorted.[15] The goods of creation are now desired badly, leading to sinful and unjust forms of moral, social, and political ordering. Affluence, then, may serve as a faint recollection of the material abundance of creation that the Genesis story conveys in its imagery of the garden of Eden. To be clear, this does not mean that globalization is *the* way of restoring the old Eden or creating a new one, a hopelessly utopian goal that Christians must resist.[16] But it does provide a theological and moral basis for claiming that an economic system promoting a widespread pursuit of affluence is more in tune with the created order disclosed in Genesis than alternative systems that, either wittingly or unwittingly, prevent or disable its pursuit.

A properly ordered pursuit, use, and enjoyment of affluence assist faithful stewardship. God created a good creation, but this does not mean that it has no need for care or tending. Eden is a garden, not a wilderness. And God created and chose humans to be its gardeners, or in more eloquent biblical language, God calls, commands, and blesses them to be its stewards, to rule over and subdue the earth.[17] The material abundance of the world is in its potential, requiring further development if humans are to flourish in accordance to God's intentions. This need to produce is reinforced in Jesus' parable of the talents.[18] A man entrusts one, two, and five talents of money,[19] respectively, to three servants or stewards. Over time those entrusted with the greater amounts double their value, while the one with the least amount adds no value whatsoever. When the master takes an accounting, the servants doubling the value of their talents are commended while the one who did nothing is condemned. Material abundance results from productivity, and is a laudable goal as portrayed in Jesus' teaching. This parable, as well as the imagery of the garden of Eden, conveys the necessity of work. The faithful servants are

15. See Schneider, *The Good of Affluence*, 45–49.
16. See Oliver O'Donovan, *Resurrection and Moral Order: An Outline for Evangelical Ethics* (Grand Rapids, MI: Eerdmans, 1986), esp. ch. 2.
17. See Gen. 1:28.
18. Matt. 25:14–30.
19. At the time of this writing, a talent is estimated to be worth between $150,000 and $360,000 (US).

expected to be industrious with the financial resources entrusted to their care, and Adam and Eve must undertake certain chores to ensure Eden's lavish fecundity. More expansively, this stewardship suggests that humans must work to shape the world into a more hospitable habitat. A pristine earth could only sustain relatively few people at mere subsistence levels. Without exercising their dominion and stewardship, creation would be devoid of abundance, delight, and leisure.

Such dominion, however, is not absolute but limited, for it is exercised under the sovereignty of God. Humans are not authorized by God to do with creation whatever they will. Stewardship entails certain expectations, duties, and obligations. Chief among them is the task of bringing forth the world's potential material abundance in ways that create sufficient affluence to enjoy a Sabbath rest; the leisure to take delight in the blessing of creation's abundance. With the fall, however, the pursuit of this requisite affluence is disfigured. On the one hand, many people are prevented from attaining sufficient affluence to enjoy creation's material abundance, while on the other hand, a few people accumulate, in comparison, exorbitant material wealth. The problem is especially acute in zero-sum economies that were predominate until roughly the nineteenth century. The ancients in particular presumed that a life of leisure—whether expended in contemplation, self-indulgent luxury, or civic benefaction—was (and should be) restricted to a small cadre of privileged families and individuals. Philosophers, aristocrats, and patrons could only pursue their lives by keeping the vast majority of laborers impoverished or enslaved. Consequently, the biblical, theological, and moral denunciations of wealth that have dominated Christian social and political thought were on target given the prevailing economic context.

But the contemporary economic context has changed. Affluence is now created or produced rather than seized and withheld from others. The moral and political challenge is not one of redistributing wealth, but creating opportunities for everyone to pursue the good of affluence. In this respect, globalization, at least ideally, helps to create a greater range of opportunities for more people to pursue affluence. The emergence of affluent societies, however, creates its own set of moral concerns. The pursuit of affluence, for example, can be corrupted into an avaricious quest for wealth; a relentless cycle of production and consumption becomes an end in its own right. But it is a quest that can never be satisfied, for there is never enough things to be produced and consumed, and never a sufficient amount of wealth to be accumulated. Consequently, Sabbath is also effectively lost, for there is not time for the leisure that is required to properly enjoy the blessing of creation's material abundance.

Again, to be clear, I am not arguing that globalization alone can end poverty, or that the emergence of affluent societies is merely exchanging one set of temptations for another. More modestly, I am suggesting that the emergence of new and expanding global markets affords opportunities, as well as challenges, for faithfully exercising the stewardship of creation in ways that more people can properly enjoy its material abundance.

A properly ordered pursuit, use, and enjoyment of affluence exhibit and express the love of neighbor. Following Karl Barth, we encounter and are in fellowship with a wide variety of neighbors.[20] There are neighbors with whom we are intimate, and those who are strangers; neighbors who are friends, and those who are enemies; neighbors who are fellow citizens, and those who are not; some are near and others are distant. Moreover, we interact and depend on neighbors in countless ways. Daily life, in short, is inconceivable in the absence of neighbors.

Christians are commanded to love God and their neighbors.[21] The two commands are inseparable—we cannot love God and hate our neighbors or love our neighbors and hate God. But who is a neighbor? In answering this question, Jesus tells the parable of the Good Samaritan.[22] The point of this familiar story is that the Samaritan is a neighbor to the man robbed and beaten by thieves. From this parable we may draw the salient principle that a love of neighbor is exhibited in helping or having mercy for those who are in dire need. To some extent, however, the parable does not answer the question, at least not entirely, for it seemingly restricts neighbor love to a unidirectional relationship between benefactor and beneficiary. The parable provides excellent guidance in respect to charity: namely, that those in dire need must be helped without expecting any reciprocity. But how is the love of neighbor exhibited in the array of relationships mentioned above, many of which are characterized by reciprocity or exchange? Surely the parable is not implying that these other relationships among neighbors are devoid of love. Consequently, more needs to be said about what neighbor love entails beyond unreciprocated benefaction.

Neighbor love is not a trite expression of superficial cheerfulness—we do not love our neighbors by hugging everyone we meet and wishing them a nice day. Neither is it mere courtesy, though this is preferable to

---

20. See Karl Barth, *Church Dogmatics* (Edinburgh: T. and T. Clark, 1961), III/4, §54.
21. See Luke 10:25–27; see also Mark 12:28–34 and Matt. 22:34–40.
22. Luke 10:25–37.

sullenness, enmity, or casual indifference. Moreover, there is no universal or generic expression of neighbor love given the wide variety of neighbors that are encountered or interacted with on a daily basis. The love of intimates differs from that of strangers; we love our friends differently than our enemies. Given these differences, some discernment is required to determine what kind of neighbor is being encountered, and what type of action or response this encounter entails.

The starting point of this discernment is to be attentive to the neighbor. Following Simone Weil, to attend to neighbors is to be attentive to their good or well-being.[23] Discerning the good of the other requires a temporary suspension of self-orientation, for the goal is to understand the particular needs, wants, and desires of the neighbor.[24] Building on Weil, Iris Murdoch insists that attentiveness is a "just and loving" gaze that seeks to know rather than manipulate or control the other, an act she depicts as "obedience."[25] To treat the neighbor one encounters morally is to respond to her good, and more broadly to the good of the world that both inhabit and share. The just and loving gaze, however, does not generate a uniform moral response in every instance, for the goods of the neighbors we encounter vary, and are to a great extent delineated by the relationship in question. The moral responses to the good of intimates, friends, and enemies, for instance, diverge, perhaps evoking such moral responses, respectively, as forgiveness, forbearance, and mercy.

Most of the neighbors we encounter on a daily basis are near and distant strangers. The vast majority of these encounters are brief, cursory, and anonymous, often occurring through exchanges and transactions. Consequently, the just and loving gaze is largely unfocused, and our attentiveness is fleeting. Yet neighbor love is not absent in encountering near and distant neighbors, and we may still attend to their needs, wants, and desires, albeit in chiefly unknown, indirect, and derived ways. In this respect, affluence may help us to express a love for unknown and anonymous neighbors.

As a means for expressing neighbor love, affluence facilitates a twofold approach. First is the approach of charity or benefaction. As the parable of the Good Samaritan makes clear, when people are in dire need

23. See Michael Ross, "Transcendence, Immanence, and Practical Deliberation in Simone Weil's Early and Middle Years," in E. Jane Doering and Eric O. Springsted, eds., *The Christian Platonism of Simone Weil* (Notre Dame, IN: University of Notre Dame Press, 2004), 45–48.

24. See Simone Weil, *Waiting for God* (New York: HarperCollins, 2001), 99–117.

25. See Iris Murdoch, *The Sovereignty of Good* (London and New York: Routledge, 2001), 34–40.

immediate assistance should be provided. Most often this assistance is provided through financial contributions or providing services, and as noted previously affluence can encourage generosity. Consequently, the beneficiaries usually remain unknown to the benefactors, but this does not diminish the importance of the act. There are admittedly individuals who devote themselves to caring for the homeless, hungry, sick, and indigent, and they attend to their needs with commendable urgency, but their efforts would be far less efficacious in the absence of generous financial support afforded by widespread affluence. It should also be stressed that the motivation for charity or benefaction is not something like pity, which can create a false sense of moral superiority in the benefactor, but the recognition that unmet dire needs prevent people from enjoying the blessing of creation's material abundance. And it is love that prompts (or should prompt) the removal of this barrier.

The second approach involves exchange and the pursuit of affluence. I produce and consume goods and services, which not only satisfy my needs and wants but also help me, hopefully, become affluent so that I may better enjoy the blessing of creation's material abundance. In participating in these market exchanges, I in turn assist largely unknown neighbors to meet their needs and wants, and, hopefully, become affluent so they may also enjoy the blessing of creation's material abundance. The reader might object that I am merely trying to justify my selfishness by masquerading it as neighbor love. No, but as the second great commandment makes clear, the love of neighbor is not unrelated to love of self.[26] This requires a proper balancing so that neither pole—the neighbor or the self—is loved inordinately. Consequently, my pursuit of affluence that also enables others to pursue affluence may be regarded as an act of neighbor love, albeit in an indirect or derived manner. This is not an attempt to baptize Adam Smith's self-interested bakers, butchers, and brewers, or to amend the second great commandment to read you shall love your neighbor as yourself, so go and endlessly produce and consume. Rather, a "properly formed pursuit of self-interest is generally good for everyone and everything concerned."[27] A mutually beneficial pursuit of affluence in and through competitive markets is not, at the very least, incompatible with Christian teaching on loving one's neighbors and may actually assist its enactment. This recognition is especially acute in light of emerging global markets in which the scope of anonymous

26. Take another look at Luke 10:27.
27. Schneider, *The Good of Affluence*, 36.

or unknown neighbors is expanding rapidly, and differentiating between near and distant neighbors grows more complex.

A properly ordered pursuit, use, and enjoyment of affluence help to differentiate between ultimate and penultimate goods. There is nothing superior to an ultimate good, and all other goods in comparison are of lesser value. For Christians, there is only one ultimate good, which is the triune God, and all other goods are thereby rendered penultimate.[28] This is not to disparage penultimate goods, for they are genuinely good. As noted above they include such things as delight, work, leisure, stewardship, love of neighbor, material abundance, and affluence. All these things are good, but not as good as God, and their pursuit, use, and enjoyment should serve to enrich our love and service of God.

Humans, however, often confuse or fail to recognize the difference between ultimate and penultimate goods. This should not be surprising, because as fallen creatures—or to use a currently unfashionable term, sinners—humans often fail to order or prioritize their desires and loves correctly. Following Augustine, we have a pronounced proclivity to desire good things badly. One may become consumed by the pursuit of a penultimate good, effectively transforming it into a false ultimate good, thereby disfiguring how one's life is lived. Or, again to use a currently unfashionable term, a consuming pursuit of a penultimate good becomes *idolatrous.* This temptation is present in pursuing the penultimate good of affluence. If one becomes consumed by a desire to produce and consume or acquire wealth and possessions, the pursuit of other penultimate goods, as well as the pursuit of the ultimate good of God, becomes distorted; one's life is out of joint. As Scripture teaches, being consumed by hoarding material possessions produces anxious fools who place their souls in peril.[29] To a large extent, this worry of an idolatrous or consuming pursuit of affluence underlies much of the biblical, theological, and moral teachings concerning riches or wealth, and the danger needs to be acknowledged. But pursuing any penultimate good involves moral and spiritual hazards, and risk alone should not preclude, much less forbid, its pursuit.

Poverty is no immunization against moral and spiritual risks. Expending nearly all of one's time and energy in barely meeting basic needs may preclude little if any consideration of ultimacy. Being involuntarily impoverished may, out of practical necessity or desperation, diminish or

28. See D. Stephen Long, *The Goodness of God: Theology, Church, and the Social Order* (Grand Rapids, MI: Brazos, 2001).
29. Luke 12:13–21.

effectively crush moral and spiritual sensibilities. As Scripture reminds us, we do not live by bread alone,[30] but those having sufficient bread to eat know, with greater certainty, that this is true. To be clear, I am *not* arguing that only the affluent can fully know God or live an abundant spiritual life, for there is ample evidence to the contrary. Rather, involuntary poverty does not incur any inherent moral virtue or superior spiritual penchant in comparison to affluence. To the contrary, a properly ordered pursuit, use, and enjoyment of affluence opens up a greater range of other penultimate goods that may be pursued, whereas involuntary impoverishment may greatly restrict the range of penultimate goods that might be undertaken. Moreover, as globalization will likely continue to engender greater prosperity for a growing number of people around the world, the moral and religious or spiritual context shifts from one of widespread poverty to that of affluence. In comparing the attendant spiritual, moral, social, and political issues in each instance, the shift should be welcomed.

To summarize, my theological and moral reasons for arguing why a properly ordered pursuit, use, and enjoyment of affluence is good, and why it is good to be affluent are that affluence enables people to take a leisurely delight in the blessing of creation's material abundance; that it demonstrates a faithful stewardship of creation; that it enacts a love of neighbor through both charity and exchange; and that it helps to differentiate penultimate from ultimate goods and order their respective pursuits. Each of these reasons are developed further throughout the remainder of the book. To this list should also be added that affluence is a prerequisite for ameliorating involuntary poverty, which is the topic of the next chapter.

---

30. See Luke 4:4; cf. Matt. 4:4.

Chapter Five

Poverty and Impoverishment

One principal reason why affluence is a good that should be pursued is that it offers the most promising strategy for ameliorating poverty on a global scale. In this chapter I argue why this is the case. The first section provides a brief overview of global poverty. In addition, I demonstrate how new and expanding global markets offer the most promising way over time of helping most people escape abject poverty, while also noting some of the more pressing social and political issues accompanying this strategy. Despite these issues, I contend that globalization is an effective practical means for enacting what Catholic social teaching describes as the preferential option for the poor.

In the following section I assert that Christian moral theology is not content with ensuring that everyone, or at least nearly everyone, achieves material subsistence, but that all, or nearly all, people should be permitted to pursue affluence, and more broadly the abundant life it affords. In making my case, I revisit the moral and theological reasons regarding why affluence is a good presented in the previous chapter, placing them in a more overtly global context. In turn, I briefly examine some of the implications and issues that are entailed in making this move from attaining subsistence to pursuing affluence. This chapter, then, also sets the stage for part 2, in which I examine both the opportunities and challenges presented by growing global affluence in respect to the abundant life, a life that is related to but greater than being materially affluent.

Global Poverty

Critics of globalization often fail to acknowledge how it has helped reduce abject poverty around the world. In 1990, 43 percent of people living in developing nations were below the "extreme poverty" line of subsisting on $1 a day. By 2010 the amount had dropped to 21 percent below the adjusted amount of $1.25. Or in other terms, the number of people living in abject poverty was reduced from 1.9 billion to 1.2 billion.[1] These reductions in the poorest regions of world coincided roughly with rapidly expanding global markets, and the rate of decline was often proportional to the extent in which nations adopted liberalized trading and foreign investment policies.

Proponents of globalization, however, often fail to acknowledge that despite this progress, extreme poverty is still pervasive in developing regions. Markets alone cannot be counted on to further reduce dire poverty at this rate, given a host of intractable social and political conditions.[2] Aggregate economic growth does not automatically diminish poverty, for other considerations, such as income distribution, also play important roles. Moreover, simply raising individuals above the global threshold of $1.25 is no panacea. As *The Economist*—the weekly newsletter of globalization—admits, "$1.26 a day is still a tiny amount."[3]

Nonetheless, the world is less materially impoverished today than it was at the end of the twentieth century, an accomplishment that should not be disparaged. This same period also witnessed the rise of a global middle class, those earning between $2 and $40 a day. Over the last twenty-five years, this class has grown to slightly under three billion people, and they are among the greatest beneficiaries of new and expanding global markets. Their status, however, is precarious. Although they have passed a subsistence threshold, they have little discretionary income, property, and savings, and are "often still struggling for the financial security that is a middle class hallmark."[4] The same dynamic global markets that enabled their relative affluence could also drive them back into poverty.

Poverty or impoverishment is a relative, particular, and subjective condition, especially on a global scale. Using raw income or assets as a baseline is to some extent misleading, because such figures often do not include factors such as regional variations in cost of living and availability of social safety nets. For example, an annual household income of $20,000 in an affluent country would be below the poverty line, often triggering both governmental and charitable assistance, whereas in most

1. See "Poverty: Not Always with Us," *The Economist*, June 1, 2013.
2. See Gideon Rachman, "Growth and Globalization Cannot Cure All the World's Ills," *Financial Times*, January 27, 2014.
3. "Poverty: Not Always with Us."
4. See Shawn Donnan, Ben Bland, and John Burn-Murdoch, "Fragile Middle: 2.8bn People on the Brink," *Financial Times*, April 13, 2014.

developing regions $20,000 would constitute affluence. The symptoms and causes of poverty are contextually particular, and vary across locales. Impoverished conditions in urban and rural settings are not identical, and circumstances in the city of Linxia Hui and the rural county Longling in China differ from those of Pine Bluff and Ziebach counties in the United States. Personal or subjective responses to available income or assets are not uniform. One household with an annual income of $20,000 may regard itself as comfortable given its particular needs and wants, while another household in the same locale regards itself as being poor with its annual income of $25,000. Moreover, most poor people in affluent societies do not suffer malnutrition or such debilitating illnesses as malaria and vitamin A deficiencies, and they live in homes with plumbing, electricity, household appliances, telephones, and televisions—luxuries the vast majority of the extremely poor in developing regions do not enjoy.

To capture a glimpse of these differences, visit the website "The Least of These."[5] On its home page you will find a "World Wealth Calculator." I entered my annual household income (two persons) and discovered, much to my surprise, that we are among the wealthiest 0.1 percent of people in the world, yet my wife and I have never thought of ourselves as being rich. I also entered the amount of $15,730, which at the time of this writing is the official Department of Health and Human Services poverty line for a two-person household in the United States.[6] I assume such households would be shocked to learn that they are among the wealthiest 14.1 percent of people on a worldwide basis.

The principal value of this exercise is that it reveals the lack of uniformity in addressing poverty on a global scale. What is meager income in one locale is prodigious in another. The exercise, however, is also a bit misleading, because income alone does not tell us everything about impoverished conditions. What is absent in this calculation are a host of other factors that are not assigned a monetary value, such as barter, informal supportive social and familial networks, and public and private assistance. This does not suggest that impoverishment is not as bad as it might appear to be, only that measuring income alone is insufficient given the relative, particular, and subjective conditions of how poverty is experienced and addressed across the world. In addition, there is no absolute correlation between relative levels of affluence and

5. World Wealth Calculator, http://www.worldwealthcalculator.org/. I am indebted to David Hogue for bringing this website to my attention.
6. Except in Alaska and Hawaii where the respective amounts are $19,660 and $18,090.

how individuals identify their own sense of well-being or happiness.[7] Nevertheless, increased income and financial assets is the most important step to be taken in ameliorating global poverty. Before exploring how this step might best be taken, a prior question needs to be asked: what causes poverty?

Identifying the principal cause or causes of poverty is a complex and contentious issue that to date has produced little consensus among economists, politicians, moralists, and policy wonks. For the purpose of this inquiry, however, three pertinent observations may be offered, particularly in respect to poverty on a global scale.

First, there tends to be a rough correlation between per capita income and levels of participation in global markets. Nations with liberal policies regulating trade, capital investment, and, to a more limited extent, immigration tend to have higher per capita incomes as compared to those nations with restrictive or prohibitive policies. For example, the three countries with the most liberal economic policies—Hong Kong, Singapore, and Australia—are also among the top ten countries with highest per capita income, whereas the three nations with the lowest levels of per capita income—Central African Republic, Burundi, and Democratic Republic of Congo—all have highly restrictive policies.[8]

Second, the poorest nations tend to have little readily available capital. Most developing countries lack the capacity to generate capital that is required for economic growth. One reason may be laws or practices restricting private ownership of property. Individuals can use their property to obtain loans in order to start businesses. Yet many developing nations have byzantine legal procedures in place that effectively prevent the acquisition of private property by the vast majority of the population.[9]

7. A rich person, for example, can be miserable, whereas a poor person might be joyous. Although it is true that money can't buy happiness, affluent people tend to identify themselves as being happy much more frequently than those who are poor. But as Arthur Brooks contends, it is not affluence per se that makes the affluent happier, but the pursuit of other goods, such as families, philanthropy, and voluntary associations that affluence affords. See Arthur Brooks, *Gross National Happiness: Why Happiness Matters for America—and How We Can Get More of It* (New York: Basic Books, 2008).

8. Data taken from the Heritage Foundation's "Index of Economic Freedom," and International Monetary Fund (IMF). It should be noted that Burundi ranks slightly higher in the Heritage Foundation's ranking than the Central African Republic and Democratic Republic of Congo. Although most of the ten wealthiest nations also ranked among the freest, Qatar (wealthiest) and Brunei (fifth wealthiest) are notable exceptions, being ranked, respectively, 30th and 40th. Moreover, per capita income does not necessarily mean that it is distributed fairly or advantageously among a nation's population.

9. See Hernando de Soto. *The Mystery of Capital: Why Capitalism Triumphs in the West and Fails Everywhere Else* (New York: Basic Books, 2000).

Access to adequate banking and financing are often unavailable or highly restrictive, or foreign grants or loans provided by public and private sources may be employed in unproductive ways. Policies may also severely restrict or prohibit direct foreign investment (DFI), or there may be inadequate legal safeguards protecting capital from being seized or confiscated, effectively discouraging potential investors.[10]

Third, the poorest nations tend to have limited employment opportunities, or large segments of the population lack skills that would better enable them to compete in global markets. It is not surprising that countries that fail to participate in global markets to any great extent or have insufficient access to capital also have high rates of unemployment.[11] If a region is not producing goods or services that consumers around the world need or want, good jobs are not usually on offer. Moreover, countries with large populations lacking sufficient literacy and skills do not attract capital investments that generate high-paying jobs.[12] Fortunate individuals who complete higher levels of education and training, typically by studying abroad, must often immigrate in order to find employment using their particular skills and expertise.

Although the causes of global poverty are more complex than indicated above, the lack of participation in global markets, unavailable capital, and inadequate employable skills are, in general, primary contributing factors. Addressing these problems, however, requires special efforts stemming from both public and private initiatives. This raises the question of why should special efforts be undertaken to help the poor on a global scale? Isn't this ultimately a waste of time and money since poverty has perennially proven to an intractable problem as even the Bible suggests?[13] There are a number of pragmatic replies that could be offered, such as diminishing poverty promotes social and political

10. DFI tends to concentrate in affluent and politically stable nations. In 2010, the United States, United Kingdom, and France were the largest recipients of DFI, whereas in 2012, the smallest recipients were Tonga, Bhutan, and Lesotho.

11. The countries with the highest rates of unemployment are Liberia (70 percent), Zimbabwe (60 percent), and Djibouti (50 percent), whereas Thailand (0.62 percent), Singapore (1.8 percent), and Hong Kong (3.2 percent) have the lowest levels. Other factors such as malnutrition, inadequate health care, and political instability may also contribute to unemployment.

12. In 2012, according to the CIA, the countries with the lowest estimated literacy rates were Burkina Faso (21.8 percent), Niger (28.7 percent), and Afghanistan (28.1 percent), whereas Finland, Greenland, and Luxembourg were all rated at 100 percent ("the World Factbook," Central Intelligence Agency, https://www.cia.gov/library/publications/the-world-factbook/fields/2103.html).

13. See Matt. 26:11; Mark 14:7; and John 12:8.

stability, or humanitarian reasons such as helping fellow humans in dire need. From the perspective of Christian ethics, however, the most compelling rationale for ameliorating poverty is biblical and subsequent theological teaching stressing a preferential option for the poor. The practical challenge is to employ the most efficacious means for exercising this option. In what follows, I argue that globalization, in conjunction with targeted aid or assistance, and suitable governmental regulations and safeguards offer the most promising strategy for assisting the poor in aggregate on a global scale. It should be stressed that I am *not* offering or endorsing any particular policies, but briefly describing some basic reasons why I believe that using global markets to pursue the good of affluence is, at present, the most effective way for exercising this preferential option for the poor.

Charity is a good place to start. Those in dire need must be helped—the starving should be fed, the homeless sheltered, the naked clothed, and the sick and injured cared for. By "charity" I am referring to contributions or gifts of money, services, expertise, and time without requirements or expectations of reciprocation on the part of beneficiaries. The sources of such charity include public and private sources such as governmental and international agencies, nongovernmental organizations (NGOs), and faith-based agencies and initiatives. Unquestionably, charitable contributions help the poor around the world. Over the past twenty-five years, public and private aid has helped lessen extreme poverty by nearly 50 percent and decreased child mortality rates. Moreover, an accusation that such aid is wasteful and ineffectual is partly true but often exaggerated, for it has also driven "improvements in health, agriculture, and infrastructure."[14] In short, charitable aid helps alleviate global poverty.

Such aid, however, is limited and should be carefully targeted in order to not only address the most immediate needs but also pave the way for long-term solutions. According to Matt Ridley, the "global-aid industry" rarely undertakes this "cost-benefit analysis," and more distressingly benefactors often impose their pet causes, such as climate change and environmental protection, that offer little direct benefit.[15] In more stark terms, William Easterly insists that aid should not indulge a "rich-world vanity that exaggerates the importance of western elites," creating

14. See Bill and Melinda Gates, "Three Myths on the World's Poor," *The Wall Street Journal*, January 17, 2014.

15. See Matt Ridley, "Smart Aid for the World's Poor," *The Wall Street Journal*, July 25, 2014.

the "condescending fantasy" that the poor will ultimately be saved by "benevolent" leaders as "advised by wise experts."[16]

Drawing upon the work of Bjorn Lomborg and the Copenhagen Consensus Center, Ridley proposes that the five most beneficial targets for aid include reducing malnutrition, preventing malaria and tuberculosis, providing better preprimary education, improving access to sexual and reproductive health, and enlarging free trade.[17] These targets illustrate that although charity is a good place to start in exercising the preferential option for the poor, it is not the end. As each of these instances indicates, the last one most overtly, enabling exchange by providing better nutrition, health care, and education is what most effectively and expansively alleviates poverty.

Ridley notes that expanding free trade is routinely dismissed by the "development industry," since it is seemingly far removed from humanitarian concerns that should prompt charitable assistance. Yet free trade "often delivers phenomenal improvements to the welfare of the poor in surprisingly quick time." The United Nations' Millennium Development Goal of reducing global poverty by one-half has been achieved ahead of schedule.[18] Additionally, Ridley estimates that a positive Doha Round of the WTO "could deliver annual benefits of $3 trillion for the developing world by 2020." As Ricardo's principle of comparative advantage demonstrates, trade benefits both parties, so the more trade occurs on a widespread basis, the more it generates aggregate affluence; and conversely the more trade is restricted the more aggregate impoverishment remains deeply entrenched.[19] Trading, however, requires that both parties have something of value to exchange. Such items include natural resources, agricultural products, manufactured goods, and services. Many of the poorest countries lack sufficient mechanisms for generating the necessary capital to exploit their comparative advantage. Aid and development programs funded by both public and private sources have admittedly generated some much-needed capital, but the lack of strategic targeting often fails to maximize the comparative trade advantages of the intended beneficiary.

---

16. See William Easterly, "Western Vanities That Do Little to Help the World's Poor," *Financial Times*, January 24, 2014.

17. Ridley, "Smart Aid for the World's Poor," and Lomborg, Copenhagen Consensus Center, http://www.copenhagenconsensus.com/.

18. See http://www.un.org/millenniumgoals/.

19. See Michael Mandelbaum, *The Road to Global Prosperity* (New York and London: Simon and Schuster e-book, 2014), ch. 2.

Moreover, aid alone cannot generate sufficient capital; invested capital is also needed. Again, many of the poorest countries effectively prevent investment. This may be due in part to laws or practices that do not adequately protect the property rights of foreign investors or restrict access to credit for potential indigenous entrepreneurs.[20] To a larger extent, the lack of capital results from policies that restrict or deter direct foreign investment, which is needed to create trade that is mutually beneficial to both rich and poor nations. As Tony O. Elumelu asserts, in respect to trade between Africa and the United States, the time has come to "move beyond the usual conversations on aid and instead to explore new opportunities to collaborate and co-invest in initiatives that generate value on both sides of the Atlantic." He adds, "America's generosity will always be welcome, but today we in Africa are most interested in your capital."[21]

Additionally, capital investment can also enhance social capital. As societies become more affluent they are in a better position to meet the basic needs of sustenance, housing, and health care that in turn allows more time and resources to be devoted to child rearing, education, and the formation and strengthening of private associations.[22] Opening a society to increased opportunities for capital investment can be especially beneficial to oppressed or stigmatized minorities. Devesh Kapur, for instance, notes that in conjunction with India's "market-based reforms in the early 1990s," the Dalits ("untouchables") have not only "advanced their economic lives," but have also made "more impressive gains in securing dignity and ending social humiliation." Kapur credits capitalism and "market forces" with creating employment opportunities that are enabling Dalits to escape their consignment to "demeaning occupations." This newfound mobility has in turn promoted greater toleration and acceptance among the larger Indian population, effectively challenging traditional "patterns of caste oppression."[23]

To state the obvious, the best way to combat poverty is to have a job. Having a source of income helps to satisfy one's material needs and wants, and without capital investment to create goods and services that can be

20. See William Easterly, *The Tyranny of Experts: Economists, Dictators, and the Forgotten Rights of the Poor* (New York: Basic Books, 2013).

21. Tony O. Elumelu, "Africa Is Open for Business, Ready for Investment," *The Wall Street Journal*, July 31, 2014.

22. See "Parenting in America: Choose Your Parents Wisely," *The Economist*, July 26, 2014.

23. Devesh Kapur, "Western Anti-Capitalists Take Too Much for Granted," *Financial Times*, July 23, 2014.

exchanged, there are no jobs to be had. It is investment and exchange, commerce and private enterprise that create and sustain jobs, and hence the pursuit of affluence.[24] What, then, are individuals to do if they find themselves in locales where, for whatever reasons, there is insufficient capital investment to produce goods and services? Presumably, if trade and capital should be free flowing, shouldn't labor enjoy similar mobility? If the goal is to ameliorate poverty on a *global* scale, then individuals, provided they have the requisite skills, should be able to migrate where capital investment and the production of goods and services are offering employment. Such labor migration is already occurring to a significant extent.[25] The last twenty years has witnessed an unprecedented growth in the population of cities. For the first time in history the majority of the world's population are urbanites,[26] and the growth of so-called megacities continues to accelerate, albeit at a slower pace. There have been steady regional migration patterns in such areas as the United States, European Union, and China, coupled with illegal migrations along the United States' southern border, the European Union's Mediterranean coastline, and Australia's northern shore.

The highly contentious issue of labor migration across national borders, and how it is linked to relatively free-flowing capital and trade illustrates how both the creative and destructive forces of a globalized economy help to alleviate aggregate poverty, albeit in an uneven manner. Opponents insist that migration or immigration promote lower wages and create greater unemployment, and there may also be fears, rightly or wrongly, that an influx of foreigners will change a society in unwanted ways. Yet migration has undeniable benefits, not only for individuals finding employment, but also for the hosting and departed regions. Migrants and immigrants benefit a local economy by enlarging the "labor pool and number of consumers," and some bring with them needed "technical expertise and entrepreneurial drive." The regions that migrants leave may also benefit from higher wages caused by a shrinking labor pool, and received remittances that exceed the "level of international economic assistance."[27] From a global perspective, labor migration helps alleviate aggregate poverty.

24. The not-for-profit and governmental sectors also provide jobs, but their respective sources of funding originate in and are dependent on investment and exchange.
25. Localized wars and political unrest also prompt migration.
26. According to the UN, the 50 percent line was crossed in 2008.
27. Mandelbaum, *The Road to Global Prosperity*, 64. According to Easterly, the total amount of remittances in 2011 was estimated to be around $372 billion; Easterly, *The Tyranny of Experts*, 207.

There is a similar pattern in capital investment. On the one hand, the foreign inflow of capital may be opposed because it diminishes indigenous control of production and employment. Corporate boardrooms in Seoul or Stuttgart rather than Detroit, for example, determine the fate of American autoworkers. On the other hand, the outflow of capital may be resisted because it diminishes local investment and employment. An auto factory built by an American firm in Mexico employing Mexicans means that a factory would not be built in the United States employing US workers. Similarly, restrictions on trade may be advocated on the basis that it protects potential lost production and jobs.

Free-flowing capital and trade, however, creates greater employment and benefits for consumers over time. Under favorable social and political conditions, capital investments tend to be widely dispersed and reciprocal. The United States, for instance, is both the largest generator and recipient of direct foreign investment. Both the inflow and outflow of capital has created new jobs at various locales around the world and lowered prices for consumers. To return to the example of automobile manufacturing, despite the perception of its collapse in the United States, the number of cars made in the United States has declined from a little over 5.5 million in 1999 to a little under 4.5 million in 2013, along with a roughly corresponding drop in sales from slightly under 17 million to slightly over 15.5 million. Moreover, the number of manufacturing jobs during the same period declined from a little over 1 million to slightly under 900,000. The principal difference is that many factories, owned by a variety of US and foreign firms, have migrated from the upper Midwest to southern states where lower wages cut production costs. At the same time China has emerged as the world's largest car maker and new sales market,[28] largely prompted by the capital investment of such foreign corporations as General Motors, Ford, and Volkswagen.

Over the last fifteen years, new and expanding global markets have helped to create new employment opportunities, thereby ameliorating poverty on an aggregate global basis as illustrated by the manufacturing and sales of automobiles as well as a wide range of other goods and services. Additionally, global markets lower the aggregate price of goods and services, thereby increasing purchasing power. Free trade, capital investment, and labor migration are the principal factors enabling a larger spectrum of individuals to pursue the good of affluence—hence,

28. In 2013, China produced 24 percent of all cars on a worldwide basis, dwarfing its principal competitor Japan at 11.9 percent (http://www.statista.com/statistics/226032/light-vehicle-producing-countries/).

the creative aspect of new and expanding global markets. Such creativity, however, has its price: namely, selective destruction. Since global markets are competitive, some individuals and communities, even societies and nations, are adversely affected through the loss of jobs, reduced income, and diminished capital investment.

Consequently, it is understandable why those adversely affected often ardently oppose globalization, in turn prompting political backlashes. Although globalization enjoys what may be characterized as "performance legitimacy," its success does not usually generate enthusiastic support or make it "immune to criticism or even opposition."[29] The benefits of globalization are widely diffuse and modest—for example, slightly lower prices for goods and services that are opaque to the public at large; whereas those suffering immediate ill effects are more concentrated and visible— for example, closed factories and unemployment lines make headlines, and therefore a potent political weapon.[30] Particularly in democracies, sufficient public support might be garnered to threaten or enact protectionist policies restricting trade, capital investment, and labor migration.

Again, establishing protectionist barriers is an understandable response, but it is a temptation that should be resisted. Governments are dedicated to promoting the prosperity of their citizens, but at present there is no realistic alternative for achieving this goal other than a globally integrated economy. The threatened immediate interests of some individuals and communities may, for a while, be shielded, but at the cost of consigning other individuals and communities across the world to prolonged impoverishment and retarding the pursuit of affluence for nearly everyone other than those selected to be protected.

Moreover, there are no easy political solutions for striking a balance between promoting affluence *and* protecting citizens from global competition. The creative forces of new and expanding global markets that are driving a widespread pursuit of affluence cannot help but create a destructive wake; the two are inseparable. As Michael Mandelbaum insists, the global economy, when it is "working successfully—indeed *because* it is working successfully—cannot help but provoke opposition to its workings, which in turn produces political conflicts."[31] Rather, the political backlashes prompted by globalization disclose the fundamental dilemma of what Philip Bobbitt portrays as the transition from nation-state

---

29. Mandelbaum, *The Road to Global Prosperity*, 3.
30. See ibid., 46.
31. Ibid. (emphasis original).

to market-state that was examined in chapter 3. The proclivity of the nation-state to protect is not compatible with the emerging market-state's penchant to promote economic opportunity. Although competitive global markets admittedly prove destructive for some in the short term, their ability to help create long-term aggregate prosperity represents, at present, the most promising strategy for alleviating poverty on a global scale.

If it is good to pursue affluence, and if a globally integrated economy is the best practical option for alleviating poverty that enables the poor to pursue the good of affluence, then enabling the poor to more fully compete in global markets is exercising a preferential option for the poor. Targeted charitable and governmental aid is needed to promote initially this participation, but the pursuit of affluence can only be sustained through exchange rather than perpetual assistance.

The present ascendancy of a globally integrated economy requires a reassessment of the dominant strand in traditional Christian moral teaching that has condemned wealth and possessions pursuit. Throughout much of its history such a sweeping judgment was often both wise and prudent counsel. In the zero-sum economies predating modern industrialization, wealth was largely acquired through seizure, and unremitting and inescapable impoverishment was the lot of the vast majority of people. Under such circumstances, hoarding and consuming more than what was needed were immoral acts that harmed the poor, and those pursuing wealth were placing their souls in jeopardy. In such a setting, charity was the only viable means of sustaining the poor.

Although contemporary economic circumstances have changed, this emphasis on charity or assistance should not be casually discarded. There are still over a billion people around the world suffering dire or extreme poverty, undoubtedly requiring the immediate assistance of their affluent global neighbors. The status of the growing global middle class is also precarious, and individuals will, from time to time, require assistance when they face the destructive forces of competitive global markets. The great strength of traditional Christian moral teaching on wealth and possessions has been its steadfast emphasis on charity as a love for needy neighbors.

This strength, however, is becoming a weakness. With its singular emphasis on charity, the dominant strand of Christian moral teaching on wealth and possessions has much to say about the necessity of subsistence but little to offer beyond it other than caution or condemnation. Given the growing ascendancy of an integrated global economy, such a moral vision is myopic, for it effectively establishes subsistence as a norm. This is tantamount to enabling the poor to rise to a certain level of material well-being but no higher, and concurrently to lower the material well-being of the affluent. Yet even on the basis of the most radical teachings against wealth and possessions it is difficult to justify such a latent strategy, particularly in light of a global economy that is increasingly predicated on the creation of material abundance rather than the distribution of scarcity.[32] Charity or assistance will often be needed to help raise the poor to a subsistence level, but it is exchange that will enable them to sustain and improve their material well-being. In short, traditional Christian moral teaching on wealth and possessions has offered and continues to offer little moral guidance on the proper uses of material abundance that the increasingly widespread pursuit of affluence enables on a global scale.

Unless this moral myopia is addressed, the Christian insistence on charity or assistance for those most in need may effectively be dismissed or muted to a trite and irrelevant mantra. Ironically, in failing to address affluence as a good that can be properly pursued, used, and enjoyed, the accompanying pleas for charity or assistance are diminished. If globalization continues apace, there is cautious optimism that by 2030 dire poverty will be even more substantially reduced[33] and the global middle class could increase to slightly under 5 billion people.[34] Given rapidly growing affluence, the remaining poor could easily be dismissed or ignored as an unfortunate minority that is unable, unwilling, or incompetent to participate in the global economy. Unless charity or assistance *and* exchange are portrayed as directly related components of both ameliorating poverty *and* enabling human flourishing, charity could be relegated to the well-meaning but ineffectual hobby of religious and wealthy eccentrics, or, more troubling, aid could become an unvarnished political tool of oppression.[35] More broadly, as the world grows more prosperous, what counsel should Christian moral teaching offer regarding the proper pursuit, use, and enjoyment of affluence? And equally important, what greater purposes should this pursuit, use, and enjoyment serve?

32. To be clear, this does not mean that scarcity and just distribution are not important issues. Obviously they are important, otherwise we would have no need for economics as an intellectual discipline or markets as a practical means of matching supply with demand.

33. See "Poverty: Not Always with Us," *The Economist*.

34. See Jose W. Fernandez, "Bridge to Somewhere: Helping U.S. Companies Tap the Global Infrastructure," *Foreign Affairs*, November/December 2013 (92:6): 111–12.

35. For some pundits, aid, or development, has almost always been such a machination; see, e.g., Easterly, *The Tyranny of Experts*, pt. 2.

The Abundant Life

The principal purpose of this section is to begin addressing the moral myopia of Christian teaching on wealth and possessions noted above, or, more accurately, to initiate a reassessment and further development of this teaching that extends throughout the following chapters. I undertake this task by briefly revisiting four theological themes that were discussed in the preceding chapter: delight in creation's material abundance, stewardship, neighbor love, and differentiating between ultimate and penultimate goods. In each of these instances I derive four corresponding principles that pertain to economic globalization: production, capital, trade, and the limits of affluence. Each of these principles in turn are applied to the issues of ameliorating poverty; the proper pursuit, use, and enjoyment of affluence; and larger purposes or goods that affluence should enable people to serve. To reiterate, the following discussions are cursory, and are further elaborated in part 2.

To enjoy God's blessing of a good creation is, in large measure, to take delight in its material abundance. As embodied creatures, physical well-being and comfort are not trivial concerns but are central theological considerations. It is through material abundance, as I argue above, that humans are enabled to take a leisurely Sabbath in order to immerse themselves in the fullness of God's good creation. This abundance, however, is latent. Consequently, *production* is required to establish and sustain human flourishing. A pristine natural environment is beautiful and awe-inspiring, but it alone can never enable humans to move far beyond physical survival.

Developing this latent potential of material abundance requires stewardship. Effort is needed to transform creation's resources into housing, clothing, food, health care, and an array of other goods and services that enhance physical well-being and comfort. Stewardship, then, is most basically undertaking action designed to foster human flourishing. Consequently, *capital* is needed to induce this action. Building houses, making clothes, farming, providing health care, and manufacturing goods and services cannot be accomplished without the investment of capital.

In fulfilling God's command to be the stewards of creation, humans interact with a wide range of neighbors in competitive, cooperative, and a myriad of other ways. In these interactions God also commands humans to love neighbors in ways that are appropriate to particular circumstances. But what is common in all concrete enactments of neighbor love is exchange; something is given and received in unreciprocated and reciprocated ways.

Consequently, *trade* is a mundane but ubiquitous expression of neighbor love. As an act of love, however, exchange cannot be divorced from charity. Neighbors in dire need must be helped without expectation of immediate reciprocity, but the goal of assisting neighbors in need is not to maintain their dependence in perpetuity.[36] Practically, in a globally integrated economy aid should be targeted in ways that enable people in dire need to become participants in reciprocal exchanges. Charity and exchange is not an either-or but a both-and proposition if it is to be a genuine act of neighbor love.

Although trade enables neighbors to flourish, exchange is not an end in itself. If this were true, then the endless accumulation of possessions or money would result in a happy and fulfilled life. This is not the case, however, because only the ultimate good of God can satisfy our hearts' desires, and penultimate goods, such as affluence, always prove to be woefully inadequate substitutes. Consequently, the *limits of affluence* must be acknowledged in properly ordering its pursuit, use, and enjoyment. Production, capital, and trade are important penultimate goods, but should be ordered as means that promote a fuller love of God and neighbor within the context of a material creation. In short, a life of material abundance is not synonymous with the abundant life, although the two are not unrelated, much less mutually exclusive.

How might these admittedly sketchy principles help ameliorate poverty on a global scale? Producing creation's material abundance requires work. Producing and delivering a good or service entails the work of a wide range of people such as laborers, managers, entrepreneurs, distributors, and sales personnel. At each stage in this process, individuals derive income from their particular work. Global markets create a greater demand for goods and services, in turn creating more jobs to produce needed and wanted items. In addition, since capital is required to produce goods and services, global markets create a greater range of potential investment opportunities that benefit an expanding range of investors, workers, and consumers. Exchange is also needed to sustain productivity and therefore jobs. Trade not only increases opportunities for economic exchange but also enables regions to maximize productivity and capital investment by utilizing their respective comparative advantages. To oversimplify, globalization promotes the pursuit of affluence that drives more expansive productivity and capital investment, and therefore greater employment opportunities as well. As workers attain

---

36. There are, of course, some individuals who for extended periods of time or over their lifetimes require the assistance of others that cannot be reciprocated.

excess economic resources, they become consumers and investors that stimulate even more productivity, investment, and trade.

In this respect, enabling the poor to more fully participate in the exchange of global markets may be regarded as an act of neighbor love, albeit in an oblique manner. In general, reciprocity enhances human relationships. The parties to an exchange simultaneously give and receive. Our most satisfying and intimate relationships are based on mutual giving and receiving, and the ancients believed that genuine friendship could only occur among equals.[37] Reciprocal exchange contributes to the well-being of both parties, and it does not need not to be perfectly symmetrical to accomplish this goal. This does not denigrate the virtue of charity in which unreciprocated giving is required to assist a person in need, nor does it diminish a response of gratitude on the part of the recipient. But prolonged unidirectional giving and receiving establishes a relationship based on provision and dependence; it perpetuates a relationship of superiority and inferiority. In contrast, trade is bidirectional, providing a basis of exchange between affluent and developing regions of the world. Again, such trade need not be entirely symmetrical to establish a mutually beneficial relationship and is preferable to any other option. Affluent nations could simply ignore and have nothing to do with developing nations, which would diminish the material well-being of both. Powerful nations could conquer or colonize weak countries, impoverishing them by seizing needed resources. Or rich nations may contribute unending aid to poor nations as a kind of neocolonial benevolence often based on racist assumptions that their beneficiaries are too stupid or lazy to help themselves. Global markets at least create a greater range of reciprocal and mutually beneficial exchanges among a larger number of people.

This is where we encounter our first problem, however, because there are many poor individuals that are unable to participate or disabled from participating fully in competitive global markets. This is why, in part, exchange as an act of neighbor love must always be complemented by charity or assistance, or in less theologically tainted terms, why targeted aid is needed. Public or private funding may be needed to build hospitals and schools, because individuals cannot be productively employed if they are ill or lack requisite skills. Infrastructure may need to be constructed to attract the necessary capital investment to produce goods and services that can be traded in global markets. It needs to be stressed again, however, that the ultimate goal is to enable the poor to pursue the good of

---

37. See Gilbert Meilaender, *Friendship: A Study in Theological Ethics* (Notre Dame, IN, and London: University of Notre Dame Press, 1985).

affluence through the means of exchange and not to keep them dependent on unreciprocated assistance.

This is where we meet our next problem: aid may not be wisely targeted, or it may be mismanaged. The health care and education offered, for example, may fail to address the most pressing needs or be inaccessible for those needing these services the most. Well-intentioned infrastructure projects may prove to be ineffectual or benefit only a small minority of poor people. Moreover, public and private benefactors may unwittingly impose unpalatable cultural and political agendas upon beneficiaries that ultimately promote material and civil impoverishment.

Even if aid is properly targeted and managed efficiently, there are still problems of policies and execution that disable the poor from fully participating in global markets. As previously noted, restrictions on trade, capital, and labor migration effectively maintain the material impoverishment of many individuals around the world by preventing them from potentially benefitting from competitive global markets. If the goal is to alleviate poverty on a *global* scale then the principal concern should be with worldwide rather than national economic development.[38] Moreover, the benefits of increased participation in competitive global markets may not be fairly dispensed or enjoyed. Employees may be subjected to exploitive practices or unsafe workplaces. Invested capital may have strings attached diminishing its potential benefit for individuals and communities, and the profit derived from trade may not be justly distributed or reinvested. More troubling, when globalization is working as it should, individuals and communities that have lost their principal means of livelihood because the goods or services they produce are no longer needed or wanted, or cannot be produced at competitive prices will need short-term assistance in order to retool. To reiterate once again, globalization has its problems.

It is likely that over the next few decades, globalization will continue to generate unprecedented affluence for an enlarging range of people across the world, barring some unforeseen or unwanted catastrophe. In anticipation of such material prosperity, does Christian moral teaching have any pertinent counsel to offer regarding the proper pursuit, use, and enjoyment of affluence? Posing this question does not mean that the problem of poverty and corresponding need of charity or assistance can or should be ignored. Even if those living in extreme poverty are reduced to 200 million by 2030,[39] that is still 200 million too many. Moreover,

---

38. See Easterly, *The Tyranny of Experts*, 205.
39. "Poverty: Not Always with Us," *The Economist*.

given the dynamism of global markets, some individuals and communities will always be in need of temporary assistance, and perhaps in some cases prolonged assistance. Asking the question of how affluence should be pursued, used, and enjoyed is needed not only in recognition of changing economic and political circumstances but also to address the problems associated with globalization as enumerated above. Consequently, the kind of counsel I am proposing is developed in tandem with addressing these issues in part 2.

Sketching out a broad premise at this juncture will serve to anticipate what this proposed counsel entails. If affluence is to be pursued, used, and enjoyed properly, then it must always be seen as a means and not an end. Affluence can help one to take delight in God's creation, but affluence is not (or should not be) the object of one's delight. More specifically, one takes delight in creation's material abundance, but that does not mean that delight is an outgrowth of an endless acquisition of material possessions. To invoke the wisdom of the ancients, surplus material possessions may help us to discover happiness, but they cannot make us happy. Such happiness has nothing to do with banal cheerfulness; rather, the truly happy person is one who desires what is good—namely, God—and aligns one's life accordingly.[40]

The reason why affluence is a *penultimate* good that should be pursued is that it enables people to participate more fully in the greater good of communication or koinonia, as I argue in chapter 7. Although communication, or koinonia, may benefit from and entails exchange, it is based on and pursues relationships that are common and shared, and it cannot be reduced to exchange. To communicate is to participate in human relationships that are not formed exclusively by what is mine becoming yours and what is yours becoming mine, but what is ours. Such relationships occur most frequently in families, friendships, churches, and nonpolitical and noncommercial associations. Much of traditional Christian moral teaching has assumed, and largely continues to assume, that affluence is either unrelated to or in conflict with koinonia. In light of changing economic circumstances, this assumption needs to be challenged and revised.

The strand of moral teaching against wealth and possessions that I have been criticizing, however, offers a prescient reminder that the pursuit, use, and enjoyment of affluence is nonetheless fraught with temptations best avoided. Arthur Brooks has captured the gist of these temptations succinctly: "Love things, use people." Succumbing to this

---

40. See Augustine, *On the Morals of the Catholic Church*, in Philip Schaff, ed., *Nicene and Post-Nicene Fathers of the Christian Church*, vol. 4 (Edinburgh: T. and T. Clark, 1991).

temptation is to traverse a "road to misery," an empty "worldly snake oil peddled by the culture makers from Hollywood to Madison Avenue." His advice for resisting this temptation is equally succinct: "Love people, use things." This proves to be a difficult challenge, requiring the "courage to repudiate pride and the strength to love others—family, friends, colleagues, acquaintances, God, and even strangers and enemies." Brooks further contends that an accompanying "condemnation of materialism" and practice of charity are required. He adds, "This is manifestly not an argument for any specific economic system. Anyone who has spent time in a socialist country must concede that materialism and selfishness are as bad under collectivism, or worse, as when markets are free. No political ideology is immune to materialism."[41]

It is good to pursue, use, and enjoy affluence when its limits are acknowledged. Affluence can help people to better communicate the goods of creation with one another, but affluence alone cannot satisfy this affiliative and spiritual hunger. As Brooks reminds, we end up loving things rather than people, much less God. Material well-being is important, but it is not the same thing as being entirely well; a life of material abundance is not the abundant life. Consequently, a properly ordered pursuit, use, and enjoyment of affluence serve the greater purpose of enabling people to participate in koinonia.

Affluence today is pursued in new and expanding global markets, replete with their creative destruction—to borrow from William Tecumseh Sherman, "there is no refining it." This economic terrain is filled with dangers and temptations, but it nevertheless offers, at present, the best way for exercising the preferential option for the poor. The task at hand, however, is not to vastly reshape the landscape, but to learn how to navigate it both wisely and faithfully. This is not unprecedented, for was this not what much of traditional Christian moral teaching on wealth and possessions was trying to do in zero-sum economies in which widespread impoverishment was presumed to be the norm? But the terrain has changed, and it is time to draw new maps.

41. Arthur C. Brooks, "Love People, Not Pleasure," *The New York Times*, July 18, 2014.

Part 2

. . . but Not Sufficient

Enabling Human Flourishing

Chapter Six

Reorienting Exchange

S ome readers may be happy to know that throughout part 2, I examine some of the more pressing problems associated with globalization. Before proceeding, however, I must request their patience a bit longer in order to emphasize an important premise underlying the following chapters. Global economic exchange is a mundane but ubiquitous activity. As Eric Beinhocker notes: "No matter where you are, from the biggest industrialized city to the smallest rural village, you are surrounded by economic activity and its results. Twenty-four hours a day, seven days a week, the planet is abuzz with humans designing, organizing, manufacturing, servicing, transporting, communicating, buying, and selling."[1] The material abundance created by exchange is a vital prerequisite of human flourishing. Moral and theological assessments that dismiss or relegate exchange as an unimportant or profane activity, and characterize business and commercial activities as tawdry affairs offer an incomplete and inaccurate account of how human life is and should be lived out within God's created order. In short, exchange is a *necessary* element undergirding human flourishing.

Since exchange is such a vital component, people should be enabled to participate freely and fully in producing and consuming needed and wanted goods and services. Policies and practices that wittingly or unwittingly prevent or restrict individuals, communities, and societies from pursuing the good of affluence within new and expanding global markets effectively diminish human flourishing both collectively and individually. The problems associated with globalization tend to cluster around,

1. Eric D. Beinhocker, *The Origin of Wealth: Evolution, Complexity, and the Radical Remaking of Economics* (Boston, MA: Harvard Business School Press, 2006), 5.

on the one hand, people who are unable to participate fully and fairly in competitive global markets, and, on the other hand, people who are unable to fully and fairly enjoy the benefits of their participation.

Although participating in economic exchange is necessary to promote human flourishing, it is *not sufficient.* Material abundance is not in itself the abundant life. Exchange is an efficient means for pursuing the penultimate good of affluence, but affluence is not equipped to be an ultimate end. One pressing moral and theological task, then, is to ask how exchange can be reoriented toward serving purposes greater than the production and consumption of material goods and services. Consequently, problems and purposes should not be examined in isolation from each other. To address or solve a problem suggests, at least in part, achieving an alternative goal. To use a simplistic example, if I want to solve my problem of never seeing a sunset because I am always facing east in the late afternoon, I must reorient my gaze toward the west. Similarly, the moral, social, and political problems accompanying globalization are best addressed by also examining what goals economic exchange on a global scale should be helping to achieve. Probing both problems and purposes also requires asking different initial questions other than those restricted to function and abstract models. Following Daniel K. Finn, asking if markets are just is to ask the wrong question, because it is unanswerable. Markets are neither inherently just nor unjust. Rather, this question can only be answered by assessing the "moral ecology" of markets consisting of particular cultural, social, and political contexts. A better question to ask involves assessing the outcomes of market exchange and to what extent they are good, or more importantly for Finn, *just.*[2]

Making this assessment, however, requires prior notions of what is good or just, resulting in highly contentious disputes over what constitutes both problems and purposes based on a wide range of differing moral, ideological, and religious convictions, and hence equally acrimonious debates over policies for resolving various issues. Although I describe a number of these issues, I do not offer or endorse any particular policy proposals. Rather, my goal is to offer a general overview based on the moral and theological themes developed in part 1 (especially chapters 4 and 5) that might serve to help reorient exchange that now occurs predominantly within a globally integrated economy. In brief, my principal thesis is that economic exchange should allow a pursuit of affluence that in turn enables people to participate more fully in koinonia, or

2. See Daniel K. Finn, *The Moral Ecology of Markets: Assessing Claims about Markets and Justice* (Cambridge, UK, and New York: Cambridge University Press, 2006), ch. 6.

communicating the goods of creation. Specifically, economic exchange should be oriented toward strengthening the flourishing of individuals, communicative associations, and civil society. Moreover, these three categories are not isolated or unrelated. Individuals cannot flourish in the absence of robust associations, and a strong civil society cannot ignore or diminish the well-being and rights of individuals. The good of the one and the many are not mutually exclusive or an either-or proposition. I initiate my argument below by describing the principal problems that an economy must address, and briefly introducing what purposes an economy should serve. These purposes are further elaborated in the following chapter in which I develop the theological concept of *koinonia as communicating the abundant goods of creation.*

Problems an Economy Must Address

Following Finn, there are four major problems that an economy must address.[3] The first is *allocation.* Markets are efficient mechanisms for determining both the kinds and quantities of goods and services that need to be produced. Additionally, consumers benefit from competition among producers and sellers in terms of available choices and prices.

The second challenge is *distribution,* or what Finn calls the problem of "who gets what."[4] Distribution is largely accomplished through income. Within labor markets, individuals are paid wages for work or services that are roughly commensurate with the demand placed on their skills or knowledge.

The third problem is *scale.* For Finn, the primary issue at stake is how best to protect the environment while also producing sufficient goods and services. An endless expansion of production and consumption is not sustainable. Unfortunately, Finn contends, markets cannot determine an optimal or "proper scale of the economy in the biosphere."[5]

The fourth problem is *quality of relations.* Economic exchange entails a wide range of formal and informal interactions, but economists have "spent very little time considering the quality of those relations."[6] An economy must address such issues as workplace conditions, relationships

3. See Daniel K. Finn, *Christian Economic Ethics: History and Implications* (Minneapolis, MN: Fortress Press, 2013), ch. 12; see also Finn, *The Moral Ecology of Markets,* ch. 5.

4. Finn, *Christian Economic Ethics,* 202.

5. Ibid., 203.

6. Ibid., 203–4.

between employers and employees, and more broadly promoting trust and developing social capital.

Markets play a substantial role in solving the problems of allocation, distribution, scale, and quality of relations, and Finn insists that in evaluating the extent to which markets either promote or hinder good or just outcomes, several fundamental economic insights must be kept in mind. The most basic insight is that "scarcity is pervasive and fundamental."[7] Production and consumption are limited, so every need and want cannot be met. Consequently, meeting some needs and wants should be assigned a higher priority than others. Self-interest is a "powerful and often positive motive," particularly within trusting and mutually caring communities. A proper self-regard is not unrelated to loving neighbors.[8] Public policies should therefore usually appeal to self-interested rather than altruistic behavior. Asking people to give generously to charitable causes, for instance, is less effective than offering tax incentives. Another important insight is that "prices matter."[9] This does not mean simply producing affordable goods and services, but also assessing the social, environmental, and behavioral costs that market exchanges entail. Additionally, generosity reacts to prices. The altruistic behavior of individuals and governments tends to respond favorably to lower prices through increased private benefaction (often stimulated by tax deduction rates), while also decreasing the costs of providing social services through increased volunteer activities (e.g., Peace Corps and Volunteers In Service To America).[10] Counterintuitively, perfection is not optimal in an economy that must deal with scarcity. Although achieving a state of perfection, however defined, would presumably be wonderful, the cost of accomplishing this goal is both prohibitive and counterproductive. For example, the cost of reducing the amount of pollution to zero (if possible) would be astronomical and would lower expenditures for many other worthwhile pursuits, whereas a 20 percent reduction would benefit many people at a much lower price. In short, the pursuit of any goal of perfection eventually reaches a point of diminishing return.

Although these economic insights are important, alone they are insufficient to assess the moral outcomes of markets. Reducing human behavior to self-interested calculation, *Homo economicus*, produces a

7. Ibid., 217.
8. Ibid., 220. See also Matt. 19:19; 22:39.
9. Finn, *Christian Economic Ethics*, 220.
10. Ibid., 222.

myopic moral vision,[11] and Finn notes some of the more troubling "concerns" stemming from this "overly simplified model."[12] Economists, Finn argues, tend to adopt "psychological egoism" as the normative basis of human behavior. Individuals always act in ways to maximize their respective happiness or utility, however variously these may differ. This implicit adoption of utilitarianism means that no sharp distinction between good and evil can be drawn; saints and sinners are merely maximizing their happiness in different ways. But such a portrayal of human behavior is misleading, because individuals make decisions that they know to be good or evil. Moreover, even if people make economic decisions on largely utilitarian grounds, their choices are not always free or rational, thereby presumably diminishing their happiness. A rich person, for instance, may be free to make decisions among a wide range of attractive options, such as buying both a fine dress and exquisite dinner, whereas a poor person may be forced to choose between equally unappealing options such as either buying a shirt or a meal. Economic choices are not always rational because desires are shaped by a number of irrational, often subliminal factors. Advertising, for example, often emphasizes vague feelings or pleasant emotions associated with a product rather than its price or utility.

According to Finn, so-called traditional or mainstream economics often confuses ends and means. A rising Gross Domestic Product (GDP), for instance, is commonly used as a measure of economic success that purportedly reflects a corresponding increase of well-being or happiness. GDP is not unimportant, but it only discloses the financial value of production and exchange while revealing very little about the presumed well-being or happiness of consumers. One example Finn uses is that purchasing extra locks for doors increases GDP, but doing so in response to "rising crime" does not represent a "rise in human welfare."[13] Economists rightfully stress the central role that efficiency plays in promoting productivity as reflected in GDP, but efficient productivity is not an end but a means to achieve some other objective. In Finn's words, "we must always ask: Efficiency with respect to what? Efficiency is never a value in itself but is only a measure of our service to other values."[14] These values include such things as "meaningful community," personal

11. On the perils of turning morality into calculated interests, see George Parkin Grant, *English-Speaking Justice* (Notre Dame, IN: University of Notre Dame Press, 1985).
12. Finn, *Christian Economic Ethics*, 224.
13. Ibid., 226–27.
14. Ibid., 228.

security, civility, physical and spiritual health, trust, and reciprocity.[15] Measuring and promoting the creation of wealth is not irrelevant, but as Finn contends, economists have become too fixated on this means and pay too little attention to the more important goal of widespread prosperity, and genuine prosperity includes, but is greater than, the aggregate value of production and consumption. Markets, then, are neither inherently moral nor immoral, and a larger cultural, social, and political ecology is needed to assess market outcomes.

Finn offers a useful framework for evaluating the moral outcomes of new and expanding global markets. Both the fundamental economic insights and their limitations must be kept in mind in determining to what extent a globally integrated economy helps or hinders in solving the problems of allocation, distribution, scale, and quality of relations. Most importantly, these determinations cannot be made in the absence of what larger purposes economic exchange can and should be serving. In the following paragraphs I note briefly some of the issues pertaining to each of these problems, as well as larger purposes.

Allocation

Global markets are efficient mechanisms for determining and enabling the production of needed and wanted goods and services. Consumers around the world benefit from a wider range of products at more affordable prices. Markets, however, cannot deliver everything that is needed or wanted. This may be due to what is desired cannot be satisfied through a material good or service. Although obtaining a material item may help make a person happy, happiness per se cannot be bought and sold. Or some individuals may not be able to participate in a market exchange. A hungry person might not have money to buy food. More typically, a variety of manipulative factors diminish the efficiency of markets in satisfying the needs and wants of consumers, particularly in respect to prices and availability of goods and services. Protectionist trade policies, monopolies, crony favoritism, cartels, and collusion harm consumers by artificially inflating prices and promoting the production of inferior goods and services. Globalization has, to some extent, lessened these problems of allocation by enabling more people to participate in market exchanges and by creating social and political pressures against manipulative policies and practices. Yet global markets alone cannot solve the problem of allocation. There are still many people who are not able to satisfy their

15. Ibid., 228–29.

most pressing needs through market exchanges, and a host of market manipulations continue to harm consumers on a global scale. And even if global markets were to maximize their efficiency (whatever that might mean), they would still be ill-equipped to deliver nonmaterial goods.

In respect to allocation, the most pressing issues are regulation and aid. In order to be efficient, markets require rules and regulations. Contracts must be honored, promises kept, and consumers protected from fraud and dangerous or faulty items. Participants in competitive markets often regulate or police their own exchanges. If, for example, a company sells expensive products of shoddy quality and offers poor customer service, consumers punish it by taking their business to competitors. Conversely, consumers reward a company offering cheaper and better products, or superior customer service by purchasing its items rather than those of its competitors. More formally, business and professional associations establish certification requirements, best practices, and codes of ethics, in turn monitoring and holding their members accountable. Governments regulate through enforcing contracts, monitoring product safety, enforcing laws and policies designed to protect consumers from fraud or other harms, and punishing violators. More broadly, such regulation is also used to promote, discourage, or prohibit certain kinds of market exchanges in respect to other values such as protecting the environment. The extent of governmental regulation varies from minimal to extensive, both among jurisdictions and sectors of an economy. In the United States, for instance, interior designers are highly regulated in Florida while entirely unregulated in other states.[16] Unfortunately, many individuals, countries, and regions are unable to adequately participate in market exchanges, thereby restricting the allocation of goods and services to meet needs and wants. It is virtually impossible to compete in and to enjoy the benefits of global markets when people do not have access to adequate nutrition, housing, health care, and reliable sources of energy. In these instances, private and public aid is needed to enable more equitable allocation of goods and services.

It should not be assumed, however, that regulation and aid are always effective. Consumers can be unwieldy, fickle, and uninformed in deciding which producers to reward and punish. Business and professional associations may prove self-serving or lax in enforcing standards. Governmental regulations may lack sufficient power to address a concern, or prove unduly cumbersome and ineffective. Or more perversely, some

---

16. See John Micklethwait and Adrian Wooldridge, *The Fourth Revolution: The Global Race to Reinvent the State* (New York: Penguin, 2014), 116.

regulation is designed not to benefit consumers but to protect special interests: to return to Florida, the goal of the tight regulations on interior designers is not to safeguard Floridians from "clashing color schemes,"[17] but to protect the interests of an influential and effective lobby.[18] Additionally, aid is often poorly targeted, and fails to help the people it is intended to benefit.

These problems are exacerbated by globalization. To some extent consumer reward and punishment has been marginally effective, given the frequency of how quickly sector leaders and losers come and go. But this is largely a reactive strategy that cannot adequately address issues of prevention and protection. To date there is little evidence that international business and professional associations are adept at either certifying or monitoring their members, or even if attempts at imposing universal standards is efficacious given the world's diverse cultures. The regulatory proficiency of international bodies is far from awe inspiring, and private and governmental aid has, at best, a mixed track record.

Moreover, myriad proposals for improving the allocation of goods and services often become fixated on questions of efficiency while failing to interject questions of purpose. To use Finn's categories, fundamental economic insights are employed while their shortsightedness is ignored resulting in a myopic understanding of the problem of allocating goods and services. In other words, the question what purpose should allocation serve is rarely asked, or in more stark terms: what *should* people want? The problem of how best to allocate goods and services on a global scale, particularly in respect to enabling those who are not able to participate more fully in global markets, cannot be adequately addressed without more overt attention being directed toward greater purposes beyond efficiency.

To be clear, in posing the question what should people want, I am *not* recommending that the state, an elite cadre of experts, renowned celebrities, or (God forbid!) seminary professors should concoct a universal hierarchy of desires to order the allocation of goods and services anywhere and everywhere around the world. More modestly, I am suggesting that a more overt deliberation regarding the normative purposes of distribution should be undertaken in order to address the issues involving regulation and aid in a more satisfactory manner. Christian moral theology can make some important contributions to this discussion if it can constructively incorporate the fundamental economic insights proposed by Finn, particularly in assessing both the promise and peril of global markets

17. Ibid.
18. The lobby in question represents established interior designers.

in distributing goods and services. Most important, it can remind that although global markets empower the pursuit of affluence, markets alone cannot allocate the greater goods that prosperity should enable and serve.

Distribution

Income, and derivatively affluence, is often distributed through labor markets. Exchange requires labor to produce goods and services. To a large extent the demand for certain skills or knowledge determines the value of labor that is most often reflected in wages, salaries, benefits, and other forms of compensation. When the supply for certain skills or knowledge is relatively low, income tends to be higher; whereas when the supply is relatively high, income tends to be lower. Income is also derived from invested capital, and investments in turn influence demand for labor. For example, increased capital investments create new jobs, whereas declining investments may result in lost jobs, or investing in technologically efficient systems of production may increase the demand for high-skilled employees while also eliminating the need for low-skilled jobs. Consequently, market-based distributions of income vary in response to both the demand for particular skills or knowledge as well as available capital, and are invariably uneven.

Unfortunately, many people are unable, constrained, or prevented from participating fully and freely in labor markets. Some people are physically or mentally disabled to such a degree that they have no skills or knowledge that are of value in producing goods and services. Other people are unable to participate in labor markets because there are no jobs available. If a locale has little or no capital investment, then few if any employment opportunities will be forthcoming, or subsequently capital may be removed and invested elsewhere, creating unemployment in the low-capital locale. Still others are constrained from taking advantage of labor markets because they lack valued skills or knowledge. Finally, some people are prevented from participating in labor markets because they are prohibited from migrating to locales where their skills or knowledge are needed, or policies or practices—such as licensing, closed shops, and tenure—effectively control entrance and create artificial labor shortages. Additionally, income is not distributed evenly. Everyone is not paid the same wage, and some investors enjoy a greater return than others. Consequently, there are fluctuating income gaps.

Again, the most pressing issues entail regulation and aid. Individuals entirely unable to work require familial or community care, or private or public assistance. In order to create or preserve jobs, governments may adopt policies that either promote or discourage investment, or prevent capital from leaving their jurisdiction. Providing individuals opportunities to acquire more valuable skills or knowledge necessitates extensive investment in education and training, requiring taxation, corporate initiatives, and in impoverished regions external private or public assistance. Various governments may adopt policies ranging from permitting or even encouraging labor migration to discouraging, restricting, or forbidding it altogether. Additionally practices controlling entrance to various sectors of the labor force may range from being prohibited or discouraged to being permitted or encouraged. In addressing the issue of "income inequality," regulatory options include government inaction, a minimum wage, price and wage controls, taxation, and redistribution through public services. Almost without exception, any intervention by the state to regulate the distribution of income triggers bitter disputes both in terms of efficacy and outcomes.

Globalization intensifies the acerbic nature of these disputes, as well as exposing the dilemmas nation-states face within a globally integrated economy. In competing for capital investment, some countries adopt attractive taxation policies, while conversely other nations impose heavy penalties on capital extraction. Some governments legislate strict laws restricting immigration with a few even preventing emigration, while others enact lax policies, in some instances actively recruiting expats, especially those with highly valued skills and knowledge. Additionally, some regimes informally encourage labor migration in order to relieve unemployment and increase income through remittances. The extent to which certain national or regional employment sectors are open or pro-tected varies widely as do policies addressing income distribution. These conflicting goals often create or amplify international tensions, as well as generating paradoxical if not contradictory political commitments within individual nation-states. In the United States, for example, some politi-cians on the left are simultaneously committed to open borders and high wages, while some on the right endorse closed borders and low prices for goods and services made in America. Or many developed nations espouse the virtues of free trade while protecting selected domestic sectors, such as agriculture, with high tariffs and generous subsidies.

The situation is equally chaotic in respect to aid or assistance. In order to compete within global markets some nations have chosen or been forced to cut back on social services or abstain from developing ade-quate safety nets, while others have maintained or expanded assistance, subsidies, and entitlements by incurring heavy debt. Additionally, private and public assistance to impoverished nations is often poorly targeted or mismanaged, resulting in little, if any, immediate value to intended beneficiaries.

Again, the problem of distribution is routinely tackled in isolation from questions of purpose. Any economy must solve the problem of how income should be distributed, but to what end? Any answer that evades this question of purpose will be truncated, further exacerbating conflicting and contradictory commitments and agendas. The challenge of addressing both the problem and purpose of distribution is even more pronounced in a globally integrated economy in which there is no universal or widespread agreement on what such a purpose might mean or entail. Income, however, depends on the production of goods and services that can be exchanged, and their production inevitably requires some kind of effort or labor. Consequently, can we not ask *what is the purpose of work?*

I am not suggesting that any singular or uniform answer can be offered, particularly in light of globalization. But work is a universal activity, and to pose the question of its purpose at least initiates a moral framework, or to use Finn's category ecology, in which to assess the outcomes of global labor markets. The principal contribution that Christian moral theology can make is to affirm, at the very least, that work should be productive and that workers should be treated in just and humane ways, despite the lack of consensus of what these ways might entail. More broadly, Christian moral theology can remind that although work produces income, its value is not restricted to financial reward. Following John Paul II, human well-being is the purpose that work serves. It is principally through work that people not only express their self-interested aspirations but also contribute to the welfare of others and fulfill, in part, their role as stewards of God's creation. This does not mean that everyone is entitled to an enjoyable job or stimulating career. Rather, it acknowledges that "work is becoming increasingly important as the productive factor both of non-material and material wealth."[19] This acknowledgment serves as a warning that any assessment of globalization that stops with production and distribution of material wealth is incomplete because it fails to account for the nonmaterial wealth that work also produces. Although globalization helps many people to pursue, use, and enjoy the good of affluence, if all it settles for is a frenetic accumulation of material wealth, then it will be a failed enterprise. Work without Sabbath is pointless

19. John Paul II as quoted in Finn, *Christian Economic Ethics*, 302.

since there is no time to enjoy both the material and nonmaterial fruits of one's labor.

Scale

Addressing the challenges of allocation and distribution requires the production of goods and services. As an economy develops it requires increasing amounts of natural resources and energy, not only to manufacture items but also to transport them to consumers and to construct and maintain their supportive infrastructures. This is particularly the case in respect to economies generating widespread affluence or prosperity. Consequently, the scale of production, consumption, and use of natural resources enlarges dramatically within growing economies.

Economic growth, however, is not free and has its costs, and these costs also increase as the scale of production and consumption enlarges. Extracting minerals and energy, for example, makes them more scarce and thereby more expensive. Industrialization and transportation also entail the costs of soil, water, and air pollution that are paid through more expensive health care, cleanup, and diminished quality of life. Moreover, natural resources and the earth's ability to absorb pollutants are not infinite, so indefinite economic growth is unsustainable. It is easy to see why globalization amplifies the problem of scale. As economic growth occurs on an expanding scale around the world, so too does pollution that is involved with the requisite processes of extraction, manufacturing, and transportation. Over the past decade China has been a leader in economic growth and the leading polluter, and many other developing nations are following its lead. Globalization simply hastens the ultimate end of endless economic growth.

Finn asserts that markets "cannot and will not" determine an optimal human "ecological footprint." This determination, he insists, can only be made by the state.[20] But since there is no world-state, his purported solution is highly problematic within an integrated global economy and shared ecology. Some countries export their pollution costs to other locales. Norway has stringent environmental protection statutes but exports its oil to other jurisdictions having little or none. Additionally, a patchwork of policies adopted by various nation-states does little to protect the world's shared ecology. It does not matter how green wealthy countries might become if developing nations pollute at voracious rates. Moreover, if wealthy nations were to attempt to impose their green

20. Finn, *Christian Economic Ethics*, 203.

agenda on others through tariffs, sanctions, or more coercive measures, not only could global unrest ensue, but the poor would be most directly harmed. To date less coercive international attempts to shrink the human "ecological footprint" through various agreements and treaties has proven futile. Whether or not the emergence of market-states as opposed to nation-states will more effectively address the problem of scale remains to be seen.

Finn's rather blithe assertion that markets cannot and will not solve the problem of scale, and that *only* the state is equipped to do so is questionable. He does not mention, for instance, how diminishing natural resources and rising energy prices may prompt new markets for alternatives based on unforeseen technological innovations. Nonetheless, Finn raises the important reminder that material economic growth is not infinite and therefore not infinitely sustainable. Consequently, even the most vociferous proponents of globalization cannot evade the issue of the limits of economic growth.

An adequate assessment of this issue requires some inquiry into its objective: *what is the end of economic growth.* "End" connotes two different but related concerns. On the one hand, since economic growth entails the production, consumption, and accumulation of material goods it cannot continue forever. At some point thermodynamics kicks in and stasis takes over. Although the fate of a static universe is so distant that it does not (or should not) prompt any immediate anxiety, it nonetheless serves as a reality check that we live in a finite rather than infinite world. More immediately it requires us to be attentive to the fact that the current forces generating economic growth on a global scale are not inexhaustible. Assuming, for example, that plentiful supplies of fossil fuels will *always* be available is foolish. Eventually other sources of energy will need to be developed.

On the other hand, "end" denotes purpose. The purpose of economic growth is not growth per se. This would be tantamount to saying that the purpose of eating is to continue eating. At some point an optimal point of satisfaction is reached in which any further consumption becomes gratuitous or worse gluttonous. Likewise with economic growth an optimal point can be reached where further production, consumption, and accumulation of wealth becomes superfluous or worse avaricious. To raise the issue of scale is, to a large extent, to pose the question: when is enough really enough?

Again, to be clear I am not suggesting that the state or any other self-appointed moral authority is in the position to determine where this line should be drawn for all individuals, societies, or nations. I am also not implying that enough material goods are already available and what is required is their equitable redistribution. To the contrary, economic growth needs to be sustained for the foreseeable future if the good of affluence is to be pursued, used, and enjoyed on a global scale.

To raise the question of the purpose of economic growth is to help individuals, societies, and nations determine when an optimal level of affluence has been reached. Failing to make this determination diminishes human well-being, because when economic growth becomes its own end, then time, energy, and resources are expended with steadily diminishing returns. One contribution that Christian moral theology can make in determining the scale and purpose of economic growth is to reaffirm the virtue of charity. Particularly when an optimal level of affluence is attained, generosity is not an accompanying duty or obligation, but a means of promoting human flourishing by enriching the lives of both givers and recipients. More broadly, Christian moral teaching may remind that the good life is not one that can be ultimately captured by an inventory or spreadsheet. The good life is lived out in relation to God, family, friends, neighbors, strangers, customers, and competitors. The good life that Christians commend is at its core relational. As I have argued, contrary to some prevalent strands in the Christian tradition, that affluence, and therefore economic growth, can strengthen rather than weaken human relationships, but GDP is not an irrelevant indicator of human flourishing.

Quality of Relations

Market exchanges create many relationships, not only between buyers and sellers, but also among employers, employees, producers, suppliers, and competitors. Most of these relationships are benign. I deposit a check at my bank and banter a bit with the teller, and I am grateful that my seminary pays me to do work that I enjoy and find fulfilling (most of the time). But not all interactions are pleasant. I would not be happy if my bank refused to give me back the money I deposited, and I would be unhappy if I worked for a taskmaster that forced me to work long hours under wretched conditions for little pay.

Governments often regulate market exchanges in order to prevent potentially unseemly relations. Banks are regulated to prevent them from defrauding customers, and laws are enacted overseeing workplace safety, time constraints, and minimum wage. These interventions are often salutary, but not always effective and at times unintentionally or willfully harmful. Regulators may prove to be inept or corrupt. A policy designed to solve a particular problem may unintentionally create others. For instance, imposing more restrictive investment and lending regulations on banks and venture capital firms may discourage the creation of new enterprises and employment opportunities. Or a regime may enact policies overtly favoring the interests of particular corporations or cronies, effectively creating state-sanctioned monopolies. At worst, a government may ignore the rule of law and rights of individuals through the seizure of property and incarceration. All of these unfavorable consequences, rather intended or not, diminish the quality of relations. In each of these instances, the state uses its coercive power to enforce these policies or preferences. In short, states have the rightful authority to coerce in order to enforce compliance, but whether or not particular states use such coercion in a just manner is a different issue.

Moreover, it should be noted that all regulatory interventions are predicated on and enforced by the coercive power of the state. This does not suggest that coercion is unsalutary, for its use or threat is needed to enforce the rule of law and protect the rights of individuals and organizations. Nonetheless, the quality of relations differs when it is voluntary as opposed to compelled. A bank, for example, cannot force me to deposit my money in its safe (or more accurately deposit my digitized financial information in its computer), but I would suffer severe consequences if I refuse or fail to pay my taxes.[21]

The effect of globalization on the quality of relations is mixed. In some instances the quality of relations has been strengthened. For example, greater affluence may enable individuals to spend more time with family and friends or participate in a wider range of activities and common pursuits beyond the workplace. In other instances, the quality of relations has been weakened or at least neglected. Given the highly competitive nature of global markets, some people are subjected to long and exhausting hours of work, under wretched conditions at meager pay. How global corporations and their suppliers treat their employees, maintain safe working conditions, and are attentive to broader community concerns varies widely among firms.[22] To some extent both the

21. Consequently, I find depositing my check in a bank account more pleasurable than sending one to the IRS.
22. For an example of how one global corporation deals with these concerns, see "Unilever: In Search of the Good Business," *The Economist*, August 9, 2014.

manicured corporate campuses and gated communities of Silicon Valley and sweatshops in a slum symbolize the mixed effects of globalization.

Regulatory responses on the part of nation-states are also uneven, resulting in localized and disparate levels of protection, uncertainty, and risk. Some governments may be either unwilling or unable to impose significant or effective regulation. One country may choose to impose few regulations in order to encourage capital investment, while another lacks the ability to adequately enforce enacted regulations. Moreover, regulatory policies and practices of particular nations, as well as their consistent and fair enforcement, vary widely, and attempts at standardization through international treaties and agreements have not proven to be uniformly successful. Some regimes may fail, disregard, or repudiate proffered safeguards protecting invested capital, property, and workers. Collectively, this cacophony of regulations affects the investment of capital, workers, and consumers in both advantageous and disadvantageous ways that in turn may strengthen or weaken the quality of relations.

In aggregate, globalization has vastly enlarged the scope of markets within which exchange takes place, as well as reconfiguring how markets operate. Global "marketplaces" are now both physical and virtual. The ensuing benefits in respect to prices and convenience cannot be denied, but there are also accompanying effects on the quality of relations, since exchanges are increasingly anonymous and distant. Traditionally, a marketplace entailed a physical locale in which exchanges required some kind of "face-to-face" interaction. Over time familiarity and trust are established among marketplace participants,[23] in turn supporting the broader civil community. In contrast, when I purchase an item on Amazon.com, no familiarity is needed or expected. So long as Amazon has the item and I have a credit card, I will get what I want, and there is no checker with whom I can banter. Additionally, the transaction does not entail any broader and shared civil community. On those rare occasions when I need to talk or chat with a customer service rep to resolve a problem, I have no idea where he or she is located.

This does not imply that globalization inevitably destroys local communities and diminishes the quality of individual lives. Rather, it acknowledges that expanding global markets change how goods and services are produced and consumed, and that these changes affect, for good or ill, the quality of relations. To use a trivial example, one day I went to the barbershop and after getting my haircut I realized I didn't have any cash and my barber does not accept credit cards. I suggested that I go to the

---

23. Or untrustworthy participants are identified.

bank to get some money, and offered my mobile phone as a hostage to ensure my payment. She rejected my offer and told me to pay her the next time I was in the area. I doubt if a similar arrangement would ever occur on any commercial website.

Although too much should not be read into this example, it nevertheless reveals an important element underpinning exchange: namely, familiarity and trust. Over the years my barber and I have become familiar to each other, and she trusts that I will pay her for a haircut as I have always done in the past. On that embarrassing day she assumed that my empty wallet was the result of my absentmindedness (I am, after all, a professor) and not a ploy to deceive her. But more broadly, we run into each other occasionally at the grocery store or some public event, and we chat about topics other than haircuts. There is a sense that we share, however vaguely and tenuously, a larger association that, although supported by commercial activities, is not entirely predicated on or determined by market exchanges.

What does this admittedly trivial example have to do with globalization? Exchanges within global markets do not build on trust and are not based on trust, but are predicated on verification and coercion. Before I purchase an item on a website my credit card is verified. More broadly, before capital is invested the reliability of governments in enforcing contracts and other assurances and safeguards are assessed. And given the increasingly remote and anonymous character of exchanges in global markets, the effects on larger and dependent associations are neither presupposed nor taken into account. An issue that is rarely addressed is the extent to which globalization tends to promote or diminish the creation of social capital. Moreover, governmental regulatory intervention alone, however effective it might prove to be, cannot create social capital. The state can adopt policies that either, overtly or inadvertently, promote or diminish social capital, but it cannot create it due to the state's necessary recourse to the threat or use of coercion. Complying with duties and obligations imposed and enforced by the state is not the same thing as acts predicated on familiarity and trust.

In brief, human flourishing occurs within associations that share goods that can be neither exchanged nor coerced, or following Augustine, they are "bound together by a common agreement as to the objects of their love."[24] Market exchange and political coercion either alone

24. Augustine, *Concerning the City of God against the Pagans*, trans. Henry Bettenson (London and New York: Penguin, 1972), 19/24; see also Oliver O'Donovan, *Common Objects of Love: Moral Reflection and the Shaping of Community* (Grand Rapids, MI, and Cambridge, UK: Eerdmans, 2002).

or in tandem can create neither this love nor its bonds. Exchange and coercion can serve to either strengthen or weaken these bonds. For example, exchange can generate affluence that provides associations with the leisure to attend to and enjoy the objects of their mutual love. Or the production and consumption of goods and services can become so overwhelming, either due to necessity or avarice, that common objects of love command inadequate attention, effectively weakening their binding quality. Likewise, the proper application of coercion can provide stable social environments that support, or at least permit, human associations to thrive through the strengthening of their shared bonds. Or coercion can be unduly asserted or withheld to such an extent that the bonds of common love are effectively crushed or wither due to insufficient support.

There are three possibilities regarding how markets and the state may serve to strengthen or weaken human associations: (1) they may be working at cross-purposes: one weakening, the other strengthening; (2) they may both weaken human associations; (3) they may both strengthen. The third option is preferable, but in order to properly orient markets and the state again requires that the question of purpose must be asked: *what is the goal of human associations?* The short answer to this question is human flourishing, and the remainder of this chapter and the next are dedicated to its elaboration.

Purposes an Economy Should Serve

Orienting markets and the coercive power of the state so that both promote human associations in which their participants might flourish requires what Finn portrays as a "moral ecology."[25] The first characteristic of any market is to set *rules* regarding what can be exchanged, how exchanges are made, and who may or may not participate. These rules are often set informally by those engaging in exchange in addition to governmental regulation that may range from negligible to extensive. *Essential goods and services* should be made available to all people regardless of ability to pay and may be provided through private assistance, taxes, or some combination. There is, however, no consensus regarding which goods and services are vital, and whether their provision should occur primarily through familial relationships, private charities, or governmental programs. Another vital component of the moral ecology is that markets require *virtuous participants*, both in terms of individuals and groups. In opposition to

25. See Finn, *Christian Economic Ethics*, 205–13, and *The Moral Ecology of Markets*, ch. 7.

current, existing economic exchange, which is based on verification and coercion, economic exchange within the moral ecology is predicated on trust, reliability, honesty, and promise keeping, and in their absence the scope and benefits of exchange are greatly diminished. Although markets are competitive, they cannot function without cooperation as well. The final component of the moral ecology is *civil society* that Finn defines as the "network of organizations larger than the family but smaller than the national government that helps organize daily life."[26] These organizations include such associations as schools, churches, service clubs and the like, which presumably promote the well-being of their members, as well as collectively promoting the common good of civil society. There is, however, little agreement over what constitutes the common good, how its promotion is best pursued, or even if this goal is best pursued through private or governmental initiatives. Although there is general agreement that the *coercive power of the state* is needed to sustain the moral ecology of markets, the extent to which this power should be asserted is ardently debated.

Although Finn's moral ecology suffers certain weaknesses that are alluded to in subsequent chapters, it nonetheless provides a useful framework for reorienting markets and the state. If an economy, through both markets and governmental regulations, is to solve the problems of allocation, distribution, scale, and quality of relations, then rules, the provision of essential goods and services, virtuous marketplace participants, a robust civil society, and the coercive power of the state are surely required. But what kinds of rules, essential goods and services, virtues, civil society, and coercive power are needed? Or more succinctly, what end or ends should markets and the state serve and promote? Answering this question is made more difficult given the complex economic and political challenges that globalization poses. Nevertheless, the question cannot be ignored, and answering it requires some recourse to purpose. The short answer, as professed previously, is human flourishing. This answer, however, is vague because it joins two abstractions into a single concept. What does "human" mean, and what constitutes its "flourishing"? Both terms require further explanation if their joining is to provide a useful shorthand reference.

26. Finn, *Christian Economic Ethics*, 207. Finn's exclusion of the family reflects, perhaps, a presumption of the so-called nuclear family as being normative. In some cultures extended families or kinship networks can exert, for good or ill, substantial influence on commercial activities, political governance, and civil society. See Francis Fukuyama, *Trust: The Social Virtues and the Creation of Prosperity* (New York and London: Free Press, 1995), part 2.

Human

We begin with human, and we need not undertake an exhaustive survey of theological anthropology given the limited scope of this inquiry into how markets and the state should be oriented toward promoting the flourishing of human beings. A precise definition of what it means to be human is not needed to initiate moral discourse on how market exchanges and political coercion may promote or hinder the well-being of consumers and citizens. Rather, we may concentrate on humans as individuals, members of associations, and participants in civil society. I have chosen these three categories because of their rough correlation across varying cultural, social, and political contexts. Although there are differing understandings of personal identity and agency, [it is ultimately individuals who produce and consume, who govern and are governed.] People around the world congregate with one another, though the scope, purposes, and opportunities for association are highly diverse. These associations in turn form, either formally or informally, licitly or clandestinely, networks for ordering a variety of daily activities that collectively may be designated as civil society. Moreover, these three categories are not discrete or insular, but interlocking and integrally related. To conceive one presupposes and reinforces the necessity of the other two. To speak about an individual is to also refer to her network of associations, and conversely to speak about civil society is to refer to the particular individuals constituting its associations. Again, globalization adds complexity toward fashioning fitting moral discourse, because although the categories of individuals, associations, and civil society are rough correlates, they are neither singular nor identical within various cultural, social, and political settings.

Individuals

To invoke the word "human" is to conjure a rather cold and lifeless image. To be human is to be something more than part of a generic or abstract species, population, or class. Following Hannah Arendt, there is no such thing as humankind, but only particular men and women.[27] To denote human is to refer to persons who experience joy and happiness, pain and suffering in particular and unique ways.[28] It is important to keep in mind that underlying all the aggregate statistics and charts measuring

---

27. See Hannah Arendt, *The Promise of Politics* (New York: Schocken Books, 2005), 61–62.
28. See Robert Spaemann, *Persons: The Difference between "Someone" and "Something"* (Oxford and New York: Oxford University Press, 2006).

economic success and failure are individuals with particular needs and wants, and distinctive desires and aspirations.

Global markets are instruments that can either enhance or diminish individual well-being. Individuals with requisite skills and opportunities can successfully compete in these markets in order to satisfy their desires and aspirations, whereas other individuals are crushed by competitors, lack skills, or are prevented from competing, while others are simply unable to use markets in meeting their most basic needs and wants. Likewise, governmental regulations can either promote or impede individual well-being. Well-regulated markets ensure equal opportunities to compete and enforce fair competition that encourages widespread prosperity, while poorly regulated markets prevent many individuals from competing or support unfair competition effectively ensconcing widespread impoverishment.

Biblical and Christian theological teachings are unapologetic in respect to the moral worth or value of individuals. Every person bears the *imago Dei*, and therefore an inherent, God-given dignity that is to be respected and protected.[29] Many of Jesus' parables and healings focus on the value or plight of a particular person; the good shepherd expends considerable time and energy searching for one lost sheep,[30] and individuals with specific maladies are made well. Subsequent moral teaching continues this emphasis on the individual, particularly in respect to charity. People who are hungry and naked should be fed and clothed through the acts of other, more fortunate individuals. The theological prospect and imperative of correcting the ill effects on a systemic basis is a recent development in Christian social and political thought. Admittedly this shift in emphasis was motivated by a genuine thirst for justice, but it too, like macroeconomics, often slips into the trap of turning humans into an abstraction, losing sight of the needs and wants, hopes and desires of particular persons. Although individual rights are often overemphasized in affluent Western societies, their importance in developing regions cannot be overestimated if poor individuals are to be genuinely helped.[31]

29. See John Kilner, *Dignity and Destiny: Humanity in the Image of God* (Grand Rapids, MI, and Cambridge, UK: Eerdmans, 2015).

30. Luke 15:3–7.

31. See William Easterly, *The Tyranny of Experts: Economists, Dictators, and the Forgotten Rights of the Poor* (New York: Basic Books, 2013), esp. chs. 9–10.

Associations

Although each person has inherent worth and dignity, individuals do not live in isolation from one another; they associate. This is due in part to the practical necessity of cooperation in order to enrich the material quality of life, a principle captured in Adam Smith's notion of the specialization of labor. More broadly, individual identity is formed in relation and contrast to other individuals. I can only be a teacher, for example, in relation and contrast to students. People form and maintain associations that range from informal friendships to highly complex and structured organizations. The purposes for which people associate vary widely, such as shared commercial or professional interests, leisure pursuits, the arts, charitable giving, sports, religious activities and the like. It is within this broad range of associations that individuals learn and practice such crucial virtues as trust, reliability, and reciprocity. Moreover, except for familial and political associations, almost all other forms are, at least ideally, voluntary or chosen. It is virtually impossible to imagine human life in the absence of associations.

Again, global markets can either strengthen or weaken human associations. As noted previously, participation in global markets can generate more widely dispersed affluence or prosperity that frees individuals to allot more time, energy, and capital to associations that are not devoted exclusively to commercial transactions. Market competition, however, can also weaken associations by requiring an inordinate investment of time, energy, and capital in the production of goods and services, depopulating local communities in response to consumer demands, and diminishing trust and familiarity that often accompanies labor migration. More broadly, the increasingly anonymous and remote character of exchange that globalization fosters often reinforces a false sense of individual autonomy.

Likewise, governmental policies and regulations also strengthen or weaken associations. Governments may permit and protect the right of individuals to associate with one another for any lawful purpose, while other regimes may place constraints on the purposes for which individuals are permitted to legally associate. Moreover, it should not be assumed that certain forms of government invariably permit or promote a wide or constrained range of association. For example, a strong sense of individualism in the United States is often attributed to its tradition of limited government. Yet people in the United States have been adept at forming a wide variety of voluntary associations. In contrast, socialist or communist regimes purportedly champion social solidarity, but their citizens have little desire or opportunities to express their camaraderie through voluntary or private associations.[32] Indeed, in totalitarian regimes individuals may strive for as much autonomy and anonymity as possible, given their mutual suspicions of one another.

In conjunction with biblical and theological teaching on the inherent worth and dignity of every individual, there has been an equally strong emphasis on the need and good of human association. The biblical story of Adam and Eve makes clear that it is not good to be alone,[33] and the church exists when two or three are gathered in the Lord's name.[34] Although there are individual believers, they are also parts of Christ's body.[35] More expansively, Christians believe in a relational rather than unitary God, a Trinitarian relation of one in three, and three in one. The Father can only be understood in relation to the Son and Holy Spirit, and the same pattern holds true for the other two persons. The influence of these biblical and theological themes on the development of Western social and political theory and practice should not be underestimated. According to Luigino Bruni and Stefano Zamagni, within the Western tradition the very notion of civil society is inconceivable in the absence of Christian Trinitarian thought.[36] These biblical and theological themes should continue to inform economic and political thought in respect to how policies and practices may assist, or at least not hinder, people from associating. More particularly, although much of Christian moral teaching on wealth needs to be revised in light of how affluence is now created, it should also continue to warn that the accumulation of material goods is not an adequate substitute for common, often nonmaterial goods that are created and shared within human associations. Consequently, how should markets and governmental regulations be oriented to meet the need of people to freely associate?

Civil Society

Civil society denotes both the network of human associations described above, and their maintenance over time. Although many informal associations are temporary or provisional, more formal associations endure over extended periods of time. Civil society in its totality provides continuity

32. See Fukuyama, *Trust*, ch. 6.
33. Gen. 2:18–24.
34. Matt. 18:20.
35. 1 Cor. 12:12–31.
36. See Luigino Bruni and Stefano Zamagni, *Civil Economy: Efficiency, Equity, Public Happiness* (Bern and Oxford: Peter Lang, 2007), 27.

while also responding to and incorporating changing cultural, social, economic, and political circumstances. The church, for example, may be regarded as a global religious association that has existed, in varying and changing forms, over the past two millennia, in turn interacting with and influencing other associations constituting civil society. Civil society is dependent on, but not reducible to, either the market or the state, in turn playing a crucial role in mediating the relations of individuals to both economic exchange and coercive political power.

The importance of this mediating role cannot be gainsaid if individuals are to avoid being reduced to little more than producers and consumers, or vassals of the state. Collective action can help people to both take advantage of and resist the corrosive effects of global markets. Through common effort, individuals can acquire skills and knowledge that promote their own affluence as well as that of others, and which in turn can be used to create social capital that promotes civil life. Such common effort can also help to preserve the enduring good of civil society in reaction to threatening market forces. A similar pattern holds true in respect to the state. Some governments may either fail or lack the ability to assert sufficient power to protect the right of association—failed states invariably lead to failed or impoverished civil societies. Or more troubling, the state may perceive civil society as a competitor for the loyalty of its citizens, and effectively discourage or overtly forbid associations that are not subject to governmental control. The coercive power of the state is always enhanced when it governs individuals who lack opportunities to associate. As Arendt contends, totalitarian regimes thrive on "isolation and lack of normal social relationships,"[37] being little more than "mass organizations of atomized, isolated individuals."[38] Civil society is a bulwark of individual freedom by preserving the right of individuals to associate.

There is much in the Christian tradition that may be taken to support civil society as a public space for individuals to associate, particularly in respect to markets and political coercion. The gospel, for instance, is a liberating message to the poor and oppressed. Both the Bible and Christian moral teaching condemn commercial and political practices that perpetuate poverty, but the harshest condemnations are aimed at governments that oppress their people, especially those who are the weakest and most vulnerable. Nevertheless, biblical and Christian moral teaching

---

37. Hannah Arendt, *The Origins of Totalitarianism* (San Diego, CA: Harvest Book, 1968), 317.
38. Ibid., 323.

also acknowledges and affirms the necessity of political governance.[39] Freedom, then, is a word that fits comfortably within the Christian moral lexicon, but it is always understood in terms of relationships. Consequently, freedom is defined and exercised within bonds of human association or fellowship, and is also never far removed from justice that delineates and constrains both exchange and coercion.

The preceding comments on individuals, associations, and civil society are admittedly cursory, but they are revisited frequently throughout the remainder of the book, receiving further elaboration. At this juncture they serve as useful categories for understanding what human flourishing comprises. In other words, to speak of human *flourishing* requires an inquiry into how individuals, their associations, and civil societies might thrive in respect to global markets and emerging market-states. The next chapter initiates this inquiry.

39. See, e.g., Rom. 13 and Augustine, *City of God*, bk. 19.

Chapter Seven

Koinonia

Communicating the Goods of Creation

The thesis of this chapter is simple and straightforward: humans flourish as individuals and as members of associations that constitute civil society. Therefore, markets and states should be ordered in ways that promote, or at the very least permit, individuals to form and freely participate in associations that collectively sustain a robust civil society. The principal reason why human flourishing occurs within these predominantly noncommercial and nonpolitical associations is because they are not predicated primarily on either exchange or coercion, but on koinonia—or communication. Human flourishing results from communicating goods that can be neither exchanged nor coerced. Although markets and states are related to and both may assist this communication, they may also prove to be a hindrance. Or worse, markets and states may attempt or be allowed to supersede communication, and neither one is equipped to be an adequate substitute, thereby effectively diminishing human flourishing. Humans do not flourish when reduced to producers and consumers or to denizens of the state. Human associations do not exist to promote the interests of markets or states; but, conversely, markets and states should enable and protect civil society.

In the remainder of this chapter I define what communication or koinonia means and why it embodies human flourishing. Although koinonia has strong religious connotations, I argue that its core principles and practices are applicable to other, nonreligious forms of association. Building on the discussion initiated in the previous chapter, I further examine how markets and states may either support or obstruct civil society, particularly in light of the globally integrated economy and emerging market-state.

Koinonia

Communication has come to mean sending, receiving, transmitting, and exchanging information or news.[1] A variety of media are employed to accomplish this task, such as correspondence, television, telephones, e-mails, texting, video conferencing, and the Internet. For late moderns, so-called information and communication technologies are becoming increasingly entwined and indistinguishable.

Communication, however, has a much richer and more interesting pedigree. It is derived from the Latin *communicare*, which means, "to share." The word also has a Greek antecedent—*koinōnia*—that, according to Oliver O'Donovan, can be variously translated as "community," "communion," or "communicate."[2] For O'Donovan, communication is not merely a descriptive term but ascribes the basic form of social life: "To 'communicate' is to hold some thing as common, to treat it as 'ours,' rather than 'yours' or 'mine.' The partners to a communication form a community, a 'we' in relation to the object in which they participate."[3] A communication is neither a one-way conferral nor a mutual exchange. The object being communicated becomes an "ours" without the parties relinquishing their respective claims. The primary purpose of communicating shared objects is to ground human equality in a specific social nexus, because in relation to God as ultimate creator or origin of these objects, no individual can be the foundation of a communication. No woman, for instance, can communicate with herself. Two or more individuals communicate such objects as gifts, meals, and property, and there are appropriate social spheres for conducting these communications such as families, religious communities, and commerce.

Consequently, reciprocity (as opposed to bestowal, exchange, or coercion) encapsulates how koinonia as the basic form of social life is enacted. Reciprocity entails various acts located between unidirectional giving or receiving, roughly equivalent exchange, and exerting or threatening coercion.[4] Moreover, such reciprocal relationships are

---

1. This section draws upon previous themes developed in Brent Waters, *Christian Moral Theology in the Emerging Technoculture: From Posthuman Back to Human* (Farnham, UK, and Burlington, VT: Ashgate, 2014), and "Communication," in Robert Song and Brent Waters, eds., *The Authority of the Gospel: Explorations in Moral and Political Theology in Honor of Oliver O'Donovan* (Grand Rapids, MI, and Cambridge, UK: Eerdmans, 2015).

2. See Oliver O'Donovan, *The Ways of Judgment: The Bampton Lectures, 2003* (Grand Rapids, MI, and Cambridge, UK: Eerdmans, 2005), 242–43.

3. Ibid., 242.

4. See Luigino Bruni and Stefano Zamagni, *Civil Economy: Efficiency, Equity, Public Happiness* (Oxford and Bern: Peter Lang, 2007), 168–69.

predicated on an ontological equality among the parties, though often expressed in asymmetrical ways. These reciprocal relationships "cannot operate without substantial equality among the parties, because neither reciprocity nor friendship can exist between a benefactor and a passive recipient."[5] In short, human associations based on reciprocity cannot be sustained exclusively on benefaction, exchange, or coercion.

Civil society comprises differentiated spheres of communication that share "enkaptic relations."[6] An *enkaptic* relation requires each sphere to have an internal order that is pertinent to the goods its members are communicating, and they also interact, overlap, and are dependent on other differentiated spheres. A family, for example, communicates a wide range of emotional and physical goods, but it also depends on such other external and overlapping spheres as schools, health care facilities, and the workplace in order to communicate its internal goods. These interactions, however, must be limited if respective social spheres are to remain differentiated. To return to the family, although it depends on other spheres to sustain itself, this does not suggest that it should model its communication in line with these other spheres. A family should not organize itself as if it were a school or business firm, and likewise schools and businesses should not communicate their internal goods as if they were families. It is precisely the differences among the various social spheres that enable communication, or koinonia, to be the foundational form of the social life.

O'Donovan uses two critical concepts in explicating a differentiated civil society. The first concept is that of a *people*. Civil society is not simply an assortment of autonomous individuals, but the outcome of beliefs, customs, and associations, of a particular people over time. A people hold in common a perception of a binding good or goods that together they pursue or should pursue. This imaginative construct is not capricious, because it stems from a binding and enduring cultural tradition. Such a cultural tradition is instantiated and preserved in a network of "overlapping and interlocking" spheres of communication,[7] confirming, to a large extent, Augustine's dictum that a people are bound together by their common objects of love.[8] A people tacitly concur on

---

5. Ibid., 184.

6. See Herman Dooyeweerd, *A Christian Theory of Social Institutions* (La Jolla, CA: Herman Dooyeweerd Foundation, 1986), and *A New Critique of Theoretical Thought*, vol. 3, *The Structures of Individuality of Temporal Reality* (Philadelphia, PA: Presbyterian and Reformed Publishing Co., 1957), pt. 1, ch. 2.

7. See O'Donovan, *The Ways of Judgment*, 150.

8. See Augustine, *City of God*, 29/24; see also Oliver O'Donovan, *Common Objects of Love: Moral Reflection and the Shaping of Community* (Grand Rapids, MI, and Cambridge, UK: Eerdmans, 2002), ch. 1.

what the goods of creation are, why they should be loved, and what social spheres are required in communicating these goods.

The second concept is that of *locale or place*. Territory and borders are decisive features of a people. Goods are communicated at particular places, and boundaries are necessary to differentiate the "you" and the "I" that become a "we." In short, the physicality of a place is required if goods are to be communicated—a family needs a house in which to reside; material goods and services are produced in a specific location. More expansively, place encompasses the totality of differing communications in which the social spheres cohere in a given locale. According to O'Donovan, it is a "high achievement to define society in terms of place, rather than blood-relationship," for such a "universal" notion embraces "all the forms of society that arise within a formally defined" place or bounded territory.[9] Civil society is not a free-floating construct, but grows out of and embodies a particular land and people.

O'Donovan draws on the work of Johannes Althusius who depicts civil society as an affiliation of associations and enkaptic social spheres rather than an alliance of autonomous individuals.[10] This affiliative alignment embodies an inherently social human nature. People cannot live a genuinely human life in isolation from each other, for God has determined that it is not good for any human to be alone.[11] Adam and Eve are *together* stewards of the garden that God planted. God did not, however, distribute the gifts or goods of creation evenly among human creatures. As a result, both labor and cooperation are needed to maintain Eden's fecundity, and it is worth quoting Althusius at length in this regard:

> [God] did not give all things to one person, but some to one and some to others, so that you have need for my gifts, and I for yours. And so was born, as it were, the need for communicating necessary and useful things, which communication was not possible except in social and political life. God therefore willed that each need the service and aid of others in order that friendship would bind all together, and no one would consider another valueless.[12]

---

9. See O'Donovan, *The Ways of Judgment*, 256.

10. See Johannes Althusius, *Politica*, trans. Frederick S. Carney (Indianapolis, IN: Liberty Fund, 1995).

11. See Genesis 2:15–25.

12. Althusius, *Politica*, 23.

Given this uneven distribution of gifts, labor and commercial exchanges—markets, if you will—are required for communicating the goods of God's creation. Since humans are "symbiotic" creatures, the chief task of the state is to support the "purpose of establishing, cultivating, and conserving social life," to the end of sustaining "holy, just, comfortable, and happy symbiosis, a life lacking nothing either useful or necessary."[13]

The principal import of O'Donovan's account of communication is its implication that human flourishing occurs most readily in communicating the goods of creation. Conversely, human flourishing is diminished when opportunities for koinonia are unavailable or restricted. Neither markets nor states can engage directly in communicating goods, because the former is predicated on exchange and the latter on coercion. Moreover, the concept of communication reinforces the notion that humans do not flourish exclusively as consumers or citizens, but as individuals embedded within a society composed of associations or spheres of communication. There must be a distinct "you" and "I" before a "we" can emerge, and there must also be social settings in which communicating can occur. As Ted McAllister contends, an "individual as a human personality emerges as a product of a social environment—without society, there are no humans,"[14] and more pointedly, that "humans have a fundamental need to be part of a community, including a community of purpose."[15] In order to flourish, a people need a place that is neither a market nor a state—hence the need for a civil society that is free from unwarranted intrusions by both.

If O'Donovan's account of communication is correct, then it would appear that human flourishing can only be diminished within a globally integrated economy. The dynamic and destructive forces of global markets are not conducive to either preserving a people or a particular place. The fluidity of trade, capital, and labor tends to promote volatile or provisional conditions in respect to associations dependent on stable locales. Global markets encourage nomadic producers, workers, and consumers since mobility provides a competitive advantage. There is little that nation-states can do to effectively counter this nomadic proclivity. If a state embraces globalization in order to improve the economic opportunities of its citizens, it cannot protect the associations or spheres of communication that constitute civil society other than providing temporary

---

13. Ibid., 17–18.
14. Ted V. McAllister, *Revolt against Modernity: Leo Strauss, Eric Voegelin, and the Search for a Postliberal Order* (Lawrence: University Press of Kansas, 1995), 11.
15. Ibid., 267.

safety nets for individuals suffering the ill effects of competitive markets. A state adopting protectionist policies may initially provide a buffer for groups and associations from the creative destruction of global markets, but at the cost of diminishing the material well-being of its citizens over time that may also serve to erode civil society. Globalization is apparently inimical to human flourishing based on communicating shared goods.

Admittedly, globalization exerts a corrosive influence on many traditional communicative associations. This challenge is examined in greater detail below, but before proceeding an interpretive lens needs to be developed. It is important to recognize that O'Donovan is a Christian moral theologian. Consequently, the church is the premier social sphere in which the goods of creation are communicated. The church, therefore, may offer an example of a communicative association that is potentially well suited for meeting the challenges posed by globalization, and perhaps even thriving in a world in which global markets and the emerging market-state are ascendant.

First, the church, through its common life, worship, and ministry, is a community centered almost exclusively on reciprocity. The church is not an association based on exchange. One cannot buy the mercy and grace of God or purchase the forgiveness of those one has wronged. The church, as an institution, does engage in exchange. It pays salaries to its ministers and other employees, hires people to maintain its buildings, invests its financial resources and endowments in financial markets, and depends on the generosity of its members who ultimately earn their incomes through market exchanges. The church participates, both directly and indirectly, in markets in order to maintain the organizational structures that fulfill its mission and ministry, but its internal life is not a marketplace. Christians do not gather on Sunday morning to exchange items, but to communicate the good of God that binds them together in fellowship.

The church is not an association based on coercion. It cannot force people to be baptized or receive the sacrament,[16] and although it may discipline its members—for example, by withholding the sacrament or by excommunication—it cannot incarcerate or seize the property of individual Christians. Moreover, it is not governed, unlike the state, through a zero-sum process of acquiring and losing power. The church, however, can be a beneficiary of governmental services such as police and fire protection, and its members are also citizens who participate in political activities or hold governmental responsibilities. The church can

---

16. I am not aware of any contemporary church teaching or theologians that condone episodes of enforced conversions that blemish the history of the church.

also be a target of repressive regimes, and its members can be victims of state-sponsored or sanctioned persecution. The church exists within states that may enable or constrain its attempt to fulfill its mission and ministry, but its internal life is not political. Christians do not gather on Sunday morning as a legislative body, but to communicate the good of God that transcends all political affiliations.

The church is not an association based on charity. This may seem to be an odd claim to make since charity plays such a central role in Christian thought and practice. And so it should. Christians are commanded by their Lord to assist those in need wherever in the world they might be. Through both ecclesiastical channels and individual efforts, the church supports endeavors to feed the hungry, shelter the homeless, clothe the naked, and heal the sick across the oceans, in nearby neighborhoods, and within its own households of faith. Markets and states may assist or hinder the efficacy of these charitable efforts, but the church's internal life is not centered around unidirectional giving and receiving. Christians do not gather on Sunday morning to only give or receive, but to communicate the good of fellowship that they share together.

The church, then, is an association that engenders reciprocity, a simultaneous giving *and* receiving that is neither exchanged nor coerced. In the life of the church what is "yours" does not become "mine" and vice versa; an "I" cannot seize what is "yours" to make it "mine" and vice versa; one cannot be solely a perpetual giver or receiver. Rather, there is a reciprocal giving and receiving in which a good is not exchanged, seized, or lost, but shared or communicated. Markets and political governance, then, are necessary in ordering human life, but neither is sufficient, and even both in tandem are insufficient, to promote human flourishing, because neither independently or together is a form of koinonia.

Second, the church, through both its theological organizational principles and historical experience, suggests some helpful ways for negotiating the volatility of competitive global markets and diffidence of emerging market-states. In many respects, the church is a unique form of human association. It is a "gathering community,"[17] whose members are drawn from every race and nation.[18] It is an association that cuts across and negates divisive social and political divisions, for unity in and obedience to Christ also entails equality in Christ. The church, then, is

17. See Oliver O'Donovan, *The Desire of the Nations: Rediscovering the Roots of Political Theology* (Cambridge, UK: Cambridge University Press, 1996), 174–78.
18. See Matthew 28:16–20.

an association of second-births rather than first-births, because no one is born into the church, but rather baptized into its koinonia.

Consequently, the church is not territorial. It exists wherever its members gather. It is not a community tied to a particular place or locale; it communicates wherever it happens to be. The church, therefore, is highly mobile. In this respect, it shares a striking similarity with late modern nomads who tend to follow, or are displaced by, free-flowing capital, production, and labor.[19] But Christians are not nomadic; pilgrimage is a more apt metaphor. To evoke Augustine's imagery of the two cities,[20] the ultimate loyalty of Christians is the heavenly city, but they are residents of its earthly counterpart. Consequently, they are always a bit restless because they are not entirely at home in the world. This restlessness stems largely from the eschatological orientation of Christian faith. Christians anticipate the Parousia of their Lord and the accompanying consummation of creation. This restless anticipation, however, does not diminish the importance of their present residency in the earthly city, inspiring indifference or loathing of their current, earthly circumstances, for the two cities do not exist side by side but are intermingled. Although Christians are not entirely at home in this world, they nonetheless love God's creation and the goods it affords. But in contrast to late modern nomads who purportedly only require the provision of goods and services enabling their mobility, the pilgrims of the heavenly city insist that such mobility should be used to promote communication rather than be restricted to exchange, or more troubling, property to be seized.

The church is also universal, but *not* homogenous. Although the church is unified in Christ, the expression of its unity is not uniform. Drawing its members from every race and nation does not entail negating their respective particularities and peculiarities. In and through its koinonia, the church is a community of variegated unity, communicating a shared faith in pluriform ways. In worshiping with fellow Christians in various locales, for instance, one simultaneously encounters elements that are familiar and unfamiliar.

In contrast, the state fosters a homogenous universality. Citizens are more easily and efficiently governed when they share uniform convictions

---

19. For an overview of the emerging late modern nomadic life, prompted in large part by new and expanding global markets, see "Special Report: Mobility," *The Economist*, April 12, 2008.

20. See Augustine, *City of God*. Allusions of the Christian life as one of pilgrimage permeate Augustine's masterpiece. See esp. bks. 15 and 29.

and practices. There is a common perception, however vague, of what constitutes a good political order that the state attempts to protect and promote. Within democracies there is disagreement over how this ordering is best achieved, but the range of policy options that are debated are remarkably narrow. Characterizing the opposition as being too radical, in either a leftward or rightward direction, is often used as a strategy for gaining power. Or on those rare occasions when a party or leader comes to power with a so-called revolutionary agenda, practice often disappoints, and a government is removed from office in succeeding electoral cycles. An authoritarian and tyrannical state forcefully imposes its ideological vision of a "good" political order on either a willing or unwilling populace through its coercive power. In each of these instances a powerful state finds it easier to manipulate or control public support or compliance by dealing directly with individual citizens to the detriment of private association to which they may belong. As noted in the previous chapter, isolating individuals from any form of association other than that controlled by the state is a central strategy of a totalitarian regime. Any state that either intentionally or unintentionally weakens civil society by proclaiming that political affiliation is a universally superior and encompassing form of human association is also taking a step down a tyrannous road, because coercion effectively displaces communication, the basic form of the social life.[21]

Markets also tend to encourage universality and homogeneity. The efficient production and consumption of goods and services requires both an economy of scale and uniformity of function. If every item were unique, then relatively little would be produced or consumed. Such commonplace items as computers, smart phones, and cars are mass-produced in order to achieve affordable prices and in turn are purchased by masses of consumers. Certain customized features may be added for individuals willing to pay the additional cost, and certain brands may command customer loyalty, but all computers, smart phones, and cars function in pretty much the same way. Globalization simply amplifies the mass production and consumption of goods and services. Local or cultural customs may prompt particular ways in which mass-produced items are used, but their design and function remains unaltered. Computers, smart phones, and cars look and perform the same way anywhere they are used in the world: for example, there is no such thing as a uniquely Icelandic or Nigerian computer, although Icelanders and Nigerians may use identical

21. See F. A. Hayek, *The Road to Serfdom* (Chicago: University of Chicago Press, 2007), and Leo Strauss, *On Tyranny* (Chicago and London: University of Chicago Press, 2000).

computers for differing purposes. Markets, then, are not attuned to the internal needs of human associations, other than as demographic data for marketing particular goods and services to potential customers. Ultimately markets are designed to satisfy the needs and wants of self-interested individuals in which other bonds of association are rendered effectively extraneous to market exchanges.[22] This appeal to individual self-interest, however, produces a population of mass consumers that are more readily controlled or manipulated by both powerful commercial and political interests.[23] In this respect, universally homogenous markets are at best indifferent to civil society other than the extent to which it promotes or discourages the consumption of goods and services or, at worst, they relentlessly erode the bonds of human association by effectively encouraging the displacement of communication with exchange as the basic form of the social life.

Both states and markets tend to promote their respective universality and homogeneity as encompassing forms of human association. The danger is that both proffer a partial and misleading understanding of the universal that leads to a destructive goal of creating, paradoxically, homogenous individuals. A universal and homogenous state and a universal and homogenous market are both perilous, because it is assumed that either political coercion or economic exchange can be substituted for communication. Such replacement is inimical to human flourishing.

Following F. D. Maurice, the longing for some kind of universal association is a good desire given the social penchants of human nature.[24] This good desire, however, can be easily corrupted, the most salient example being that of a quest for universal empire. The centripetal force of imperial power destroys the particular customs, traditions, and identities of vanquished nations. The goal is to homogenize conquered lands and peoples into a singular artifact of imperial will and power. Although late modern nation-states and emerging market-states have ostensibly repudiated any interest in establishing empires, they nevertheless assert universalizing and homogenizing tendencies. The encroachment of the state, in both its liberal and authoritarian manifestations, into

22. Organizations also engage in market exchanges, but for purposes of production and consumption these corporate needs and wants are effectively regarded as being roughly analogous to those of self-interested individuals.

23. See Hannah Arendt, *The Human Condition* (Chicago and London: University of Chicago Press, 1998), pts. 1–4, esp. chs. 17 and 22; William T. Cavanaugh, *Being Consumed: Economics and Christian Desire* (Grand Rapids, MI, and Cambridge, UK: Eerdmans, 2008); and George Grant, *Philosophy in the Mass Age* (Toronto: University of Toronto Press, 1995).

24. See F. D. Maurice, *Social Morality* (London: Macmillan and Co, 1869).

virtually every aspect of daily life has a withering effect on symbiotic and communicative associations, effectively distorting civil society into an instrument of political control and manipulation. A rapidly expanding labyrinth of laws, policies, and regulations produces bloated and clumsy bureaucracies that effectively impose universal and homogenous compliance. The danger is not only that governmental encroachment tends to discourage potentially more efficient and efficacious initiatives originating in the private sector,[25] but more troubling, the tendency conflates public and political. The two spheres are certainly related, but not synonymous. The state, for instance, protects the rights of citizens to gather in public places and forums, but such gatherings are not properly organs of the state. In its most debased form this conflation is expressed in the sentiment that politics is the only thing that people do together publicly.

In many respects, new and expanding global markets have helped to resist or even reverse the state's encroachment. Competitive global markets pressure states to adopt less intrusive policies and leaner bureaucracies. Yet displacing the universal and homogenous state with the universal and homogenous market is not a good exchange. As noted above, markets tend to reduce individuals and communities to mass producers and consumers. More expansively, and more disturbing, this reductive tendency disperses the public sphere into a series of private exchanges. The goods of creation are not communicated but transformed into commodities to be bought and sold. Associations are therefore no longer symbiotic and communicative, because their only value is the extent to which they promote this process of commodification. A family, for instance, becomes not an association for communicating shared goods, but a unit consuming goods and services. In its most perverse form, this dispersal of the social sphere into markets is captured in the sentiment that the only things people hold in common are working and shopping.

The church satisfies this healthy longing for universal association; hence its emphasis on being catholic. Yet unlike the state and markets, its universality is not achieved at the cost of homogeneity. Again, the church is gathered from every race, nation, and culture. Although becoming one in Christ relativizes and redefines these identities and allegiances, it does not negate them. Rather, as Maurice insisted, these differences are both recognized and strengthened within the church's koinonia. The church's unity is expressed in pluriform ways, for it is out of the one that the many

---

25. See John Micklethwait and Adrian Wooldridge, *The Fourth Revolution: The Global Race to Reinvent the State* (New York: Penguin, 2014), esp. pts. 2 and 3.

come and not vice versa. In communicating its inherent goods, the church protects and strengthens both the freedom of individual believers *and* the unity of the community. The church's unity is composed of its parts, for every individual, in virtue of being one in Christ, is of equal value. And the church in turn provides a social setting in which communication, as opposed to exchange or coercion, exhibits the basic form of the social life. The individual is not amalgamated into the collective, and conversely, neither is the community a haphazard assortment of individuals. In short, the "I" and "You" become "We" without negating either "You" or "I." In this respect, the church exemplifies, in an admittedly crude way, the triune God.

Additionally, the church has endured for over two millennia as a communicative association. Consequently, it has a rich storehouse of practical experience, both good and bad, upon which to draw in light of changing economic and political circumstances. The church has both flourished and floundered in affluent and impoverished societies. The church has also prospered and faltered under conditions of political privilege, indifference, and persecution. Although the church has adapted to a wide range of changing cultural, economic, and political circumstances, certain core beliefs (such as the incarnation and the Trinity) and practices (such as charity and neighbor love) have endured, albeit in differing ways over time and in response to particular contexts. This history also discloses the church as being an imperfect exemplar of a communicative association, for it has often been unfaithful in both faith and practice. The church has hopefully learned valuable lessons from both its successes and mistakes, lessons that others can also learn from, on how best to protect and enable koinonia in a changing world.

In regard to the topic of this book, the preceding discussion suggests two important questions: (1) Can the church, as a communicative association, provide some suggestive ways for how other human associations, and more broadly civil society, might resist the universalizing and homogenizing tendencies of markets and the state? (2) Can the church, as a communicative association, provide some suggestive ways for how other human associations, and more broadly civil society, might flourish within the context of a globally integrated economy and emerging market-state?

Communication, Markets, and the State

In the remainder of this chapter I explore some ways that the church, as a communicative association, might assist other forms of human association to both resist unwarranted encroachments of markets and the state and how the terrain of an integrated global economy and emerging market-state might be navigated in ways that promote human flourishing. The first step in this exploration requires some initial clarification.

Koinonia is admittedly a heavily freighted religious, indeed Christian, concept and practice. How, then, can the church serve as a helpful model in a world that does not share its confession that Jesus Christ is the way, truth, and life?[26] To insist that the goods of creation can only be properly communicated exclusively within the church would be to slip into a false imperial universality. This confession is not made in a way that is somehow separate from or incompatible with the world as God's good creation that sustains and is shared by all its inhabitants. It is not only Christians who are created in the image and likeness of God, but all human beings.[27] This religious insight is encapsulated in the Augustinian dictum: out of the one, many. Consequently, we may speak of universal goods that cut across various societies and cultures that are pursued and enjoyed in pluriform ways, and misused in pluriform ways. Moreover, within the Christian tradition it is recognized that the various social spheres are grounded in the order of creation and have their respective internal orderings that cannot be replaced by an ecclesial substitute. Christian parents and business owners, for example, do not organize their families and firms as miniature churches.[28]

The church, then, can offer suggestions for how a broad spectrum of communicative associations might resist the corrosive universalizing and homogenizing tendencies of markets and states without imposing an ecclesial structure. And the same applies to suggesting ways that might enable such associations to flourish within a globally integrated economy and the emerging market-state. What are these promptings, particularly in light of globalization?

In addition to the preceding discussion on pluriform universality, the following brief dicta distilled from the previous section are most pertinent. (1) The emphasis on *reciprocity* resists the reductionist tendencies of markets and the state. Human flourishing is diminished when people are effectively reduced to being only consumers or citizens, either discretely or in tandem. Humans, as both individuals and communities, flourish in

---

26. John 14:6.

27. C. S. Lewis contends that the *imago Dei* is not limited to humans but includes, to a lesser extent, all of creation; see *Beyond Personality: The Christian Idea of God* (London: Geoffrey Bles, 1944), ch. 1.

28. See pertinent references in Brent Waters, *The Family in Christian Social and Political Thought* (Oxford and New York: Oxford University Press, 2007).

communicating goods that are shared, mutually given and received but not exchanged or coerced.

(2) The imagery of a *gathering community* resists artificial barriers that restrict or prevent communicating the goods of creation that diminish human flourishing. Culture, religion, race, ethnicity, and nationality are admittedly important sources of personal and social identity, but they can also be used in divisive ways to prevent new ways of communicating shared goods. The significance of these sources of identity should not be degraded through the homogenizing forces of markets and the state, but neither are these identities definitive or decisive in promoting human flourishing. In this respect, the dynamism of global markets offers potential new ways of creating and participating in communicative associations that transcend many traditional and artificial barriers without necessarily negating them, and governments may either enable or resist this potentiality.

(3) The notion of *nonterritorial association* is particularly pertinent to the contemporary circumstances of the new and expanding global markets. Mobility is a fitting symbol of globalization, because global markets are predicated on the rapid, and ideally unrestricted, movement of trade, capital, and labor. Consequently, communicating the goods of creation occurs increasingly by who is present at varying locales rather than in a given and fixed time and place. This mobility, however, helps to create the illusion that place and physical proximity are entirely irrelevant, in turn reinforcing the more pernicious deception of autonomous individuals who only need to exchange and not communicate. The emerging market-state can adapt to and utilize the dynamism of global markets, but it can also serve as a reminder that individuals are not simply free-floating consumers, but are also people bound by given social and political ties that cannot be entirely separated from particular locales. In this respect, the emerging market-state can exert a centripetal force against the centrifugal forces of global markets to create a healthy tension in which new forms of communicative associations might flourish.

Based on these three dicta—reciprocity, gathering community, and nonterritorial association—two closely related observations can be made regarding both the challenges and opportunities accompanying a globally integrated economy and the emerging market-state. These observations serve as basic premises that are developed in subsequent chapters.

First, the creative destruction of global markets offers, at least potentially, greater opportunities for a larger range of people to pursue and enjoy widespread affluence. In turn, this prosperity may serve to strengthen the communicative associations that constitute civil society. However, enabling people to take advantage of opportunities afforded by global markets presents a dilemma for political governance. Presumably, civil society cannot flourish within a political order that is limited to a minimalist protection of individual civil rights, but requires governance designed to promote a common or communicative identity of a people. Communicating shared goods, however, must also resist unwarranted encroachments by the state that smother the common identity of a people under the weight of bureaucratic regulation and control accompanying the false homogeneity and universality of the state. In short, the state does not create civil society, but "discovers and defends the social order" it governs. Government represents a people, and they see themselves in that representation, thereby repelling the "State-totalitarianism" endemic to late modernity in both its authoritarian and liberal manifestations.[29]

Herein lies the challenge of political governance: how does the state represent a people that is more dispersed in respect to the wide variety of goods they wish to communicate? In response to the fluidity of trade, capital, and labor generated by dynamic global markets, individuals are increasingly nomadic rather than settled. Moreover, this nomadic orientation is not restricted to physical mobility. People in place, so to speak, conduct commercial activities and benefit from the labor of others in distant locales. At any given time, a state's territorial jurisdiction may include a fluxionary collection of citizens, guest workers, foreign-owned firms, tourists, resident aliens, and illegal immigrants, whose interests also extend beyond its borders. The dynamism of global markets apparently erodes the state's ability to represent a people, given the nomadic pursuit of disparate interests. If human flourishing occurs in communicating shared goods, then presumably the best political option is to either resist participating in global markets through protectionist policies, or impose a global empire. Neither option is palatable, for both fail to represent those it claims to govern. Protectionism, regardless of any benevolent motivation, ultimately imposes involuntary impoverishment, and exerting any kind of imperial rule[30] is to enforce a counterfeit universality. In both instances, human flourishing is effectively diminished.

29. See O'Donovan, *The Ways of Judgment*, 155–57.

30. Imperial rule may be effectively exercised through the influence of international bodies, treaties, and agreements rather than military conquest and occupation; see George Grant, *Lament for a Nation: The Defeat of Canadian Nationalism* (Montreal and Kingston: McGill-Queen's University Press, 2000), and George Grant, *Technology and Empire: Perspectives on North America* (Toronto: House of Anansi, 1969).

As the historical experience of the church demonstrates, however, communicating shared or common goods are not restricted to particular places or physical locales. The church is a nonterritorial people. The mobile and nomadic character of participating in a globally integrated economy does not preclude forming and sustaining communicative associations. But they will take on more temporary, fluid, and plural structures, more akin to a gathering association drawing its members, in many instances, from multiple cultures, races, and nations. Civil society will comprise increasingly, though not entirely, associations that exist whenever and wherever two, three, or more are gathered to communicate, for a time, shared goods rather than more static and fixed institutions and organizations. The principal challenge of the emerging market-state—and it is a daunting one—is to simultaneously embrace the dynamism of global markets in order to promote more widespread prosperity, while at the same providing sufficient political stability for communicative associations to flourish. In this respect, the creative destruction of global markets is not a problem to be solved, but a force to be reckoned with and channeled in ways that promote human flourishing. This will require striking a proper balance for asserting the coercive power of the state that is designed to maintain a healthy tension between the centrifugal propensities of global markets and centripetal penchants of political governance. What might be entailed in creating and sustaining this tension is investigated in more detail in the following chapter on civil society and political ordering.

Second, the affluence generated by global markets is predicated on the mobility of capital, production, and labor. The nomads of a globally integrated economy create and follow economic opportunities wherever they might present themselves. This mobility, however, does not negate the necessity of place or physical locale. Even the most mobile nomads must land somewhere for a time. The constraints on exchange that are imposed by place and time are admittedly eased in a globally integrated economy, particularly in respect to recent advances in information and transportation technologies, but place and time are not rendered entirely irrelevant. Nomads must reside somewhere, however temporally, and all goods and services are produced and consumed in particular places and at particular times. Although communicative associations may become more fluid and temporary, they nevertheless require some place to communicate their shared goods. If civil society is to flourish within a globally integrated economy, then its inhabitants will need to be more akin to pilgrims than nomads. To evoke ecclesial imagery again, the church is a nonterritorial people, but they require territory in which to congregate.[31]

The mobility afforded by global markets cannot be fully dislodged from particular places and people associated with those locales. Markets are venues designed to facilitate predominantly commercial exchange, but no exchange is exclusively commercial. A commercial exchange is predicated on production and consumption that are already embedded within various communicative spheres. Individuals do not exchange merely for the sake of trading, but for the purpose of procuring goods and services that are required to sustain the social spheres in which the respective parties communicate. I exchange my money with the grocer to put food on my family's table. Exchange is required to maintain a market, but it is "not fundamental to community."[32] Markets are instrumental devices enabling people to communicate common goods, thereby tacitly acknowledging that communication, as opposed to exchange, is what fulfills human flourishing. Producing and consuming goods and services are indispensable in meeting the underlying material needs of communicative associations, but they are not the defining features of civil society. Moreover, markets do not sustain civil society through exchange itself, but in providing a "common space" into which people enter and meet. A market is ultimately the "sign of a local society," where goods and services are actually produced and consumed.[33]

Highlighting locality invalidates the myth that place has been rendered irrelevant. With technologies offering speedy transportation and instantaneous information, the ideal lifestyle is nomadic in which the constraints of place are nonexistent. Nomads are free to wander (or not) where they will. It is a fraudulent freedom. Locality has not been vanquished, but rendered less visible and immediate, creating the illusion of unencumbered mobility. In O'Donovan's trenchant words: "For me, as for slave-owners of the early modern colonies, it is all too easy to overlook those on whom the gratifying of my desire depends, and to succumb to the illusion that the tips of my fingers on keyboard and mouse have freed *them* from the constraints of place too!"[34]

---

31. I am not going to enter the debate over whether or not the church can congregate and communicate virtually as well as physically. For an argument favoring the church's virtual presence, see Douglas Estes, *SimChurch: Being the Church in the Virtual World* (Grand Rapids, MI: Zondervan, 2009); for a more critical appraisal, see Tim Challies, *The Next Story: Life and Faith After the Digital Explosion* (Grand Rapids, MI: Zondervan, 2011).

32. See O'Donovan, *The Ways of Judgment*, 246–47.

33. See ibid., 255.

34. Ibid., 260.

Despite the mobility and ability to conduct exchanges at a distance that characterizes global markets, these exchanges affect particular individuals and their communicative associations in beneficial or harmful ways. The following simple example illustrates how communicating common or shared goods remains inextricably tied to a particular place and people. Niall Ferguson notes that when he bought a new seaside home he was dismayed by the amount of rubbish on the beach. Each day when he took a walk he filled a trash bag, but this did little to solve the problem. He recruited a few volunteers to clean up the beach, but even collectively they were not up to the task. It was only when the local Lions Club "got involved" that the beach was cleaned up and kept clean, and he doubts if the "new social networks of the internet are in any sense a substitute for real networks."[35]

What should be stressed in this example is that the unorganized efforts of individuals were not able to communicate the shared good of a clean beach. What was required was an association (the local Lions Club) that was dedicated to community service. For Ferguson, this episode disclosed the "power of the voluntary association as an institution. Together, spontaneously, without any public sector involvement, without any profit motive, without any legal obligation or power, we had turned a depressing dumping ground back into a beauty spot."[36] More broadly, Ferguson is concerned that voracious consumerism is diminishing the capacity of people to undertake these voluntary corporate activities, and he fears that this growing void will be filled by governmental regulations and programs that often prove to be overly intrusive and overbearing, further eroding the capability for voluntary action. He worries if any "truly free nation" can "flourish" without a "vibrant civil society."[37]

Ferguson's emphasis on a vibrant civil society is welcomed, because it is primarily within the communicative associations constituting civil society that human flourishing occurs. Additionally, his worry of an intrusive state filling the void of a declining civil society should be taken with great seriousness. Nevertheless, maintaining the vibrancy of civil society requires governmental action in the face of issues that local associations are ill-equipped to address given their limited scope. This is where O'Donovan's emphasis on a landed people is instructive, particularly in respect to the corrosive effects that global markets assert against civil

35. See Niall Ferguson, *The Great Degeneration: How Institutions Decay and Economies Die* (New York: Penguin, 2013), 111–13.
36. Ibid., 112–13.
37. Ibid., 113; see also ch. 4.

society. A landed people serves as a reminder to avoid the trap of confusing ends with means. Producing and consuming goods and services are important instrumental activities, but production and consumption are *not* ends in themselves. GDP, for instance, discloses rates of productivity, but reveals little about whether these activities are aiding or diminishing the communication of the goods of creation. That determination is a normative judgment based on the tradition and culture of a particular people, and the ensuing political question is the extent to which the state should regulate markets to ensure that the communicative associations constituting a people are well served, sustained, and protected. Although O'Donovan shares Ferguson's concern about the intrusion of the state, he also worries that in light of the potential prosperity that global markets offer, states may also choose to do too little, thereby diminishing the vibrancy of civil society because of their inaction.

The principal challenge for civil society—and it too is daunting—is how to simultaneously enable the freedom of individuals to participate in competitive global markets while also maintaining the vibrancy of civil society. This challenge entails a twofold dilemma. On the one hand, enabling greater participation in global markets can generate more widespread prosperity that can in turn strengthen communicative associations, but such participation can also become a nearly all-consuming activity, thereby weakening civil society. Consequently, a creative tension between centrifugal market forces and centripetal needs of civil society must be struck. On the other hand, the coercive power of the state is needed to help preserve and protect civil society, but in limited ways that do not effectively smother or displace communicative associations. Consequently, a robust civil society must also resist unwarranted intrusions by the state. Resolving this twofold dilemma requires some inquiry into the relation between freedom and justice, for resolving the challenge faced in maintaining civil society may require enabling greater individual freedom in some instances, while restricting it in others. This inquiry is undertaken in chapter 9 on freedom and justice.

Chapter Eight

Civil Society and Political Ordering

One of the most vexing questions posed by globalization is, How can political ordering embrace the creative destruction of global markets in ways that simultaneously promote widespread prosperity while also providing sufficient stability for communicative associations to flourish? This chapter addresses this question, but offers no definitive answer. Rather, the goal is to provide some provisional guidelines for how the Christian theological and moral tradition might help to conceive a relation between civil society and political ordering that fosters human flourishing within the context of dynamic global markets. Some readers might complain that what follows is too general and imprecise. I am admittedly using very broad strokes to depict a highly complex issue, but I would point out that broad paintbrushes perform a useful function: namely, to provide an undercoat upon which more intricate embellishment is added. Similarly, my intent is to invite, perhaps even provoke, further inquiries requiring greater precision.

The following sections on civil society and political ordering tie together selected themes I have alluded to in previous chapters. Additionally, I draw out some implications in each instance to lay the groundwork for the final section in which I examine the illustrative issues of market regulation and enabling competition within global markets.

Civil Society

As noted previously, Daniel K. Finn defines civil society as a "network of organizations larger than the family but smaller than the national government that helps organize daily life."[1] Finn's definition is expansive but not sufficiently capacious, for if civil society comprises communicative associations, then the family needs to be included. Moreover, within the vast literature on civil society there is no consensus regarding a specific definition.[2] Such ambiguity, however, captures rather nicely the untidy condition of civil society. People associate for a wide variety of purposes that are achieved through both informal and formal means, and are accomplished over brief and extended periods of time. Communicating the good of friendship, for example, requires no formal organization; whereas communicating the good of knowledge is best pursued within schools that are organized to teach successive generations. Moreover, associational patterns or structures evolve over time—the friendships of late moderns are not identical to their ancient counterparts, and the lecture hall of the early twentieth century is not the same as the virtual classroom of the early twenty-first century.

As I argued in the previous chapter, it is this scruffy collection of associations that best promotes human flourishing, for it is within these reciprocal affiliations that shared goods are communicated, goods that cannot be bought and sold, or forcefully seized or surrendered. To return to Niall Ferguson's filthy beach, it was cleaned not in response to any profit motive or governmental compulsion, but by the cooperative efforts of people who believed that a clean beach is a good they share in common. Consequently, in order to communicate shared goods, people must have the opportunity and ability to associate. Taking advantage of these opportunities and abilities, however, requires supportive markets and governments, markets to provide for the material well-being of individuals and governments to protect their right to associate. Consequently, markets and states are necessarily interlaced throughout civil society, and the ensuing challenge is to ensure that neither becomes too deeply invasive or determinative. In either instance, the resulting autonomous individuals can be easily manipulated as mass consumers or as dependent and compliant wards of the state.

If the associations that compose civil society are to flourish, then it is crucial to strike a proper balance or tension to prevent unwarranted intrusions. Ferguson worries that over the last fifty years the state has encroached far too deeply into civil society, becoming effectively its "real

1. Daniel K. Finn, *Christian Economic Ethics: History and Implications* (Minneapolis, MN: Fortress Press, 2013), 207.

2. See, e.g., Alison Van Rooy, *The Global Legitimacy Game: Civil Society, Globalization, and Protest* (Houndmills, UK, and New York: Palgrave Macmillan, 2004), ch. 1.

enemy."[3] He believes "that spontaneous local activism by citizens is better than central state action not just in terms of its results, but more importantly in terms of its effect on us as citizens."[4] It is through participating in a variety of associations, as opposed to governmental programs and agencies, that people learn how to govern themselves. This does not imply, however, that there is no need for the state, because it is better equipped to undertake certain tasks and responsibilities that voluntary associations are simply incapable of performing. I assume, for instance, that if a hostile flotilla were on its way to invade Ferguson's cherished beach, he would not entrust its defense to the local Lions Club but would prefer that the state send its armed forces. Less dramatically, Ferguson is fortunate to reside in a country in which the state protects his right to associate. Under certain circumstances, John Micklethwait and Adrian Wooldridge contend that "too little government is more dangerous than too much."[5]

The principal task at hand is to create a proper tension between markets and the state that enables civil society to flourish. Too much governmental encroachment disables individuals from utilizing the competitive dynamism of global markets to their advantage, not only diminishing the prospect of greater prosperity and material well-being, but also weakening, as Ferguson fears, the capacity for self-governance. In contrast, too little governmental regulation and support is to leave individuals to their own devices in weathering the creative destruction of global markets, effectively reducing them to producers and consumers. In both instances, opportunities for people to associate beyond market exchanges or governmental activities are diminished.[6]

Achieving this proper tension is particularly difficult because it lacks a conceptual basis in much of late modern social and political discourse. Society is often neatly divided between the private and public realms. The private realm consists of individuals engaging in commercial transactions and whatever other legal activities and relationships they might choose to pursue. The public realm is synonymous with government effectively operating, endorsing, or permitting various forms of association. This bifurcation, however, is artificial, often encouraging extreme and

---

3. See Niall Ferguson, *The Great Degeneration: How Institutions Decay and Economies Die* (New York: Penguin, 2013), 123.

4. Ibid., 132.

5. John Micklethwait and Adrian Wooldridge, *The Fourth Revolution: The Global Race to Reinvent the State* (New York: Penguin, 2014), 21.

6. See Robert D. Putnam, *Bowling Alone: The Collapse and Revival of American Community* (New York: Simon and Schuster, 2000).

acrimonious political disputes. To oversimplify, one side insists that the market can solve virtually any problem, while the other demands that government must be involved in every solution. And both sides fight to either defend or seize turf from their opponent. Pitting private (read markets) and public (read political) against each other creates farcical solutions when pushed to their respective logical conclusions. For instance, shopping for a court that would render a favorable decision is preposterous,[7] while requiring a judge's permission to send a text message to a friend would be equally ludicrous. In respect to markets and government, every option is not either-or, but in some instances both-and, and in other instances neither. Ironically, although a number of business leaders, politicians, pundits, and academics champion and bemoan the decline of civil society, they offer it no space in which it might flourish, for it is not the creation of either markets or states.

If civil society is to flourish, it requires its own sphere, one that is genuinely public because it is neither entirely private nor political.[8] I am not suggesting that the public sphere is somehow indivisible from the private and political spheres. To the contrary, a public requires the support of, overlaps, and is intertwined with the private and political spheres, but cannot (or should not) be reduced to either. Following Oliver O'Donovan, the public sphere is where the identity of a people is formed and sustained.[9] Within the context of globalization, however, the public sphere is increasingly fluid and protean. Individuals compete within global markets to meet their material wants and needs, and in turn participate within communicative associations. People simultaneously enact their private, political, and public identities, and one particular identity should ideally not trump the others. It is within the turbulent confluence of these overlapping identities that erratic tensions form that will either strengthen or weaken civil society, and hence the identity, life, and well-being of a people.

Unfortunately, the dominant forms of late modern political and moral discourse largely fail to capture this dynamism, reverting instead to the artificial division between private (read markets) and public (read political). In the 2012 US presidential election, it was reported that, while stumping, President Obama said, "If you've got a business—you didn't

---

7. Although some judges accept bribes and some courts are more favorably disposed to accepting class action suits.

8. For a more detailed account of a genuinely public sphere, see pertinent sections of chs. 3, 6, and 10 in Brent Waters, *Christian Moral Theology in the Emerging Technoculture: From Posthuman Back to Human* (Farnham, UK, and Burlington, VT: Ashgate, 2014).

9. See ch. 7 above.

build that. Someone else made that happen."[10] The statement was made to highlight the many services government provides that businesses depend on—such as schools, infrastructure, fire departments—which is certainly true. The declaration was nonetheless incomplete and disingenuous. Someone owning a business did in fact build it. He or she envisioned it, took a risk investing time and money, and is responsible for its profitable operation. To imply that a business is a creation of the state is to denigrate the countless private initiatives that undergird civil society.

To suggest, however, that a business is exclusively the result of individual initiative is to evoke a false sense of autonomy that is also incomplete and misleading. If you've got a business—you built it. But you were not alone. Contractors, suppliers, employees, and customers are all needed to start and make a business successful. And it is successful businesses that generate the tax revenue to pay for the supportive infrastructure and governmental services championed by President Obama.[11] In brief, it is both competitive markets *and* governmental services that promote the interdependent and cooperative associations constituting civil society. More broadly, it is in and through the confluence of the private, political, and public spheres that a people form and maintain themselves over time.

The principal challenge is how can civil society flourish in the face of the growing fluidity and mobility of global markets? This challenge appears, at least initially, to be insurmountable since, as O'Donovan noted,[12] being a people over time has been traditionally interlocked with a particular place, seemingly requiring a degree of stability and relative permanence that is antithetical to the creative destruction of global markets. Globalization, then, appears to be the enemy of civil society. Yet as I argued previously, communicative associations are not necessarily confined to particular locales. As the church demonstrates, a people can flourish without being territorial; it communicates its shared goods wherever two or three are gathered. Although a globally integrated economy diminishes the importance of place, it does not render it irrelevant.[13] Again, the church is not composed of nomads

10. See Eugene Kiely, "'You Didn't Build That,' Uncut and Unedited," FactCheck.org, updated on July 24, 2012, http://www.factcheck.org/2012/07/you-didnt-build-that-uncut-and-unedited/.

11. Businesses generate cascading streams of tax revenue. In the United States, for instance, a business typically pays taxes on its profits, property, and user fees. Through its suppliers, employees, and customers, additional tax revenue is generated by a wide-ranging combination of taxing income, sales, and energy usage.

12. See ch. 7 above.

13. Ironically, the development of mobile technologies has increased the importance of particular locales. See Patrick Lane, "A Sense of Place: Geography Matters as Much as Ever,

who wander aimlessly, but pilgrims who are headed somewhere. They stop from time to time along their pilgrimage, and are advised to settle down for a while to build homes, engage in commerce, and communicate goods wherever they might be and for however long or short time their sojourn proves to be. Returning to Ferguson's beach, there is no reason why people cannot join the local Lions Club[14] or similar organizations to promote communicating the good of a clean beach regardless if their stay in a particular locale is relatively short or lengthy.

Most important, globalization offers opportunities for new and unforeseen forms of human association to emerge, perhaps transcending political, cultural, and ethnic identities that have proven divisive in the past. In this respect, new and expanding global markets, complete with their creative destruction, may offer the prospect of bringing in something new regarding how the goods of creation might be better communicated. Christians in particular might see this task of finding new wineskins for the new wine as a work of the Holy Spirit, and a task that political ordering should also embrace rather than resist.

Political Ordering

A vibrant civil society requires political ordering. There are certain tasks and problems that neither markets nor voluntary associations are equipped to undertake or solve. The public sphere requires not only markets enabling individuals to engage in exchange but also the protection to associate. Material goods and services are best exchanged, and shared human goods are best communicated under lawful and orderly conditions. Shopkeepers could not stay in business if there was no compulsion requiring customers to pay for the items they want, and individuals would be loath to gather if there were no safeguards against others preventing or disrupting their gatherings.

Ideally, political ordering is exercised under the rule of law. There is a vast philosophical and theological literature on what constitutes the rule of law, its sources, and its proper execution. A critical summary of this literature cannot be undertaken within the limited scope of this book. Given my limited purposes, I use the rule of law to indicate that good

---

Despite the Digital Revolution," *The Economist*, October 27, 2012; see also Wilfred M. McClay and Ted V. McAllister, eds., *Why Place Matters: Geography, Identity, and Civic Life in Modern America* (New York and London: Encounter Books, 2014).

14. The Lions Club and other similar service clubs are often international organizations composed of local chapters.

governance serves to delineate and limit the actions of the state as opposed to asserting the arbitrary will of rulers over the ruled. Law delineates the appropriate tasks that government is to undertake in maintaining peaceful and orderly conditions in which people under its jurisdiction, and more broadly the communicative associations constituting civil society, can flourish. Law also constrains government in order to protect people and their communicative associations from arbitrary interventions and restrictions that effectively diminish human flourishing.

The rule of law is a crucial concept, for government both exercises its duties and honors its constraints through what O'Donovan characterizes as acts of judgment.[15] A judgment is essentially *"an act of moral discrimination that pronounces upon a preceding act or existing state of affairs to establish a new public context."*[16] This act has four successive stages. First, "Judgment is an act of *moral discrimination*, dividing right from wrong."[17] For example, it is judged wrong to restrict women to working only within their households and right that they should be permitted to seek employment within the marketplace. Second, "Judgment *pronounces upon a preceding act*, or on an existing state of affairs brought about by action."[18] Men preventing women from entering their place of employment are arrested and incarcerated. Third, "Judgment *establishes a public context*, a practical context, that is, in which succeeding acts, private or public, may be performed."[19] More specific laws are enacted protecting the right of women to work outside the home. Fourth, "The object of judgment is the *new public context*, and in this way judgment is distinct from all actions that have as their object a private or restricted good."[20] It is determined that women, both individually and collectively, and the public more broadly are better served by offering greater educational opportunities to women to assist them in acquiring more completive skills and knowledge required by the workplace.

Making such judgments are controversial and contestable. Virtually any judgment will be assessed by some as being wrong, particularly those against whom a judgment is made. In the United States, for instance, bartenders and their patrons had no doubt that prohibition was a wrong judgment. Over time, judgments that have proven to be wrong can be

---

15. See Oliver O'Donovan, *The Ways of Judgment: The Bampton Lectures, 2003* (Grand Rapids, MI, and Cambridge, UK: Eerdmans, 2005), esp. ch. 1.
  16. Ibid., 7 (emphasis original).
  17. Ibid. (emphasis original).
  18. Ibid., 8 (emphasis original).
  19. Ibid. (emphasis original).
  20. Ibid., 10 (emphasis original).

revisited and amended. In thirteen years, bartenders and their patrons were back in business. It is the imprecision of judgment that makes the rule of law indispensable in order to provide a standard against which judgments are both made and amended. To return to the example in the previous paragraph, the judgment that previously prohibited women working outside the home was determined to be wrong because it violated, say, the principle of individual freedom, and it is therefore right to repeal this prohibition. Moreover, the rule also serves as a check against arbitrary judgments—for instance, extending a right to work outside the home only to blue-eyed women. Additionally, the rule of law is imperative since judgments are almost always zero-sum, entailing subsequent coercion (or its threat) in enforcing them. Men presumably suffer lower wages or unemployment with the influx of women entering the job market, and men attempting to prevent women from entering their places of employment experienced the coercive power of government firsthand through their arrest and punishment.

Coercion, then, is a fundamental prerequisite of political ordering, and this power is typically entrusted to the state. Through its formal legislative, executive, and judicial functions, the state enacts and enforces a plethora of judgments. Consequently, the power to render lawful judgments and coercively enforce them is confined to agencies of the state. These judgments affect both private individuals and their commerce and associations, for both good and ill, but universal compliance is required to maintain the peace and order of civil society. Those harmed by particular judgments are not entitled to form alternative legislative, executive, and judicial bodies authorized to exercise coercive power. Men, for instance, cannot form an alternative government that prohibits women from entering a parallel workplace, capable of arresting and punishing women attempting to do so.[21]

Since the state is entrusted with a monopoly on coercion, it must use this power wisely, in ways that benefit the people it governs, and conversely either inadequate or excessive coercion harms civil society. What principle or objective, then, should guide the proper use of coercion by the state? The coercive power of the state should be employed to maximize opportunities for individuals to participate in markets in order to

---

21. The right of a private firm to be discriminating in hiring employees is contentious. It can be argued, however, that since a private firm benefits from services provided by government, it should not be lawful to arbitrarily discriminate against people because of their race, gender, or religion, provided they possess the requisite skills or other necessary qualities. An airline, for instance, should not be coerced into hiring a "pilot" who knows nothing about flying a plane, and a church has the right not to hire an atheist priest.

provide for their material well-being, and to associate with one another to communicate shared goods. A simple observation by C. S. Lewis illustrates this principle:

> [The State exists simply to promote and to protect the ordinary happiness of human beings in this life. A husband and wife chatting over a fire, a couple of friends having a game of darts in a pub, a man reading a book in his own room or digging in his own garden—that is what the State is there for.] And unless they are helping to increase and prolong and protect such moments all the laws, parliaments, armies, courts, police, economics etc. are simply a waste of time.[22]

This does not imply that when people chat, play a game of darts, read a book, or tend a garden all will be well. But it does serve to illustrate that achieving the objective of meeting material needs and wants, and communicating shared goods require both action and restraint by the state. The state must ensure sufficient stability and order so that market exchanges can be made to obtain wanted goods and services such as darts and books. Government must also ensure that contracts are honored so that a firm manufacturing darts pays its employees, and publishers pay their authors. The state must also provide adequate policing so that robbers do not routinely assault dart players and people reading books. If the state fails to act in such instances both the material well-being and ability of people to communicate are diminished. Restraint, however, is also required. There is no compelling reason why government should determine which player will win a game of darts, which books people are required to read, or insist that a husband and wife sit in separate chairs while chatting over a fire.

Although active participation by the state is required to maintain the public sphere within which civil society might flourish, such interventions do not entail direct or overwhelming bureaucratic control. Promoting such goods as dart games, book reading, and chatting over a fire does not require the state to own and operate factories manufacturing darts, publishing firms, or houses with fireplaces. [Government, however, performs a useful function by ensuring safe workplaces, promoting literacy, and enforcing building codes.[23] Since the public sphere is intertwined with markets and

---

22. C. S. Lewis, *Beyond Personality: The Christian Idea of God* (London: Geoffrey Bles, 1944), 43.

23. Whether or not governments tend to undertake these tasks in an efficient or inefficient manner is a different issue.

the state, there is no reason why political mandates and goals cannot be achieved through a combination of governmental and private initiatives. Various regimes around the world are experimenting with cooperative arrangements with private firms in such areas as transportation, prisons, medical care, welfare, and education.[24] But as noted previously, the state needs to maintain an exclusive coercive monopoly in such areas as the judiciary and military.[25]

The principal challenge is how can the emerging market-state enable civil society to flourish in the face of the growing fluidity and mobility of global markets? Or to use O'Donovan's terms again, how can government represent a people that is often dispersed, and those residing under its jurisdiction often in flux; how does it govern an increasingly nomadic people? The market-state will properly continue to possess a great deal of coercive power, but how it should be used to benefit the people it represents and governs needs to change given the dynamism of competitive global markets. As noted in previous chapters, the state could use its coercive power to implement protectionist policies, but rather than benefitting civil society they would likely diminish the material well-being of many individuals. Conversely, short of resorting to war, one state cannot force another to open its borders to trade, capital investment, and migratory labor. Consequently, the coercive power of the market-state should not be used to protect its citizens from competitive global markets, but to enable opportunities to successfully compete. This again requires a rule of law, but a rule agreed to by emerging market-states competing within global markets. Negotiated rules will be needed to regulate trade, commerce, finance, taxes, and labor that regularly flow in and out of jurisdictions. The coercive power of states is limited in enforcing these agreements, for short of a world government, there are no direct ways to coerce compliance. Consequently, the rule of law on a global scale will need to be based on consent, compromise, and mutual self-interest rather than coercion. This scheme is admittedly fraught with uncertainty,

24. The success rate of these experiments is mixed.

25. The simultaneous transition from nation-state to market-state and return of geopolitics is producing a number of pressing political, legal, economic, and moral issues in respect to the contemporary declaration and waging of war. A vast literature on various aspects of these issues has already been written. For general overviews, see Nigel Biggar, *In Defence of War* (Oxford and New York: Oxford University Press, 2013); Philip Bobbitt, *Terror and Consent: The Wars for the Twenty-First Century* (New York: Knopf, 2008); Jean Bethke Elshtain, *Just War against Terror: The Burden of American Power in a Violent World* (New York: Basic Books, 2003); David Fisher, *Morality and War: Can War Be Just in the Twenty-First Century?* (Oxford and New York: Oxford University Press, 2011); and Oliver O'Donovan, *The Just War Revisited* (Cambridge, UK: Cambridge University Press, 2003).

because consent can be withdrawn in light of changing perceptions of
self-interest. This uncertainty and limited use of coercion, however, is
preferable to the distasteful options of protectionism or universal empire.
Moreover, abiding by whatever rules are negotiated will create a series of
tensions both within and among emerging market-states.

Tensions

Since both markets and the state should promote human flourishing, and
since such flourishing occurs predominantly in communicative associations, then inevitable tensions exist both within and between the tasks of
economic and political ordering. The goal, however, is not to eliminate
these tensions, but to maintain a proper or creative balance that serves to
strengthen the associations constituting civil society. Achieving this goal
entails both an internal ordering within particular states, and its external
ordering to other states within competitive global markets. A comprehensive survey of the most significant tensions, as well as what might
constitute a proper balance in each instance, is beyond the scope of this
chapter. Rather, I focus on two illustrative issues of market regulation
and enabling competition within global labor markets.

Market Regulation

Some governmental regulation of markets is both necessary and desirable.
Even the most fervent libertarian favors the coercive power of the state to
enforce contracts made between private individuals as opposed to using
personal violence. And even the most ardent statist does not insist that every
contract should be made between individuals and the state. Regulation
is also not an either-or proposition in which the state either regulates
extensively or not at all. Rather, the extent of desirable regulation varies
from market to market. Very little regulation, for example, is required in
a clothing market, because there is no compelling reason why the state
should dictate what people should wear or how much they should pay for
particular garments.[26] In contrast, extensive regulation and oversight of
pharmaceuticals is needed to protect consumers from potentially harmful
drugs.[27] Some regulations may also reflect the moral values of a society

26. The state may inspect the premises where clothing is manufactured and sold to ensure
that working conditions are safe, that employers are complying with labor regulations, and that
workers are lawfully eligible to be employed.

27. Even when extensive regulation is warranted, however, a radical application of the

that are expressed through market suppression. There is, for instance, a market for child pornography, but governments prohibit its production and consumption.

All regulations produce good or bad consequences. Few would quarrel with the state requiring banks to distribute or return deposited funds upon the lawful instructions of the account holder. Some regulations are discriminatory, intended to harm particular individuals or groups, such as prohibiting members of certain races or ethnicities from buying property or owning a business. Other regulations are designed to benefit the interests of particular groups, such as Florida's required licensing of interior designers. Many regulations produce mixed results. Imposing fuel consumption standards on automobiles, for example, has improved energy efficiency while also lowering tax revenue generated by diminished gasoline sales. Many regulations have unforeseen or unintended consequences, such as requiring minimal ethanol additives to gasoline, which drive up the price of food products using corn. Still other regulations are contradictory to stated policies; for instance, a government striving for energy independence while effectively discouraging the extraction of fossil fuels. Moreover, the extent of market regulation often waxes and wanes in response to perceived public preferences or ideological commitments of governments. In the United States, for example, deregulation of the airline and telephone industries has generally proven popular, whereas increased federal regulation of health care has been largely unpopular.

The issue, then, is *not* whether or not the state should regulate markets, but the extent to which various markets need to be regulated in order to promote widespread prosperity, and the flourishing of communicative associations. Determining the extent of such market regulations is not made solely in every instance to maximize economic exchange, but also to achieve other social and political goals, such as protecting the environment. Moreover, these determinations vary from state to state, reflecting differing cultures, traditions, values, and interests of the people they govern. For example, one state might impose highly invasive environmental safeguards, while another has few if any. Additionally, regulations may change over time in reaction to changing circumstances, unintended consequences, or the ideological commitments of a new gov-ernment. A state with extensive environmental safeguards may relax them

---

so-called "precautionary principle" should be avoided since risk can never be entirely eliminated for prevented. See Roger Scruton, *How to Think Seriously about the Planet: The Case for an Environmental Conservatism* (Oxford and New York: Oxford University Press, 2012), ch. 4.

to encourage developing cheaper sources of energy, while another with minimal regulations may enact more restrictive regulations to encourage the development of alternative sources of energy. Intrastate regulations are established in light of competitive global markets, and some political calculus must be made to determine if a people are best served through relatively open or protectionist policies regarding inflowing and outflowing trade, capital, and labor. Again, these determinations vary from state to state and are not necessarily uniform: for example, one state might engage in free trade, while imposing tight restrictions against labor migration, while another state may have opposite emphases.

The emerging market-state has determined that the interests of the people it governs are best served by affording them opportunities to compete in global markets. Some agreed-upon standards are thereby required to govern interstate relations: a minimal rule of law. Such agreements are established through formal treaties or membership in organizations that include procedures for responding to violations and mediating disputes. These agreements include designating which goods and services can be traded and at what tariff rates, if any; protecting invested capital from arbitrary seizure or preventing it from being extracted in the future; and assurances that foreign firms and workers will be subject to the laws of host states, and that host states in turn extend legal protections to guest firms and workers.

Although the purpose of these interstate agreements is to promote fair competition, they need not impose uniform models of social and political ordering on particular states. Rather, each state will, at least ideally, enact intrastate regulations and policies that will maximize their respective comparative advantages within global competitive markets in respect to trade, capital, and labor.[28] It might be objected that without uniform policies and regulations, competition is unjust because some states would enjoy unfair advantages. For example, a state with low corporate tax rates would attract much more capital investment than states with higher tax rates. This is not necessarily true, however, because other considerations such as political stability, a skilled workforce, quality of infrastructure, geographic location, environmental safeguards, and the like also inform where investments are made. Some states may implement policies and regulations that are purportedly designed to maximize their respective comparative advantages within competitive global markets but fail to do so due to unforeseen consequences. To return to the example of corporate

---

28. Ineffective regulation or corruption, however, may fail to maximize these comparative advantages.

tax rates, a particular state might possess many favorable features to attract or retain capital investment, and believes it can impose a high rate in order to increase tax revenue. The offsetting factors, however, prove less attractive than assumed, not only discouraging an inflow of capital but also encouraging capital outflows resulting in less tax revenue.

Finally, as noted previously, certain policies and regulations may be enacted that do not encourage participation in competitive markets in order to achieve other, more valued social and political objectives. In respect to intrastate political ordering, this in not inherently objectionable so long as the judgment made by a state truly represents the good of the people it governs and enables them to communicate these goods. But should such goods be imposed by some upon others through interstate agreements regulating trade, capital, and labor? Beyond the minimal standards noted above, such impositions are hazardous because they are fraught with unintended consequences. For example, many if not most people believe that breathing clean air and the education of children are goods that should be enjoyed by all people. Suppose a developed nation is negotiating a trade agreement with a lesser developed counterpart. The former insists that the latter adopt stricter environmental regulations and prohibit child labor. Although each of these requirements is arguably good, imposing them might actually harm the less affluent trade partner. Renewable sources of energy are more expensive and less reliable than fossil fuels thereby blunting the pursuit of affluence, and if schools are not readily available children might be subjected to more dangerous circumstances than those of the workplace. A people may be better served by first achieving a higher level of material prosperity before it can afford the goods of clean air and prohibited child labor.

To summarize, some degree of interstate and intrastate regulation of global markets are needed if they are to be genuinely competitive. Ideally, such political ordering is exercised under the rule of law for the purpose of promoting widespread prosperity, which enables people to meet their material wants and needs. Such intrastate ordering does not entail imposing or adopting uniform policies by each particular state, thereby resisting a false universality. Again ideally, particular market-states participate in global markets in pluriform ways. As noted, both intrastate and interstate regulations may either succeed or fail to meet their objectives, may be administered well or badly, are fraught with unintended consequences, and in some instances restrict the pursuit of affluence to achieve other social and political objectives that a particular people value more highly. So long as the intent of these regulations is to offer people

opportunities to compete in global markets in order to meet thei
rial wants and needs, and provided they are administered justly—and the
outcome of both of these conditions will undoubtedly prove imperfect,
thereby requiring frequent amendment—there is no compelling reason
why, on Christian moral grounds, one should object. Perhaps. A more
expansive issue needs to be addressed: unlike the nation-state, the
emerging market-state enables people to compete in global markets
as opposed to protecting them from their potentially destructive
consequences. Can such a shift in emphasis promote *both* a pursuit of
affluence *and* the flourishing of communicative associations? Or, is the
former achieved at the expense of the latter?

Enabling Market Competition

Enabling people to compete in global markets necessarily exposes them
to risks. Although competing successfully within global markets creates
greater affluence for more people over time, some individuals and
communities necessarily suffer adverse consequences. Moreover, these
consequences cannot be prevented, because the success of globalization
is predicated on the creative destruction of its markets. The emerging
market-state governs people who are rightfully anxious and uncertain
about the future of their material well-being. Such apprehension, however,
need not be debilitating, but may serve to stimulate individuals to be more
competitive, and as argued in chapter 2, such competition is not inimical
to greater cooperation and may even serve to enhance it. Consequently,
the task at hand for the emerging market-state is how it should go about
enabling the people it represents to compete in global markets.

Although emerging market-states compete for trade and capital
investment, I will focus on labor. As noted previously, the value of work
is determined primarily by supply and demand. Jobs requiring few
skills, for example, pay little because there is an abundance of potential
workers; whereas jobs requiring highly specialized skills and knowledge
command high salaries due to a smaller pool of qualified individuals.[29]
Globalization is often caricatured as a process in which corporations
headquartered in wealthy nations build factories in poor countries with
plentiful unskilled laborers who are paid little to manufacture such items

---

29. This pattern is often distorted by governmental employment practices. For instance,
combat skills are scarce but military personnel tend to be paid relatively little, whereas other
governmental employees are often compensated at higher levels than those performing similar
services in the private sector.

as clothing or Christmas decorations of questionable taste. These items are in turn exported back to wealthy nations where shoppers voraciously consume cheap shirts and baubles. Corporations and newly employed workers benefit from this process, while unemployed factory workers in wealthy countries suffer. Additionally, highly skilled and well-paid jobs in wealthy countries are unaffected, and even benefit from this process through the availability of cheaper items.

There is admittedly some truth in this portrayal of globalization, creating a number of pressing issues in regard to displaced workers. This popular portrayal, however, is incomplete and misleading for two reasons. First, the process of "offshoring" manufacturing or provision of services does not lead to a permanent loss of jobs, nor is it confined to a relation between rich and poor countries. If an economy is growing, displaced workers may find comparable jobs in other sectors,[30] or be retained and retrained to perform other, related tasks. For example, some European firms are starting to manufacture steel in the US Gulf region because natural gas is cheaper than European coal or coke. This move has created jobs in the United States, as well as shipping and transport jobs, and many of the former factory workers have been retained to furbish the imported steel into finished products. Nonetheless, this process of creative destruction proves disruptive for many workers, generating a sense of insecurity and anxiety. Moreover, this uncertainty is no longer confined to jobs requiring relatively few skills. Increasingly, more specialized skill or knowledge-based professions are facing global competition, particularly in such areas as financial, legal, and medical services, a trend exacerbated by rapid advances in digital technologies.[31]

Consequently, if individuals are to compete successfully within competitive global markets, they must acquire requisite skills and knowledge. At the most basic level, this requires rudimentary literacy and numeracy. More specialized skills and knowledge are also needed to obtain better-paying jobs, and new ones will be needed in response to changing markets and technological advances. How do individuals acquire such basic and more specialized proficiencies? The obvious answer is through

---

30. Sometimes individuals will be forced to take, at least temporarily, less skilled and lower-paying jobs, particularly in anemic or contracting economies.

31. See, e.g., "Wealth without Workers, Workers without Wealth: The Digital Revolution Is Bringing Sweeping Change to Labour Markets in Both Rich and Poor Worlds," *The Economist*, October 4, 2014; "The Onrushing Wave: The Future of Jobs," *The Economist*, January 18, 2014; see also Erik Brynjolfsson and Andrew McAfee, *The Second Machine Age: Work, Progress, and Prosperity in a Time of Brilliant Technologies* (New York and London: Norton, 2014).

experience and education, but experience can often not occur without education. In short, schools are required to teach individuals what they need to know in order to compete in global labor markets.

But what do individuals need to know? Answers to this question vary widely across particular contexts. Many people in poor nations have few opportunities to learn elementary reading, writing, and mathematics, much less more specialized knowledge and skills. Some rich nations, however, offer compulsory educational curricula that often lack pertinent proficiencies in respect to the labor market. In the United States, merely 2 percent of "high school students concentrate in vocational educational programs" even though it is estimated that in the "near future, two-thirds of jobs will not require a four-year college degree."[32] Additionally, continuing or lifelong educational opportunities need to be offered in order for individuals to update or learn new skills.[33]

What is the best way to offer educational opportunities that enable people to compete in global labor markets? Again, specific answers to this question vary widely in response to particular circumstances. In general, however, a variety of approaches and organizations are needed that can adapt and respond to rapid changes in global labor markets. Providing such diverse educational opportunities enables people to take advantage of dynamic employment opportunities, as well as leveling the field among competing workers.

The most pressing issue is how to provide equitable or just access to appropriate educational opportunities. Or in more practical terms, how should education be funded? To some extent incurred expenses should be borne by individuals and their families as an opportunity cost. Like any exchange, selling one's labor requires offering something of value, and increasing the value on offer requires a greater initial cost of invested time and money. The opportunity cost for becoming a rubbish collector is very low, whereas the cost for becoming a surgeon is very high.

The principal flaw with this scheme is that it effectively prevents poor individuals from obtaining more valuable skills and knowledge, and within global labor markets this places people in impoverished regions at a distinct disadvantage. Intrastate solutions for addressing the issue of

32. Carrie Sheffield, "Skills-Based Education Can Help Solve the Inequality Puzzle," *Forbes*, Dec. 18, 2014. In comparison, between 40 percent and 70 percent of students elect vocational tracks in such countries as Austria, Denmark, Switzerland, Germany, Norway, and Japan. Youth unemployment in these countries is roughly half that of the United States (ibid.).

33. I am not proposing that vocational tracks should displace the humanities or liberal arts, but that the humanities should not be emphasized to the detriment of vocational tracks.

access often entail a combination of funding schools or students through taxation and private philanthropy. Interstate solutions require more elaborate schemes of targeted aid from both governmental and private sources, philanthropic initiatives such as providing scholarships for students to enroll in schools in wealthier nations, and encouraging dependent states to assume greater responsibility for funding the education of their citizens as they become more affluent.

Enabling people to acquire marketable skills and knowledge thereby requires that the opportunity costs for most individuals should be paid collectively. The state organizes this payment by both redistributing financial resources (taxes), and encouraging private philanthropy (e.g., tax-deductible tuition payments and/or contributions to schools or scholarship funds). There are good reasons why society as a whole should pay a significant portion of the opportunity costs for people to acquire at least a minimal floor of marketable skills and knowledge.

First, at the intrastate level, civil society benefits when its individual members enjoy greater and more widespread affluence as a result of the more valued proficiencies they bring to competitive labor markets. Consequently, sharing opportunity costs helps individuals to meet material wants and needs that in turn encourage the flourishing of communicative associations. In this respect, these redistributive measures and private initiatives to pay opportunity costs for a wide range of people may also be seen as an investment in social capital. Again, there is wide variation among particular states on how they provide educational access. Some states, for instance, may concentrate on primary education while providing little, if any, assistance for secondary or postsecondary schools or students. Such a strategy may provide far more immediate benefits to an impoverished nation with high rates of illiteracy. Or some states may enact policies affecting a much more extensive range of educational opportunities. This strategy may prove more beneficial to a wealthy nation requiring many highly skilled or knowledgeable workers. In short, enabling people to compete in global labor markets is to simultaneously create social capital that potentially strengthens civil society over the long term.

State-sponsored, private, and philanthropic initiatives to help create social capital in poor regions or sectors can be justified on pragmatic grounds. As individuals procure more competitive skills, impoverished regions can become locales for future capital investment. Additionally, such investment will also strengthen civil society, thereby promoting human flourishing on a more global scale. From an overtly Christian perspective, helping impoverished people to pay the opportunity costs for future employment is justified broadly by the love of neighbor, and more specifically represents a practical and effective way of exercising a preferential option for the poor.

In enabling people to acquire employable skills and knowledge, the state should play a prominent role in organizing these efforts in an equitable, efficient, and efficacious manner. As noted above, however, the false dichotomy between the so-called private (read market) and public (read state-controlled) domains must be overcome to achieve both equity and efficiency. An educational system based exclusively on the market might prove efficient and efficacious for those who can pay the cost, but inequitable to those who are unable to pay. In contrast, a state-controlled system may prove more equitable, but not necessarily more efficient or efficacious.

To reiterate, the state should play a prominent role in organizing educational opportunities, but this does not mean that it should necessarily operate or fund schools on an exclusive basis. Such a state-run monopoly is often ill-equipped to provide people with the skills and knowledge they need to compete in competitive labor markets. Many of the world's top-rated universities, for example, are located in the United States and include a mixture of private and state-funded institutions, whereas primary and secondary schools are operated predominantly by states and rank poorly in comparison with other wealthy nations.[34] In contrast, Scandinavian educational systems are highly equitable, as well as efficient and efficacious, largely as a result of recent reforms in how students and schools are funded. In Sweden and Denmark, vouchers have helped create a rich mixture of competitive state, nonprofit, and for-profit schools.[35]

A variety of educational systems and institutions are needed in order to provide people with the skills and knowledge they need to compete in global labor markets. Moreover, educational providers must have the ability to adapt to the rapidly changing demand of these markets. Enabling a wide variety of schools and curricula is a superior option to that offered by monopolistic systems dictated by either the ability to pay or the state, for neither faces competitive pressures to respond to the most pressing demands of individuals, and more expansively the needs of civil society.

---

34. Ferguson notes that in the United Kingdom the opposite trend is true. Secondary schools rank high on international tables but British universities, which are almost uniformly regulated by the state, with the exceptions of Oxford and Cambridge, rank poorly. See Ferguson, *The Great Degeneration*, 126–27.

35. See Micklethwait and Wooldridge, *The Fourth Revolution*, ch. 7; see also Ferguson, *The Great Degeneration*, 128–29.

Again, various states will devise educational systems in particular ways, but it is not surprising that the pursuit of acquiring competitive skills and knowledge is best served by competitive educational systems. As Ferguson contends: "All over the world, smart countries are moving away from the outdated model of state education monopolies and allowing civil society back into education, where it belongs."[36]

In this chapter I have argued that political ordering should promote the flourishing of civil society. In light of globalization, this requires striking a fruitful tension between the creative destruction of global markets and governmental regulation on both an intrastate and interstate basis. In respect to labor, this entails providing individuals with competitive skills in order that they might satisfy their material well-being that in turn serves to strengthen the communicative associations that constitute civil society. This admittedly idealized scheme, however, raises three important issues. First, to what extent should people be free to associate in order to communicate shared goods, particularly if such goods appear to be inimical to broader social and political goods? Second, as individuals acquire competitive skills and knowledge, to what extent should they be free to migrate to locales where appropriate jobs are offered? Third, to what extent should income and wealth be redistributed in order to enable fair competition and mitigate its ill effects? Each of these questions point toward the greater concern of how freedom and justice should be related, the subject of the next chapter.

---

36. Ferguson, *The Great Degeneration*, 128.

Chapter Nine

Freedom and Justice

Human flourishing requires both freedom and justice. Without them the ability to communicate shared goods is severely restricted. Ideally, freedom and justice are mutually reinforcing. Provided I have the requisite qualifications, I should be free to teach, and it is just if I find a school willing to hire me. Conversely, it would be unjust to inhibit my freedom to teach because of my race, gender, or other arbitrary factors. Freedom, however, is not without necessary constraints, and justice often entails honoring and enforcing these limitations. Simply because I am qualified to teach, I am not entitled to demand that a school give me a job, and no injustice is committed if I cannot find employment as a professor in a tight job market. Additionally, since I am a seminary professor, I am not free to teach that core Christian beliefs and doctrines are false, and it would be unjust to both my students and the church to allow me to do so. Moreover, freedom necessarily entails restricted choices rather than unlimited options. I cannot simultaneously be a teacher, fund manager, and rubbish collector, for in trying to do all these things I sacrifice my freedom to do any of them well.

Freedom and justice are expansive and complex subjects that have prompted many lengthy and learned treatises. The limited scope of my inquiry does not permit a critical survey of the vast corpus of philosophical and theological literature, because that would require still another lengthy and (hopefully) learned treatise. Rather, I develop some basic theological suppositions regarding what freedom and justice entail in response to the questions posed at the conclusion of the preceding chapter, and that are relevant to the broader issue of globalization. In the section about freedom I argue that people should be free to associate, compete, and communicate. In the section on justice I contend that it is just to permit and protect the freedom to associate, communicate, and compete, and that it is also just to require people to share, to a limited extent, the risks and benefits of competitive markets. In the final section, I demonstrate how freedom and justice should be related, in terms of enabling, restricting, and compelling action, by examining the issues of property, labor migration, and redistribution of wealth and income. As will be apparent, this chapter builds on and expands some key themes developed in the previous chapter on civil society and political ordering.

Freedom

Since humans are finite creatures, their actions must be constrained if freedom is to be effectual. Unlike God, people are not free to do anything and everything they might want. But in recognizing these creaturely limits, humans are liberated to obey their Creator, and in such obedience are made free. This life of free obedience is captured in Martin Luther's paradoxical assertion that a "Christian is a perfectly free lord of all, subject to none," *and* a "perfectly dutiful servant of all, subject to all."[1] One is free both to act and not to act in obedience to God, which in turn frees people from the bondage of their sinful will. Consequently, genuine freedom decays by an "incapacity to obey."[2]

Since freedom entails action both undertaken and not taken, then every affirmation requires a prior negation; one must say no to that in order to say yes to this. For example, I first had to say no to other career options before I could be free to teach. Although it is individuals who negate and affirm, they do not do so as isolated beings. Rather, people exercise their freedom within a series of concrete roles and relationships such as friends, spouses, parents, workers, employers, rulers, and citizens. Consequently, following Karl Barth, freedom is lived out in relation to authority and fellowship.[3]

Authority is not the power to impose one's will upon another. Rather, we cannot act freely unless we are authorized to undertake certain kinds of action. Properly ordered authority serves to constrain arbitrary acts of power, because one exercising authority is also under authority.[4] The

---

1. Martin Luther, *The Freedom of a Christian*, in Harold J. Grimm, ed., *Luther's Works*, vol. 31 (Philadelphia, PA: Muhlenberg Press, 1957), 344.

2. Oliver O'Donovan, *Resurrection and Moral Order: An Outline for Evangelical Ethics* (Grand Rapids, MI: Eerdmans, 1986), 23.

3. See pertinent sections of Karl Barth, *Church Dogmatics*, III/3 and III/4.

4. See Matt. 8:5–13.

president of the United States, for instance, has a great deal of power, but is only free to exercise what is lawfully authorized. Additionally, authority may be informal. Parents appeal to parental authority in their childrearing, which serves to both empower and constrain what they do and refrain from doing. Without such authority they are not free to be good parents. More broadly, as Oliver O'Donovan contends, "Authority is the objective correlate of freedom."[5]

Freedom, then, entails the power or ability to either act or not to act in certain authorized ways. Yet if freedom is understood only as power, then it is reduced to an abstraction; and a "more substantial sense of freedom"[6] is only operative in *fellowship*. A purportedly autonomous individual does not enjoy freedom. To be free requires association with neighbors; Robinson Crusoe, for instance, is not free until Friday arrives. People exercise their freedom through a series of overlapping spheres of associations involving such relationships as family, worship, commerce, and political governance. Personal freedom, then, depends on and is derived from fellowship with others. I am not free to be a husband without the fellowship of my wife; I am not free to worship God without the fellowship of other believers; I am not free to be a consumer without producers; I am not free to be a citizen without rulers. Most important, we cannot be free to communicate shared goods without others, and to freely act or refrain from acting in authorized ways that promote the communication of these goods.

In tandem, authority and fellowship enable people to enact their freedom through a series of corresponding negations and affirmations. Yet how is freedom best supported by economic and political ordering, particularly in light of globalization? A comprehensive answer is clearly beyond the scope of this chapter, but some suggestive contours can be offered by focusing on the freedom to associate, compete, and communicate. The normative content of these freedoms, as well as the social and governmental processes for implementing them, vary widely across differing cultural and political traditions. Despite these variations these notions of freedom represent basic concepts that are best suited for enabling human flourishing within the contemporary context of globalization.

Association is a fundamental freedom. If humans were unable or unwilling to associate, they could not engage in either exchange or political governance. Indeed, they could not survive for very long as a species, for, as Althusius and others have argued, sociality is an indispensable human

5. O'Donovan, *Resurrection and Moral Order*, 122.
6. See Oliver O'Donovan, *The Ways of Judgment: The Bampton Lectures, 2003* (Grand Rapids, MI, and Cambridge, UK: Eerdmans, 2005), 67–68.

trait. From both a theological and moral perspective it is important to stress that it is through association, with both God and neighbor, that people are given their freedom. Individuals are not simply free to associate, but rather discover and affirm their freedom in associating with others. Consequently, prohibiting or arbitrarily restricting people from associating is tantamount to waging a war against human nature.

In order to meet their material wants and needs, people must be free to *compete*. Humans are embodied creatures and must satisfy the necessities of sustenance, shelter, rest, and health care. Material well-being, however, is not confined to meeting basic needs but is enriched through the pursuit and enjoyment of greater affluence. Widespread prosperity is best promoted through competitive global markets, which many people encounter most directly through work or labor. If people are not free to compete in global labor markets, then they are also less free to meet their material wants and needs, much less pursue and enjoy greater affluence. This freedom to compete neither contradicts nor diminishes the freedom discovered in association but rather supports and enables it, because competition and cooperation are not antithetical but complementary activities.[7]

If people are to flourish, then they must be free to *communicate* shared goods. The freedom to communicate is most directly linked to the fundamental freedom to associate, but with an important codicil: the freedom to associate for the purposes of conducting exchange and political ordering is necessary, but it is not sufficient to promote human flourishing. Neither markets nor the state, either individually or in tandem, are equipped to provide or enable the goods of creation to be communicated by the human creatures created by God. To use a simple example, a family uses various markets to provide for its material well-being while also enjoying protections and services provided by the state. Yet neither of these activities is directly the cause of a family's flourishing. Rather, this occurs through family members communicating shared goods. Consequently, safeguards are needed to ensure that communicative associations do not suffer from either too much intrusion or too little attention by the state, or inadequate access to or domination by markets.

Finally, pursuing and enacting the freedoms to associate, compete, and communicate should be based on consent instead of compulsion; otherwise the acts are not fully free. In other words, negations and affirmations are ideally, but certainly not always, chosen rather than compelled. To return to a previous example, I chose to be a teacher and consented to

7. See ch. 2 above.

the requisite training, opportunity costs, and accompanying risks; no one compelled me. Freedom, therefore, entails risks. In retrospect, one may negate and affirm the wrong available options.[8] I could have chosen to pursue a different profession for which I was ill-suited or no employment opportunities were available. Although freedom is best enacted through consent, compulsion is nonetheless required in order to enable some to act and to constrain others from acting. It is in these moments when compulsion is needed that the issue of justice is most clearly raised.

Justice

I am using "justice" to refer to a condition or action that promotes freedom in terms of either enabling or constraining certain kinds of conditions or actions that are judged, respectively, to be good or bad. To determine what is good or bad, however, is not an exclusively subjective judgment but requires some criterion against which a certain or proposed act or constraint is evaluated. The criterion I employ is human flourishing. Acts or constraints that promote human flourishing, either directly or indirectly, may be judged to be good; while acts or constraints that prevent or diminish human flourishing, either directly or indirectly, may be judged to be bad. Human flourishing occurs predominantly in communicating shared goods. Although what constitutes shared goods and how they are best communicated requires a normative argument, I do not undertake this task. Rather, I assume that such an argument can, in principle, be made, and that it can be expressed in pluriform ways across various social and political contexts and cultural and religious traditions.

Many freely chosen acts or constraints are just, requiring no external compulsion. For example, my choice to become a teacher rather than a farmer or banker was both free and just because it has enabled me to meet both my material wants and needs and has, in turn, allowed me to participate more fully in various communicative associations. Although a particular uncompelled act may be initially free and just, some subsequent compulsion is often required. In order to teach, I was required to master a certain discipline, and I am compelled to demonstrate ongoing competency. Such compulsion is just, for if I were an incompetent teacher I could potentially diminish the future material well-being and flourishing of my students.

8. I am not assuming that a person has an infinite capacity to negate and affirm any and all options. Options are limited by such things as locale, social position, physical and mental abilities, luck, and political contexts.

The kind of act described in the preceding paragraph, one that is simultaneously free and just and uncompelled, is predicated on negations and affirmations made by virtuous persons. Such virtues as prudence, self-control, tolerance, and generosity, as well as the Christian virtues of faith, hope, and love, inform what kinds of acts and constraints people should impose on themselves within a particular set of circumstances. For example, I am free, perhaps even justified, to say things designed to provoke a strong emotional reaction from other people, but I instead impose constraints on my speech for the sake of prudence and love of neighbor.[9] Virtuous people, then, not only appeal to their own goods and well-being, but also to the good and well-being of neighbors in determining which acts and constraints constitute a fitting response to a given set of circumstances.[10]

The problem is that people do not always perform or constrain their actions in virtuous ways. This is not because most people are vicious or wicked[11] but because they tend to act in thoughtless, foolish, or venal ways, resulting from what Augustine labeled disordered desire. In short, societies comprise sinners rather than angels, so it is not surprising that their actions often fail to be virtuous. Consequently, some acts and constraints must be compelled if justice, or at least some semblance of it, is to prevail.

Such compulsion is often reinforced through various interactions. For example, a manufacturer may be tempted to increase profits by producing shoddy items, but is compelled not to do so by the prospect of losing customers. In other instances, incentives or disincentives may be employed to achieve desirable or just outcomes. A student who writes an excellent essay is awarded an A, while a student failing to write an essay receives an F. On other occasions, the threat of coercion by the state is needed to compel acts or constraints that are determined to be just. It is doubtful if individuals were asked by the state to pay taxes that many would voluntarily comply. Rather, people are compelled to pay taxes because if they fail to do so or evade them, then their property may be seized, or they may be fined or incarcerated. Finally, recourse to coercion may be required to establish just conditions. Dangerous criminals and terrorists

9. This does not imply that it is always right or good for individuals to impose constraints on provocative speech as witnessed by the prophets of the Old Testament.

10. See H. Richard Niebuhr, *The Responsible Self: An Essay in Christian Moral Philosophy* (Louisville, KY: Westminster John Knox Press, 1999).

11. Although some people are vicious or wicked.

need to be forcefully constrained both to protect innocent people from harm and to punish those who have willfully harmed others.

In each of the preceding instances a condition of justice is established through potential consequences that compel certain kinds of acts or constraints. This outcome can be demonstrated by indicating the obverse. It would be unjust if consumers could only purchase shoddy items at exorbitant prices. It would be unjust if all students received an A regardless of the quality of their work or whether or not they completed all their assignments. It would be unjust if only a few individuals paid taxes. It would be unjust if people were not protected from criminal and terrorist acts, and unjust if criminals and terrorists were not punished for their acts.

Moreover, in each of these instances the resulting condition of justice that is established reinforces freedom that results from compelled acts and constraints. The freedom of consumers is enhanced when they can choose among items of higher quality and lower cost. The freedom of students to achieve genuine academic excellence is enhanced through a series of incentives and disincentives. The freedom of all citizens collectively is enhanced when tax burdens are equitably distributed. The freedom of people to participate more fully in civil society is enhanced when protected from criminal and terrorist acts.

In respect to externally imposed constraints, justice is best served by the free acts it permits and enables rather than the enforced restrictions that are required to achieve this goal. In other words, externally imposed constraints are means rather than ends, and should be evaluated as such. This is an important principle, because it places the onus on justifying the imposition of external constraints, particularly those by the state, given its monopoly of coercive power. It should be clearly demonstrated why proposed constraints are needed to enable human flourishing, particularly in respect to the freedoms to associate, compete, and communicate. The imposition of external constraints, then, should serve to expand opportunities and settings in which individuals select the negations and affirmations that form and constitute their freedom.

The normative determination of what kinds and range of external constraints that are justified varies widely across particular cultural traditions and political jurisdictions. Such determinations inevitably generate both intra and international disagreements. For example, many people around the world disagree with Saudi Arabia's restrictions on women drivers, and presumably some Saudis see these restrictions as unnecessary restraints imposed by the state. Moral and political disputes over particular imposed constraints, however, do not disqualify nations from participating in global markets, as Saudi Arabia clearly demonstrates. Despite the myriad differences regarding what constitutes freedom and justice, and how they should be related, there are nevertheless certain basic standards of justice that can and should be affirmed *if* people around the world are to more fully enjoy the benefits of participating in global markets. For the purpose of this inquiry, there are three basic affirmations.

First, *it is just to permit and protect people to freely associate and communicate*. As I argued above, the ability to associate is a fundamental prerequisite of both human freedom and flourishing. If constraints are imposed on people that severely limit their ability to associate, then their freedom and ability to communicate shared goods are diminished. The freedom to associate, however, is not absolute. There are good reasons to prevent criminals and terrorists from associating, and the scope and severity of these imposed constraints rightfully varies in response to the threats that particular political jurisdictions face. Governments have a duty to be wary of potential enemies congregating for the purpose of creating mayhem. But this is not the same as a regime imposing constraints on association for the purpose of maintaining its tyrannical or illegitimate rule. In these instances, globalization may be used to perpetuate injustice rather than a liberating or liberalizing force promoting greater human freedom and flourishing.

Second, *it is just to permit and enable people to freely compete*. Participating in competitive global markets, particularly labor markets, best promotes the material well-being of people. Moreover, a subsequent pursuit of affluence can also enable people to participate more fully in a range of communicative associations, in turn promoting human flourishing for a greater number of people. It is therefore unjust if people are prevented from competing in global labor markets. This constraint may be imposed in two ways. On the one hand, people may not have adequate opportunities to acquire requisite skills and knowledge, and on the other hand, people may not be permitted to utilize the skills and knowledge they acquire. In the first instance, some nations may lack the financial resources to provide educational opportunities. In the second instance, employment utilizing acquired skills and knowledge may not be readily available due to restrictions upon invested capital or migration to where appropriate jobs are on offer. Exercising this freedom to compete, however, is not unconditional. Some individuals, for example, do not have the requisite abilities or realistic opportunities to master highly valued skills commanding lucrative compensation. Additionally, there are legitimate reasons for constraining labor migration to ensure that some jurisdictions do not become overwhelmed by a sudden influx of migrants. As noted above, the issue of enabling free labor competition requires extensive political ordering on both an intra and interstate basis, but in both instances the onus should be placed on justifying imposed constraints on people acquiring employable skills and knowledge, and their mobility to take advantage of employment opportunities.

Third, *it is just to require people to share, to a limited extent, the risks and benefits of competitive global markets.* Competition always entails winners and losers. It is no different in global markets, and the enlarged field of competitors intensifies both the potential rewards and risks. This turbulence is experienced most directly in global labor markets as investors, businesses, and governments seek their respective competitive advantages in reaction to changing market conditions. Consequently, many workers will be adversely affected for short or extended periods of time. It is both necessary and just that such persons be assisted until such time that they are able to compete for a job or otherwise lawfully provide for their material well-being. Unless a society is willing to allow people to perish if they are not able to meet their basic needs, then it is necessary to expend supportive material or financial resources on their behalf. Such assistance is also self-interested, for it is similar to the previous discussion of sharing educational opportunity costs that ultimately benefits the individuals and communicative associations constituting civil society. The same can be said for assisting those adversely affected by competitive labor markets, for it reinforces social bonds of affinity and reciprocity. Sharing the benefits and risks of competition reinforces the notion that I help someone in need with the expectation that my act will be reciprocated in kind by someone else. This is not an exchange, because I help John but at a later date it is Jane who helps me when I am in need. Moreover, such reciprocity is not necessarily equivalent or of equal value. I gave John a sandwich when he was hungry, whereas Jane gives me a jacket when I am cold. Moreover, for Christians, charity demands that neighbors in dire need must be helped.

At the macro level, such assistance and reciprocity is accomplished primarily through a redistribution of income and wealth. Distributive channels include personal and familial assistance, private aid, philanthropy, and taxation. Although all of these measures are justified not only by the practical necessity, self-interest and charity, there is an important caveat that redistributive efforts should be limited. There is both a practical and moral reason for this limitation. Practically, a tipping point is reached when there is little incentive to be either generous or productive. Taxation policies and rates, for instance, may effectively discourage the creation of wealth to such an extent that the wealth to be redistributed diminishes over time. Such tipping points vary across cultural and political traditions, but in any instance killing geese laying golden eggs does not help those in need of assistance. Assisting those disadvantaged by competitive labor markets should also be limited in order to encourage people to return to productive labor as soon as possible. It is unjust to keep people dependent on the generosity and productive labor of others for any longer than is necessary. Such dependency may restrict the ability of people to participate more fully in communicative associations, thereby diminishing human flourishing. Consequently, there should be incentives and provisions that reward individuals who expeditiously acquire and use skills that enable their competitive advantages in global labor markets.

Although justice may at times require the imposition of external constraints, justice is not thereby inimical to freedom, but ideally supports and strengthens it. If external constraints effectively diminish freedom, then they are not just, and unconstrained freedom, which is not really freedom at all, diminishes or distorts justice. But how are people encouraged and enabled to act both freely and justly, particularly within the highly volatile context of dynamic global markets?

Enabling People to Act Freely and Justly

I have argued that since people should be free to associate, compete, and communicate, it is therefore just to permit and protect people to associate, compete, and communicate, and require them to share, to a limited extent, the risks and benefits of competitive markets. Striking the proper balance between negations and affirmations that both freedom and justice require raises a number of often contentious moral and political issues, particularly in light of globalization. In the remainder of this chapter I briefly examine three illustrative issues involving property and association, labor migration, and the redistribution of wealth and income. My investigation of these issues is far from comprehensive.

To reiterate, the ability to associate and communicate is a fundamental prerequisite of human flourishing. Egregious violations of this freedom demonstrate its unjust consequences. As Hannah Arendt contends, totalitarian regimes maintain their control over captive people by isolating and restricting their opportunities to associate, thereby establishing conditions of mutual suspicion and mistrust, which in turn thwarts human flourishing by diminishing opportunities to communicate shared goods.[12] Yet even some states that purportedly permit their citizens to associate may effectively restrict them through various policies and practices. A prominent example involves the ownership of property. Although a communicative association needs a place in which to congregate, this does not imply that the ability to associate and communicate is directly proportional to the property owned by those associating or communicating. Two or three gathered in Christ's name could communicate their fellowship in a municipally owned park as well as a cathedral owned by the diocese. Rather, private property helps to protect the freedom to associate and communicate, and it is therefore unjust to effectively prevent or discourage people from owning property.

The freedom to own property is not absolute. There are good reasons why governments own certain properties in order to protect their citizens and promote their well-being. Nor are people entitled to own property; the freedom to own property does not authorize one to seize the property of another or to take on debt that one is unable to repay. Policies or practices that effectively and extensively restrict the ownership of property, however, diminish the material well-being of many people. Throughout the world individuals often remain impoverished because they lack access to capital that would enable their participation in global markets. Yet substantial capital is readily available that could be used by the poor if laws regarding the ownership, transfer, and collateral status of property were reformed in most of the poorest nations.[13] Poor people often improve the value of the property in which they live or work, but have no legal deeds or protections, and therefore cannot use property as a source of capital. Hernando de Soto contends that "even in the poorest countries, the poor save." Writing in 2000, he estimates that "the value of savings among the poor is, in fact, immense—forty times all the foreign aid received throughout the world since 1945."[14] In the absence of legal policies and protections that enable the widespread acquisition and trading of private property, the poor are saddled with "dead capital."

---

12. See Hannah Arendt, *The Origins of Totalitarianism* (San Diego, CA: Harvest Book, 1968), 323–24; see also Francis Fukuyama, *Trust: The Social Virtues and the Creation of Prosperity* (New York and London: Free Press, 1995), 54–55, and relevant sections of Francis Fukuyama, *Political Order and Political Decay: From the Industrial Revolution to the Globalization of Democracy* (New York: Farrar, Straus and Giroux, 2014).

13. See Hernando de Soto, *The Mystery of Capital: Why Capitalism Triumphs in the West and Fails Everywhere Else* (New York: Basic Books, 2000).

14. Ibid., 5.

The significance of private property is not restricted to its potential for generating capital. More importantly, private property helps to protect the freedom of people to associate and communicate. When property is owned predominantly by the state or a few institutions, families, or individuals, it constrains a widespread pursuit of prosperity, in turn diminishing the communicative associations constituting civil society. In short, preventing individuals from acquiring property is to consign them to perpetual impoverishment, and such consignment is unjust because it diminishes human flourishing. The rule of law that protects the freedom of the many to own property is needed to rectify this injustice.

William Easterly contends that poverty does not result from a "shortage of expertise," but a "shortage of rights," or more provocatively, that the "real cause of poverty . . . is the unchecked power of the state against poor people without rights."[15] From a global perspective, the right to own property is in especially short supply for the poor, depriving them of the "remarkable ability to generate prosperity and to solve the problems of poverty."[16] Easterly characterizes this shortage of rights as a form of "oppression" that restricts true development, because it "promotes a lack of trust that inhibits trade and facilitates more oppression. It entrenches a hereditary political and economic elite that blocks the creative destruction necessary for development."[17]

The reasons for shorting the poor of their rights range from willfulness to ineptitude. At one extreme, corrupt officials and private interests may collude to enrich themselves at the expense of impoverishing others. Traditional Christian moral teaching condemns such acts because they harm the material well-being of others, thereby diminishing their flourishing. At the other extreme, some states are ill-equipped to come to terms with and take advantage of globalization. As Francis Fukuyama argues, states decay over time, a symptom of which is a plethora of outdated laws and contradictory polices that cater to various clients and special interests, as well as bloated and ineffectual bureaucracies that are used as instruments to restrict rather than enable freedom.[18] Such incompetence is objectionable not only because it directly harms the poor but also because it prevents them from taking advantage of global markets,

15. William Easterly, *The Tyranny of Experts: Economists, Dictators, and the Forgotten Rights of the Poor* (New York: Basic Books, 2013), 6–7.
16. Ibid., 175.
17. Ibid., 158–59.
18. See Fukuyama, *Political Order and Political Decay*, esp. pt. 4.

and therefore it is unjust because it restricts their freedom to compete, associate, and communicate.

Some critics contend, however, that enabling greater participation in global markets diminishes human flourishing because it weakens traditional social bonds and associations. Social solidarity is sacrificed for a self-interested or even selfish individualism that competitive markets tend to encourage and reinforce. Yet as Easterly insists, individualistic societies are not necessarily atomistic. Individuals are free to form associations, and tend to be more tolerant of other associations, particularly those based on ethnicity, than is the case in more collectivist societies.[19] The legal protection of individual rights generally, and property rights more particularly, actually stimulate greater cooperation that benefit the poor. These rights offer incentives to individuals to form associations to solve immediate problems. Drawing on F. A. Hayek and Adam Smith, Easterly insists that the "spontaneous solutions" undertaken by these cooperative efforts are more effective than those imposed by so-called development experts, because it is difficult to predict what a fitting solution might entail, and who will have the most appropriate knowledge to solve it.[20] These spontaneous solutions undertaken by the poor often involve commercial or market-based activities that are admittedly self-interested. But in respect to Smith's often misunderstood notions of the invisible hand and self-interest: "The suppliers who provide any goods that are profitable in the marketplace do so only to get the profit, but they wind up unintentionally meeting many of our most pressing needs. Our demand to get our most urgent needs met is what makes the goods profitable."[21] This is not an endorsement of selfishness or greed. Indeed, Smith was adamantly opposed to monopolies and greedy merchants that do not promote the common good. His intent was to prevent monopolies driven by greed, which would effectively help the poor. "Self-interest was not greed, it was not pursuing monopolies; it was honorable dealing and freedom of entry to whomever could deliver the goods."[22]

Paradoxically, permitting and protecting the freedom of *individuals* to associate enable koinonia and therefore human flourishing. One way to secure this freedom is by allowing individuals to acquire, trade, and use property to generate capital. Yet equally puzzling is the need of individuals to be mobile within competitive global markets. If people should be

19. See Easterly, *The Tyranny of Experts*, 183–85.
20. See ibid., ch. 11.
21. Ibid., 243.
22. Ibid., 244.

free to compete, then it is just to permit them to participate freely in competitive markets. This is especially true in respect to global labor markets. People cannot pursue greater prosperity or affluence if they are not permitted to seek opportunities for doing so, and such opportunities may sometimes require relocating temporarily or permanently. *Labor migration* is thereby both a significant consequence and key component of globalization. It is also a highly contentious political issue. To mention the word "immigration" is to spark strong reactions over whether restrictive or open laws and policies should be enacted.

I am purposely using the phrase "labor migration" to dispel many of the assumptions that often underlie heated political rhetoric. It is often assumed, for instance, that immigrants intend to reside permanently in the country to which they have immigrated. In many cases this is true, but in other instances there is a strong desire to return at some future time to the lands from which they have emigrated. Workers may take jobs in foreign lands for a while in order to send money back to their families, and many immigrants are refugees who have been forced to flee their homelands due to war, civil unrest, or persecution, and their ultimate place of settlement is unknown. In short, there are many reasons why people relocate, and a wide range of expectations regarding whether these relocations are temporary or permanent. In the following discussion, I concentrate exclusively on people relocating in order to work or take advantage of certain opportunities to engage in commerce that are not afforded in their present locale, and some issues that such migration creates in respect to globalization.

Since people should be free to compete, then it is just to permit and enable people to compete in global labor markets. This freedom is often enabled through domestic or foreign capital investment that creates jobs to produce goods to be traded or the provision of services. If such opportunities are not available in a particular locale, then people should be afforded the opportunity to migrate, either intra or internationally, to locales where such opportunities are offered. The freedom to migrate is not absolute. For example, migration may be restricted for reasons of security or preventing social services from becoming overwhelmed. Additionally, except in the case of accepting refugees, migration may be restricted to workers with applicable or needed skills. The freedom to relocate is not accompanied by an entitlement to have a job created for each migrant after they arrive. I assume that as local economies and markets grow increasingly integrated, more elaborate regulatory treaties and agreements will need to be enacted that oversee global labor migration, and protect some basic rights and privileges of guest workers that accord with those afforded to the citizens of host countries.[23]

It is understandable why the prospect of labor migration generates strong defensive or protectionist reactions. It might be feared, for instance, that the influx of new workers will drive down wages or take away jobs from locals. In some instances these fears have proven to be well-founded. Yet there is strong evidence that labor migration tends to promote economic growth in host countries. Michael Mandelbaum contends that "immigrants enhance the welfare of the places to which they immigrate. They expand the labor pool and the number of consumers. They sometimes bring technical expertise and entrepreneurial drive."[24]

Labor migration also benefits countries that workers leave. "Workers who remain in countries that immigrants leave enjoy higher wages because the labor force shrinks." More broadly, "emigration can also increase total wealth, particularly in very poor countries, when emigrants send back money—remittances—to family and friends they have left behind."[25] The amount of these remittances is much larger than that provided by aid or private philanthropy; Easterly estimates that the total amount of remittances worldwide in 2011 was around $372 billion.[26] More broadly, permitting greater labor migration is potentially a powerful force for promoting both economic growth and diminishing poverty on a global scale. Mandelbaum insists that political opposition should be resisted since the "gains" labor migration "brings are large and consistent enough that immigration qualifies as the greatest underutilized resource." Citing a 2005 World Bank study, an annual 3 percent increase in labor migration "would deliver $300 billion annually in benefits to the low-wage countries and be worth $51 billion to the countries to which they emigrated."[27]

It may be objected that encouraging greater labor migration ultimately hurts poor countries because of the "brain drain" it creates. It is understandable that individuals who have acquired valuable skills and knowledge want to leave locales where their expertise is underutilized and valued, thereby diminishing a poor country's productivity. Easterly,

---

23. This does not imply that a full range of rights and privileges should be given to guest workers, and that some legitimate restrictions, such as voting or holding a governmental office, do not violate or unduly constrain the freedom to compete in global labor markets.

24. Michael Mandelbaum, *The Road to Global Prosperity* (New York and London: Simon and Schuster e-book, 2014), ch. 2.

25. Ibid.

26. Easterly, *The Tyranny of Experts*, 207.

27. See Mandelbaum, *The Road to Global Prosperity*, ch. 2.

however, dispels this objection, particularly when economic development is viewed in global rather than national terms.[28] When so-called "drainers leave low-wage jobs for high-wage jobs, they increase their productivity. They benefit not only themselves but world development as a whole."[29] Moreover, remittances demonstrate that a supposed "brain drain" benefits rather than harms poorer regions.

To reiterate, it is understandable why labor migration generates impassioned opposition. Nonetheless, this hostility should be resisted, for it "blinds us to the possibility that migration itself could be a powerful vehicle for *both global and individual development*."[30] Within a globally integrated economy, mobility is required in order for individuals to be free to compete, and it is therefore just to permit labor migration on a global scale. More important, such migration promotes the pursuit of affluence as well as potentially creating more opportunities for communicating shared goods, both of which promote human flourishing.

Although it is just to permit and enable people to compete, it is also just to require people to share, to a limited extent, the risks and benefits of competition. Such sharing requires *redistributing wealth and income*. This is due in part to sheer practicality. Social and political ordering would prove dysfunctional if certain public services were provided on a strictly fee basis. Police officers, for example, do not require direct payment before responding to a call. Rather, policing is funded on a broad basis in which the amounts individuals pay are often disproportional to actual utilization of service. Some redistribution is needed due to dire necessity. Some people are unable to care for themselves either permanently or for indefinite periods of time, while others may require assistance for relatively brief durations in response to misfortune or changing economic conditions. In many of these instances, personal financial resources are not available to pay for such care and assistance. More broadly, redistributing wealth can contribute to the future flourishing of civil society. As I argued above, sharing the opportunity costs of education can ultimately benefit the communicative associations that constitute civil society. Additionally, growing income inequality may diminish economic growth.[31]

Some redistribution of wealth and income is also justifiable on moral grounds. Although individuals should be expected to meet their needs and

28. See Easterly, *The Tyranny of Experts*, ch. 9.
29. Ibid., 208–9.
30. ibid., 205 (emphasis added).
31. See, e.g., Martin Wolf, "Why Inequality Is Such a Drag on Economies," *Financial Times*, Sept. 30, 2014.

wants through their own initiative, they cannot fulfill this expectation on their own. As marketplace exchange makes clear, people need other people in order to pursue material well-being and affluence. Redistributing wealth and income acknowledges both the interdependency of exchange and the social bonds of civil society. Consequently, sharing the risks and benefits endemic to competitive markets supplements and complements exchange with a more widely dispersed sense of reciprocity that strengthen the bonds of civil society. Theologically, redistributing wealth and income enacts a concrete love (*caritas*) of neighbor.

There are two prevalent ways of redistributing wealth and income. Private philanthropy and charitable donations are one method. Individuals, corporations, and foundations provide support or aid to individuals or organizations that address particular issues or support various causes. For example, a student may be the recipient of a scholarship, a local shelter may receive cash or in-kind services to provide housing and food for the homeless, or an NGO may be the beneficiary of donated funds for the purpose of promoting a particular cause.

The second prevalent way to redistribute wealth and income is through taxation. Imposing higher taxes on the more affluent, such as progressive rates on income and taxing inheritances, produces revenue that is then redistributed to those in need, most often through the provision of various social services and safety nets. For example, in the United States these services include such programs as welfare, Medicaid, and food stamps. Revenue is also collected from a wider range of taxpayers to provide services benefitting civil society broadly but some individuals less directly. A childless couple owning a home, for instance, pays property tax to support public schools that more directly benefit a large family.

Although redistributing wealth and income helps to share the risks and benefits of volatile global markets, there are a number of problems that need to be noted. Private philanthropy and aid may not be well targeted and charitable giving may prove self-serving, effectively diminishing the purported redistributive benefit for those in need. Donating to my alma mater, for instance, is a way of redistributing my wealth and income, but its benefit for those in need is incidental.[32]

Redistributing tax revenue can also be poorly targeted and ineffectual. Redistributed funds may disproportionally benefit the relatively affluent as opposed to the poor; higher taxpayers often redistribute their taxes

---

32. An example of an incidental benefit is affluent graduates who presumably will support more directly beneficial causes, as well as generating greater tax revenue that can be redistributed.

to themselves rather than those in need. Imposing increasingly higher taxes on the rich and affluent may effectively discourage the creation of wealth. A tipping point may be reached when there is an incentive to be less productive or unproductive past a certain point, and if wealth is not continually being created, then neither can it be taxed and redistributed. These tipping points vary across cultures and political jurisdictions, but if productivity is effectively punished, then an injustice is committed directly against those willing to take the initiative and its risks, and indirectly against those in need.

Globalization exacerbates these problems and issues on both an intra and international basis. As argued previously, private philanthropy and governmental aid are notoriously ineffectual and poorly targeted.[33] In order to compete in competitive global markets some nations may not be able to collect and redistribute what relatively little wealth and income they have. For instance, to attract foreign capital investment a country may offer such low tax rates that insufficient revenue is collected that could in turn be redistributed.

In respect to international relations, the challenge is even more formidable. As the global economy becomes increasingly integrated it is arguable that the risks and benefits of competing in global markets should be shared across political jurisdictions. In short, a case could be made that wealth and income should be redistributed on both an intra and international basis. It is doubtful, however, that such an argument would, at present, prevail. A nation-state collecting taxes from its citizens and then redistributing the funds to other nation-states would be, to say the least, both politically unpalatable and difficult to justify. Additionally, the prospect of establishing some kind of international taxing authority to accomplish the redistribution of wealth is even more unlikely and ominous: unlikely because there is no compelling reason for a nation-state to subject its citizens to a foreign taxing authority, and ominous because a taxing authority with a global reach would likely discourage the creation of wealth by diminishing both the creative and destructive forces of competitive global markets. Consequently, proposals for imposing worldwide confiscatory taxation on wealth and income[34] are not only fanciful but also unjust since they would ultimately diminish human flourishing by effectively constraining the freedom to compete.

---

33. See ch. 5 in this volume.

34. See, e.g., Thomas Piketty, *Capital in the Twenty-First Century* (Cambridge, MA, and London: Belknap Press, 2014), pt. 4.

Nevertheless, some redistribution of wealth and income on a global scale needs to be undertaken. The transition from nation-state to market-state may suggest some potentially promising approaches. In the emerging market-state the sharp dichotomy between private and governmental sectors is replaced by a more fluid public sphere constituting civil society. It is within this public sphere, which both markets and the state ideally enable and support, that the freedom to compete, associate, and communicate is exercised. Consequently, the task of redistributing wealth and income is not lodged exclusively in either the private domain or political sphere or in tandem, but includes addressing the needs and preserving the freedom of people participating in competitive global markets in ways that share the risks and benefits of such competition, while utilizing the strength and support of both private and governmental initiatives.

This public approach toward redistribution, as opposed to private and governmental approaches, was hinted at in the previous chapter's discussion on sharing the educational opportunity costs entailed in providing more competitive skills and knowledge. As demonstrated by recent reforms in Sweden, promoting competition among state-sponsored, nonprofit, and for-profit schools simultaneously meets the needs of students in a more effective manner while also promoting greater freedom and responsibility for students and parents. What I am calling a "public approach," then, entails a three-way relationship among private initiatives, governmental policies, and personal freedom and responsibility in ways that both harness and mitigate the creative destruction of global markets.

Another example of a public approach is seen in how Singapore funds its welfare, or safety net program. "Singaporeans pay a fifth of their salaries into the Central Provident Fund, with their employers contributing another 15.5 percent. That provides them with the wherewithal to pay for their housing, pensions, and health care and their children's tertiary education."[35] Additionally, there is a minimal safety net provided for the "very poor and the very sick."[36] By empowering individuals to expend funds as they see fit within designated minimal parameters, they are free to use markets to get the best return on their expenditures.

Admittedly, this model is based on self-reliance, but *not isolated selves*. The state administers a program requiring contribution by both employees and employers that promotes the freedom of individuals to expend

35. John Micklethwait and Adrian Wooldridge, *The Fourth Revolution: The Global Race to Reinvent the State* (New York: Penguin, 2014), 140.
36. Ibid.

funds in a manner that best meets their perceived needs in response to changing personal circumstances. Such a public approach avoids the ineffectiveness of exclusively private solutions stemming from their patchwork-like quality, while also avoiding the inefficiency and escalating costs of governmental welfare and educational systems. Similar public experiments are occurring in many of the Nordic countries as well as other Asian nations in which the goal is not to expand the state's control over markets, but to extend markets into the state in ways that promote both individual freedom and a flourishing civil society.

Admittedly, Singapore, as well as Sweden and other Scandinavian nations, are small countries whose models cannot be simply replicated by larger ones. But they do provide inspiration for larger nations to begin experimenting along a range of public solutions, as witnessed by China's growing interest in adopting Singaporean approaches of governance.[37] What these experiments demonstrate is that a number of public goods such as health care and education are made widely available, while using "'capitalist' methods of competition to ensure that public goods are delivered as successfully as possible."[38] More broadly, they also demonstrate that within an increasingly globally integrated economy the emerging market-states must become leaner in order to become better. In this respect, greater globalization may potentially enhance freedom and justice, given the needs of individuals and societies to harness the creatively destructive forces of global markets, while also sharing the accompanying risks in a manner that does not diminish personal responsibility.

37. Ibid., ch. 6.
38. Ibid., 187.

Chapter Ten

Stewardship

In this chapter I weave together some themes that have appeared in previous chapters in making my concluding argument. Succinctly, that argument is that globalization, at present, offers the best possible means of exercising limited human dominion over and stewardship of creation. As I argued in chapter 4, creation is a realm of material abundance. This abundance, however, is one of potential and must be developed if it is to provide a suitable habitat in which humans might communicate created goods and thereby flourish. Eden is a garden, and not a wilderness.

Human dominion over a *finite* creation is *not* absolute. There are physical limits regarding the production and consumption of material goods. More important, there are moral considerations regarding the purpose of such production and consumption. Although affluence is a good to be pursued and enjoyed, it should be pursued in ways that enable the poor to fully participate, and it should be enjoyed in ways that promote charity and koinonia. Exchange is a necessary prerequisite of both human survival and flourishing by satisfying material wants and needs. Affluence, however, is not an end in itself, but a means for supporting the communication of shared goods. Consequently, stewardship oriented toward promoting communication and human flourishing on a global scale requires regulating markets and political ordering in ways that strengthen the communicative associations constituting civil society. Such regulation and political ordering in turn permits and protects freedom and justice as a series of requisite negations and affirmations. Freedom, then, is not license to do whatever one wills, and justice at times requires constraining the will in order that humans are free to be the good stewards God calls them to be.

Stewardship entails many things, such as allocating time, knowledge, and attentiveness, but this chapter concentrates primarily on the provision and utilization of material goods and services. I argue that the proper stewardship of creation entails the development of natural resources not only in ways that promote a global pursuit of widespread prosperity but also in ways that protect creation's ability to promote human flourishing. Although it is true that the material abundance of creation must be developed in order to instrumentally promote human flourishing, the natural beauty, sustenance, and fecundity of creation are also goods to be communicated and should be honored and protected.[1] To reiterate, Eden is a garden to be tended, but without adequate safeguards it could become a wasteland. Consequently, stewardship also entails preserving the world as an *oikos*, the Greek word for household. Creation is a fitting habitat for its creatures and not merely a storehouse of raw material to be carelessly plundered and exploited. *Oikos* is the root of both "economy" and "ecology," and both should be kept in mind in exercising the stewardship that God has entrusted to humans. Although the material abundance of creation must be developed, the "sentiment of oikophilia" must inform and temper such development.[2]

Throughout the remainder of this chapter I focus on the interrelated issues of energy and climate change. I have chosen these issues not only because of the wide-ranging and contentious public and political debates they have generated, but also because they are crucial to the argument I have been developing throughout this book. The pursuit of affluence on a global scale requires the expansive use of vast quantities of energy. If such energy levels cannot be developed and employed reliably over time, or if their development and employment prove unsustainable in respect to the environment, then my argument is moot. Indeed, many criticisms of globalization hinge on claims that the scope of economic development it engenders cannot be sustained by either available sources of energy and natural ecologies.[3] In each case I compare two broad approaches and assess each in respect to their potential effects on economic growth in general and the poor in particular.

1. See, e.g., Roger Scruton, *How to Think Seriously about the Planet: The Case for an Environmental Conservatism* (Oxford and New York: Oxford University Press, 2012).
2. See ibid., ch. 1.
3. See, e.g., Jeff Rubin, *The Big Flatline: Oil and the No-growth Economy* (New York: Palgrave Macmillan, 2012), and Peter Christoff and Robyn Eckersley, *Globalization and the Environment* (Lanham, MD, and Plymouth, UK: Rowman and Littlefield, 2013).

Energy

The industrial revolution that has helped create great wealth and widespread affluence in developed economies has been largely driven by fossil fuels. Since 1900 it is estimated that around 40,000 exajoules of oil, gas, and coal have been consumed globally.[4] Even with recent advances in efficiency and the development of alternative or renewable sources of energy, the global economy remains heavily dependent on fossil fuels. In 2013, for example, the total global consumption of all sources of energy was over 500 exajoules, of which 86 percent came from coal, oil, and natural gas. Moreover the demand for fossil fuels has grown dramatically over the past five decades, and is projected to continue, nearly unabated, for the next few decades.[5]

If globalization is to continue spurring the creation of wealth, capital, and more widespread prosperity, it will presumably need to consume fossil fuels at increasingly voracious rates. Two general objections are raised against this dependency. First, there are insufficient sources of fossil fuels to generate levels of economic growth that are required to promote widespread prosperity on a global scale. Second, the extraction and use of fossil fuels at current and projected rates inflicts catastrophic damage on the natural environment. The first objection is examined in this section, and the second is addressed in the following section.

No one disputes that fossil fuels are finite.[6] Given current consumption patterns, the world will eventually run out of oil, gas, and coal. Alternative sources of energy will need to be developed and used. The issue, then, is if there is sufficient time to develop these alternative sources before fossil fuels are effectively exhausted. Predictions of when the world will use up its deposits of carbon-based energy have proven to be notoriously unreliable. In 1972, for instance, the Club of Rome predicted that extractable oil and natural gas would be exhausted in 1992 and 1993 respectively.[7] Why did the prediction prove to be so

4. Gail Tverberg, "Our Finite World" (ourfiniteworld.com), based on BP Statistical Data.
5. See *BP Statistical Review of World Energy*, June 2014 (http://www.bp.com/content/dam/bp-country/de_de/PDFs/brochures/BP-statistical-review-of-world-energy-2014-full-report.pdf), and *Shell Energy Scenarios to 2050* (Shell International BV, 2008).
6. Technically fossil fuels are renewable sources of energy since their source is decomposed organisms, but given the long time span required they should be regarded as finite or nonrenewable sources of energy for practical purposes.
7. See Donella H. Meadows et al., *The Limits to Growth: A Report for the Club of Rome's Project on the Predicament of Mankind* (New York: New American Press, 1972), ch. 2; see also Alex Epstein, *The Moral Case for Fossil Fuels* (New York: Penguin, 2014), ch. 1.

patently mistaken? The Club of Rome based its prediction on what in 1972 were known reserves of oil and gas that could be extracted with current technological capabilities. Given the trajectories of rising demand, these reserves would be exhausted within twenty years. What the Club of Rome did not foresee were technological advances in the discovery and extraction of oil and gas. Not only did supply keep pace with rapidly rising demand, it surpassed it. In 2003 known reserves of extractable oil were around 1,041 thousand million barrels, and gas was slightly over 118 trillion cubic meters; whereas in 2013 known reserves were slightly over 1,687 thousand million barrels and 185 trillion cubic meters respectively.[8] Over this twenty-year period, roughly coincidental with rapid expansion of global markets, the consumption of oil and gas grew to unprecedented levels, but supplies actually increased rather than diminished. With the employment of current technologies and potential further advances, known reserves could continue to increase.[9]

Inaccurate predictions are also often caused by failing to take into account not only the prospect of technological innovations but also economic factors promoting both the sources and extraction of energy. This failure is operative, for example, in the concept of "peak oil." As Daniel Yergin has written, the "peak theory in its present formulation is pretty straightforward. It argues that world oil output is currently at or near the highest level it will ever reach, that about half the world's resources have been produced, and that the point of imminent decline is nearing."[10] The theory was propounded initially by M. King Hubbert, a leader of the technocracy movement of the 1930s, and a geologist who taught briefly at Columbia University before working for Shell Oil and later the US Geological Survey.[11] In 1956 he predicted that oil would hit its peak production between 1965 and 1970, and thereafter steadily decline. Declining oil production in the United States in tandem with Middle East embargoes in the early 1970s seemingly verified his prediction, yet by 2010 US "production was almost four times higher than Hubbert had estimated,"[12] and production continued to steadily increase.

8. See *BP Statistical Review of World Energy*, June 2014.
9. See, e.g., Samuel Thernstrom, "The Next Shale Revolution? The Astonishing Promise of Enhanced Oil Recovery," *The Weekly Standard*, December 29, 2014.
10. Daniel Yergin, *The Quest: Energy, Security, and the Remaking of the Modern World* (New York: Penguin, 2011), 233.
11. See ibid., 233–35.
12. Ibid., 236.

Although peak theory is seemingly little more than common sense—somewhat like drinking from a glass full of water: it eventually runs out—it does not take into account that oil reserves can be replenished and also increased in response to a variety of factors. Not only did Hubbert fail to foresee impending technological advances for discovering and extracting oil, he stubbornly insisted that energy market prices were irrelevant. Hubbert simply extrapolated from the mid-1950s when the price for oil was relatively flat. The rising price of oil in the 1970s provided incentives for developing innovative ways for finding and extracting new sources of oil, thereby increasing the supply. Hubbert—as well as the Club of Rome—was not the first to predict the imminent end of oil. According to Yergin, its demise has been confidently pronounced at least five times since the first commercial oil well was constructed in 1859, and those continuing to propound dire warnings about when the peak will be reached keep pushing the date further out.[13]

Yet is this combination of technological innovation and market forces sufficient to sustain global economic growth long enough to promote widespread prosperity? It is estimated that by 2035 total global energy demand will rise by 37 percent from current levels and will then begin to decline slightly.[14] Again, most of this demand will be met by fossil fuels (around 80 percent), with the use of natural gas increasing and coal and oil declining. The use of renewable sources of energy will increase to 15 percent (up from current 10 percent), while nuclear sources will remain a flat 4 percent. Other scenarios project flat total demand for energy between 2035 and 2050, a steeper use of renewables, and a decline of fossil fuels, especially oil.[15]

If these projections prove correct, then there is sufficient energy to sustain global economic growth at current or slightly increased levels for the foreseeable future, and fossil fuels will continue to play a dominant role. As Yergin contends "the world is clearly not running out of oil,"[16] and the same can be said for coal and gas. Future supplies of energy are even more promising when greater efficiency and development of alternative sources are added. But some important caveats need to be added. The projections may not prove to be accurate for a variety of reasons. Market forces driving technological innovation cannot be

13. Ibid., 227–33.
14. See *BP Energy Outlook 2035*, January 2014 (http://www.bp.com/content/dam/bp/pdf/energy-economics/energy-outlook-2016/bp-energy-outlook-2014.pdf).
15. See *Shell Energy Scenarios to 2050*.
16. See Yergin, *The Quest*, 239.

predicted with much certainty, anticipated technological developments may not prove feasible, and political policies or instability may greatly restrict accessibility to energy sources. Optimistic predictions are not necessarily more accurate than pessimistic ones.

Moreover, eventually alternative sources of energy will need to be developed on a large scale as fossil fuels become more scarce and costly to extract. Although there are some promising initial signs for this development, particularly in respect to solar power,[17] it will take time to complete this transition, probably well into the twenty-first century. Does continued dependence on fossil fuels provide an adequate transition or bridge, particularly in promoting economic growth and pursuit of widespread prosperity on a global scale? With the preceding caveats in mind, the answer is presumably yes. As I argued previously, over roughly the past two decades, globalization has helped to reduce dire poverty by nearly half, while promoting the emergence of a global, albeit fragile, middle class. Sustained global economic growth over the next few decades could solidify, strengthen, and enlarge these gains.

My hope that there is sufficient energy to fuel sustained economic growth is admittedly optimistic. Even if sources of energy are easily available, there are no guarantees that they will be readily accessible, or that economic growth will occur in the future in ways that continue to alleviate poverty and promote a widespread pursuit of affluence. There are many unknown factors, and things could go badly wrong. I hope my optimism proves true, for otherwise it will be the poor and fragile global middle class that will suffer disproportionally. Reducing global poverty requires such basic things as improving nutrition, health care, and education. Stabilizing these gains is best enabled through greater participation in global markets, particularly trade. Effectively participating in competitive global markets requires in turn reliable communication and transportation infrastructures, both of which entail plentiful and affordable sources of energy. For an extended period of time, fossil fuels are the only realistic options in respect to supply and cost. To unduly restrict the exploration and extraction of coal, oil, and gas is tantamount to consigning much of the world to perpetual impoverishment, and foreclosing any prospect of pursuing the good of affluence; it would effectively diminish human flourishing.

---

17. See, e.g., "Let the Sun Shine: The Future Is Bright for Solar Power, Even as Subsidies Are Withdrawn," *The Economist*, March 8, 2014; see also Yergin, *The Quest*, pt. 5.

Environment

Although fossil fuels are plentiful and relatively inexpensive, their extraction and use are nonetheless costly in respect to the impact on the natural environment. Pumping oil and gas, and mining coal can disrupt fragile ecologies, endanger wildlife, release pollutants into the air, as well as deface beautiful landscapes. Elaborate transport infrastructures involving pipelines, tankers, and trains are also needed to refine and deliver fossil fuels, entailing such risks as breakages, spills, and accidents. Despite recent technological advances, finding and extracting fossil fuels incurs both environmental hazards and social costs that can diminish the quality of life for an extended period of time for those most directly affected.[18]

Burning coal, oil, and gas releases copious amounts of carbon dioxide (CO_2) into the atmosphere. CO_2 emissions have risen dramatically since 1900, from less than 2,500 teragrams to over 30,000 teragrams in 2008.[19] Given the projected use of fossil fuels as indicated in the previous section, it is likely that emissions will continue to increase throughout much of the twenty-first century. Although CO_2 is not toxic unless highly concentrated, it can irritate eyes, nose, and throat, make breathing difficult, and cause or contribute to a range of other ailments. In short, it is not healthy to breathe smog.

More ominously, over time CO_2 emissions affect global climatic conditions. CO_2, and to a lesser extent methane, become lodged in the atmosphere, limiting its ability to disperse heat. Since heat is effectively trapped, it creates a "greenhouse effect," or what is now known as "global warming," or "climate change," as popularized by Al Gore[20] and others.[21] According to the United Nations,[22] the direst consequences involve destroying fragile ecosystems,[23] the loss of biodiversity, and

18. The Deepwater Horizon oil spill in April 2010, e.g., adversely affected people living on the Gulf coast.

19. See Oak Ridge National Laboratory, US Department of Energy (http://cdiac.ornl.gov/trends/emis/meth_reg.html).

20. See Al Gore, *An Inconvenient Truth: The Crisis of Global Warming* (New York: Viking, 2007).

21. A vast literature has been written describing global warming or climate change, as well proposing political and economic policies for addressing its most deleterious consequences. See, e.g., Bill McKibbin, ed., *The Global Warming Reader: A Century of Writing about Climate Change* (New York: Penguin, 2011), and Mark Maslin, *Climate Change: A Very Short Introduction* (Oxford: Oxford University Press, 2014).

22. See "UN and Climate Change," http://www.un.org/climatechange/blog/2014/03/ipcc-report-severe-and-pervasive-impacts-of-climate-change-will-be-felt-everywhere/.

23. Such as artic-sea-ice and coral-reef systems.

more frequent extreme weather events such severe heat waves, flooding, and intense storms. The risks and impacts will not be evenly distributed, and adversely affect disadvantaged people disproportionally. If global average temperatures continue to rise, the world will suffer increasingly frequent episodes of political instability, social unrest, economic decline, and degradation of particular cultures throughout the remainder of the twenty-first century and beyond. Since fossil fuels are the greatest emitters of CO_2, their use should be severely restricted as quickly as possible and eventually replaced altogether by green or renewable sources of energy. In short, most of the presently known reserves of gas, and especially oil and coal must remain in the ground if the grim consequences of climate change are to be averted.

In the previous section I argued that unduly restricting the exploration and extraction of abundant sources of fossil fuels would be tantamount to condemning much of the world to ongoing impoverishment. Yet if the use of fossil fuels is the principal cause of climate change, then my argument appears to be reckless. Since the poor will suffer the most from climate change, my advocacy of fossil fuels will eventually worsen their plight. So long as the kind of global pursuit of widespread affluence I am championing remains dependent on fossil fuels, it will ultimately diminish human flourishing. How might I respond to this objection?

First, I do not deny that fossil fuels are a factor in contributing to climate change over time. It seems reasonable to assume that emitting copious amounts of CO_2 (and methane) into the air year after year is bound to have some effect on the climate. Yet even among proponents, the extent, and thereby consequences, of this effect remain disputed.[24] These disputes, however, do not necessarily invalidate that the direst predictions are possible. Possible, but *not* certain. Some of the most ardent exponents portray, at times with a nearly religious fervor, the worse possible outcomes as if they are fixed.[25] The fate of the earth has been sealed unless drastic measures are taken immediately, and those opposing such measures should be regarded as simpletons, ideologues, or worse.[26] Such tactics may even prove counterproductive by inspiring public reactions that resist, and thereby delay, a transition to alternative

24. See, e.g., Yergin, *The Quest*, pt. 4; see also Steven E. Koonin, "Climate Science Is Not Settled," *The Wall Street Journal*, September 19, 2014, and Judith Curry, "The Global Warming Statistical Meltdown," *The Wall Street Journal*, October 9, 2014.

25. See Scruton, *How to Think Seriously about the Planet*, chs. 1–3.

26. Robert F. Kennedy Jr., e.g., was quoted as saying that so-called climate change deniers should be arrested for "treason." See Carol K. Chumley, "RFK Jr. Wants Law to Punish Global Warming Skeptics," *Washington Times*, September 23, 2014.

sources of energy. This fated and fearful portrayal of climate change should be resisted for two reasons.

On the one hand, predictions are possibilities or probabilities and not inevitable outcomes. The worse possible predicted consequences of climate change may not come true because of inadequate data or the ways it is analyzed, ideological skewing, or inability to incorporate unforeseen technological advances that greatly reduce CO_2 emissions, and a variety of other unanticipated events. Scientific expertise may prove highly beneficial in solving immediate or short-term problems, but its accuracy declines dramatically in respect to long-term forecasting.[27]

On the other hand, even if the direst consequences come true, it does not necessarily follow that severely curtailing the use of fossil fuels as quickly as possible is the only or best response, particularly if the preferential option for the poor is taken into account. Adapting to climate change may actually prove more beneficial for the poor, at least in the short term.[28] Continuing to reduce dire poverty on a global scale requires improvements in such basic areas as housing, nutrition, health care, education, and trade. These improvements in turn require broad-based energy, transportation, and information infrastructures, and at present the only realistic, reliable, and affordable energy sources are fossil fuels. In short, some environmental degradation may be the requisite cost for improving the physical and material well-being of the world's poor.[29]

Second, the prospect of alternative or renewable fuels to provide necessary and reliable sources of energy is presently at best uncertain, and at worst unlikely. Wind and solar power generation, for example, is both geographically limited and unreliable. It makes no sense to construct such generators in locations where windy or sunny days are infrequent. Moreover, windy and sunny days are not consistent and must be compensated by other forms of energy generation, most quickly and reliably by gas, to prevent electrical grid failures.

In respect to liquid fuels, ethanol and other biomass alternatives have proven less energy efficient than gasoline or diesel, expensive to produce, difficult to transport, and have created unintended consequences. Ethanol, for instance, cannot be transported in pipelines, raises the price

27. See Friedrich A. Hayek, "The Use of Knowledge in Society," *American Economic Review* (35:4), September 1945.
28. See, e.g., International Housing Coalition (IHC), "Adapting Climate Change: Cities and the Urban Poor," August 2011, and The World Bank, *Economics of Adaptation to Climate Change: Synthesis Report*, 2010.
29. Although admittedly short-term benefits could be offset by long-term costs associated with adapting to climate change.

of food, and contributes to greater land erosion. Rapid conversion to hybrid or electric cars might seemingly help to lessen dependence on oil and ethanol, but might also prove to be less environmentally friendly than first assumed. More hybrid and electrical vehicles may require the construction of additional electrical generation plants, and it should not be assumed that this new demand would necessarily be met by renewable sources of energy given current technological limitations. A case in point is that Germany is building new coal-firing power plants to replace, in part, the electricity lost in its planned phase-out of nuclear power plants.[30] Additionally, producing the batteries used in hybrid and electrical cars may increase mining to secure the various rare minerals required for their manufacture, and recycling and disposal will incur both environmental and financial costs.

Moreover, a rapid transition to renewable sources in order to greatly reduce CO_2 emissions may not be able to meet growing demands for energy, particularly in rapidly developing economies such as China and India. Deficient supplies of energy would restrict, if not diminish global economic growth. If current projections for the development of alternative or renewable sources of energy hold true, then they cannot replace the growing demand for energy as quickly as many environmentalists and policy makers might prefer. Without readily available and affordable energy, developing and impoverished economies will be hit the hardest. Admittedly, the development of alternative or renewable sources of energy may occur more quickly and efficiently than predicted in response to unforeseen technological advances or market conditions, but this eventuality is far from certain. It is more probable that global economic growth over the next few decades will, through the necessities of both supply and cost, be driven by fossil fuels, and without them the continuing amelioration of global poverty initiated by globalization will stall or be thrown into reverse.

If the extraction of fossil fuels can be criticized for disrupting fragile ecologies, endangering wildlife, and defacing natural landscapes, then the same can be said for providing many renewable sources of energy. Solar collectors and wind generators, for example, require a great deal of dedicated land that must be developed and cleared of any obstructions that might diminish their efficiency.[31] As with any construction project,

---

30. The new coal-firing plants will have stringent regulations regarding CO_2 emissions, and renewable sources of energy will play a significant role in this transition. Whether or not the plan is feasible is open to debate, and only time will tell.

31. The development of ethanol and biomass also requires vast areas of land.

natural ecologies are disrupted and wildlife displaced or threatened. It is also arguable that distant horizons dominated by huge wind-driven turbines, or solar panels lined along a hillside or on a prairie are not any more attractive than oil derricks or pumping stations. Although reducing CO_2 emissions is admittedly a good worth pursuing, it is far from a cost-free pursuit.

Third, affluence may be a necessary prerequisite for becoming greener. In 2014 the twelve most energy-sustainable countries were members of the Organisation for Economic Co-operation and Development, a club of primarily wealthy nations.[32] Additionally, over the past five years the GDP of all rich countries has risen 7 percent while CO_2 emissions have declined by 4 percent.[33] This concentration of using renewable sources of energy in predominantly wealthy nations is due, in part, to greater technological efficiencies, and policies mandating greater use of renewables. Affluent consumers can afford to pay higher prices for the energy they consume. For example, the cost of producing electricity using fossil fuels ranged from 6.3 (natural gas) to 13.6 (coal) cents per kilowatt-hour, whereas the cost for renewables ranged from 8.6 (hydro) to 31.2 (solar) cents per kilowatt-hour.[34]

It is understandable why developing nations or regions turn to fossil fuels—it's cheaper. China's rapid economic growth, for instance, has been fueled primarily by coal. China is the world's largest consumer of coal, accounting for 80 percent of global growth in demand since 2000. And India's demand for coal is not expected to peak until the 2030s at the earliest.[35] The economic growth needed to both ameliorate dire poverty and promote widespread affluence depends on easily accessible and affordable sources of energy. Fossil fuels, at present, most readily address this dependency.

There are admittedly exceptions to this energy dependence in developing economies, and a preference for fossil fuels over renewables is not necessarily universal. For example, nearly 45 percent of energy

32. The countries, in order of rank, include: Switzerland, Sweden, Norway, United Kingdom, Denmark, Canada, Austria, Finland, France, New Zealand, Germany, and the United States. See World Energy Council, "Energy Trilemma Index," http://www.worldenergy.org/data/trilemma-index/.

33. See "Flatlining: A Ray of Hope in the Debate about Climate Change," *The Economist*, March 21, 2015.

34. See David Coil, "True Cost of Electricity Generation," http://www.groundtruthtrekking.org/Issues/OtherIssues/True-Cost-Electricty-Generation.html.

35. See "In the Depths: As More Countries Turn against Coal, Producers Face Prolonged Weakness in Prices," *The Economist*, March 28, 2015.

consumed in Brazil comes from renewable sources.[36] China is the largest producer of electricity from renewable sources,[37] and although it remains highly dependent on coal, its use declined by around 3 percent in 2014, prompting, in part, a slight drop in CO_2 emissions.[38] Ironically, China is simultaneously the world's leading producer of renewable energy and the largest emitter of CO_2.

As indicated previously, the practicality of utilizing renewable sources of energy is dictated by particular geographic or climatic circumstances. Most of the renewable energy produced in China and Brazil, for instance, is hydro. Both countries are blessed with bountiful supplies of water that are used to produce electricity that is both reliable and affordable. This option is simply not available for arid regions. Even in poor regions with ample supplies of water, hydro may not be an attractive alternative given the extensive capital investment required to construct dams and generators. Moreover, some environmentalists would object because of the disruption of natural ecologies entailed in the production of hydroelectricity. Similar limitations and objections also apply to other renewable sources such as wind, solar, and biomass.

The advantage of fossil fuels, particularly for less affluent countries, is not only cost but also portability. Unlike most renewables, coal, gas, and oil can be transported virtually anywhere in the world. Consequently, fossil fuels provide both more affordable and reliable sources of energy for developing economies. To suddenly restrict the supply of fossil fuels would effectively, and perhaps severely, restrict economic growth and pursuit of affluence, thereby also effectively diminishing human flourishing on a global scale.

To be clear, I am not arguing for unrestricted exploitation of fossil fuels. The eventual goal—if for no other reason than the supply of fossil fuels is finite—is renewable sources of energy. In this respect, fossil fuel is a bridge to the future. But it may need to be a very long bridge. Although some promising initiatives are already underway for developing renewables in both developed and developing economies, it is likely that fossil fuels will play a dominant role throughout much of the twenty-first century, especially if affluence is to be pursed on a global scale. If recent experience is a reliable guide, then affluence is the best way to go

36. See SugarCane.org, "Brazil's Diverse Energy Mix," http://sugarcane.org/the-brazilian-experience/brazils-diverse-energy-matrix, citing Balanço Energético Brasileiro BEN (2015).
37. See Simrah Khosla, "This Chart Shows Which Countries Produce the Most Electricity from Renewable Energy," *Global Post*, June 23, 2014.
38. See "Flatlining."

green. And for most developing and poor regions of the world, fossil fuels are the most accessible and affordable sources of energy for alleviating poverty and pursuing prosperity. Building too short a bridge could prove disastrous, particularly for the poor. If, as I have been arguing throughout this book, affluence is a good that should be pursued because meeting material wants and needs can assist communicative associations and thereby enable human flourishing, then readily accessible, reliable, and affordable sources of energy are required. Hopefully technological advances and market conditions will prompt the development of renewables that will shorten the fossil fuel bridge.[39] But to plan on building a short rather than long bridge would be to commit an injustice against poor and developing countries. If the supply of energy becomes more scarce and expensive, then the amelioration of poverty and pursuit of more widespread prosperity grows increasingly difficult.

Is building a long rather than short fossil fuel bridge risky? Yes.[40] If global economic growth continues at current intensities or accelerates, the demand for energy in either case will also increase. Most of this increased demand will likely be met through fossil fuels, and demand may not peak until the mid-twenty-first century or even longer. The release of CO_2 into the atmosphere will also likely increase as a consequence despite anticipated technological advances for improving efficiency and diminishing emissions. I have little doubt that a more ambitious pursuit of global affluence will contribute to climate change, though the extent and consequences of this change are uncertain. Societies, however, can adapt to these changes, and rich ones can better afford the costs of adapting than their poorer and less affluent counterparts. Even when the short and long-term costs for adapting to climate change are factored in, fossil fuels may still prove to be the most reliable and affordable energy source for promoting global economic growth. There are undoubtedly risks in building a long fossil fuel energy bridge. But as argued above, there also risks involved in building a short bridge, and those risks fall disproportionally on the poor and less affluent. Going green too aggressively or prematurely is effectively placing the greater risk on the poor and less affluent rather than the wealthy and prosperous.

39. And more efficient ways for lessening or capturing CO_2 emissions in the meantime may be discovered.

40. The prospect of risk is not a condition that automatically prevents some course of action as often propounded by advocates of the so-called "precautionary principle." See Scruton, *How to Think Seriously about the Planet*, ch. 4.

My reason for placing the potentially greater risk on the already wealthy and prosperous (long bridge) rather than the poor and less affluent (short bridge) comes from two themes I have visited frequently in previous chapters. First, it exhibits a love for neighbor, albeit in a broad and oblique manner. I am not suggesting that the slogan "drill, baby, drill" is a synonym for "love your neighbor." Yet if neighbor love entails the meeting of material wants and needs that in turn promotes the pursuit of affluence and human flourishing, then the most practical means for achieving this goal must also be willed or allowed. For the foreseeable future this will likely require the increased use of fossil fuels.

Second, the best way for exercising the preferential option for the poor currently on offer is to increase their participation more fully in the current round of globalization. This increased participation entails the creation, expansion, and creative destruction of global markets. These markets are driven by a profuse consumption of energy. If relatively accessible, reliable, and affordable sources of energy—in short, fossil fuels—are unduly restricted or withheld, then the best possible option at present for ameliorating poverty and promoting more widespread affluence may be effectively rendered inoperative.

Additionally, the long bridge approach might prove to be a more effective strategy in making a transition to alternative energy in a quicker and less belligerent manner. Advocates of the short bridge approach are urging the adoption of radically altered and less affluent lifestyles that many throughout the world will undoubtedly resist. More troubling, such an approach may strip away resources that have served humans well in adapting to change in the past. Market forces, for instance, are one such resource that many of the most vocal proponents of climate change often dismiss or decry. Yet as Scruton contends, markets "are not the simplest, but certainly the clearest, forms of social network in which individual responsibility is the binding principle. They are the cause of some environmental problems, but also the solution to others. And they illustrate the way in which, when costs are borne by those who create them, human beings exercise responsible stewardship over the goods they enjoy."[41] Markets, especially global markets, are undeniably competitive, but "competition in a market depends on co-operation, and it is only co-operatively disposed beings that can make markets work."[42]

Moreover, with the emergence of the market-state, big governmental solutions of the kind required by a small bridge approach are both

41. Ibid., 137.
42. Ibid., 143.

unaffordable and ineffectual. As opposed to fear or coercion, Scruton's "oikophilia" as the "love and feeling for home" is a better tack with its stress on "local initiatives against global schemes, civil association against political activism, and small-scale institutions of friendship against large-scale and purpose-driven campaigns."[43] Choosing in favor of exercising a stewardship that promotes communicating shared goods is preferable to enforcing many to forgo such sharing by consigning them to material impoverishment.

Stewardship entails developing creation's potential affluence in ways that promote both material affluence and communicating the goods of created life. Without both, human flourishing is diminished. This is not a license for unrestricted or ruinous exploitation. Unwittingly transforming the earth into a wasteland would certainly not promote human flourishing. Consequently, if technological advances and market conditions make possible a shortening of the energy bridge, then there is no reason to oppose it. More broadly, there is also a responsibility to preserve the world as a place of awe and wonder, if for no other reason than natural beauty is a created good to be communicated. This will undoubtedly require striking some balance between the need for producing energy and preserving selected ecologies. There are admittedly tensions, often severe but not necessarily incompatible, between the goods of economic growth and preserving the natural environment; affluent societies, after all, tend to be more adept at maintaining such things as national parks and wildlife reserves. Stewardship is needed to keep a proper balance between these two tensions. As I have argued throughout this book, global economic growth and the affluence it promotes are necessary but not sufficient to promote human flourishing. Yet *both* are needed. As Scripture reminds us, we cannot live by bread alone,[44] but it is often those who have more than enough bread to eat who know this to be true.

43. Ibid., 3–4.
44. See Matt. 4:4.

Afterword

It is 2016, and the citizens of the United States are once again enduring another presidential election. As I write these words neither of the two major parties has yet chosen their candidates. The leading candidates still currying votes have often attacked some of the more prominent features of a globally integrated economy, frequently employing intemperate or facile rhetoric. They accuse investors, free trade, or migrants as *the* source of our problems, and they propose isolationism, protectionism, and tighter regulations as easy solutions. If only Wall Street was put in its place, or tariffs raised, or a wall built on the border, then all would be well. Moreover, these sentiments are not confined to the United States but are becoming endemic in various regions around the world.

Many pundits contend that politicians are tapping a deep-seated fear and anger within the electorate, and globalization, and capitalism more broadly, offer convenient targets for venting this anxiety and rage. The pundits may be right. Globalization has lost some, if not much, of its luster in the eyes of the public. Yet convenient targets are not always the right ones, and the simple solutions being proffered are not necessarily the correct ones, because they often obfuscate rather than clarify. Now is not the time to retreat from globalization, for it would exacerbate the adverse economic conditions that are fueling voter unrest. Isolationism, protectionism, and unnecessary regulations ultimately do not protect jobs, spur economic growth, or create opportunities, but do quite the opposite. For example, over the last few years global trade has slowed, and in some sectors stagnated or declined. Is it merely coincidental that global economic growth remains anemic?

Pandering to fear and anger is not a solid foundation for building a just social, political, and economic order, because they cannot sustain for very long the bonds of human association. These fragile bonds require exchange in order to remain vibrant, and erecting restrictive or preventative barriers will not make the world a better place. A competitive global marketplace is admittedly a rough and risky way to pursue such exchange, but on a global scale it is preferable to the other options on offer. A competitor is less menacing than a real or imagined enemy that is perceived to be taking away or withholding your material wants and needs. I am not suggesting that history always repeats itself, but it should give some pause to recall that when a previous era of globalization came to an abrupt end in 1914, the ensuing decades were far from edifying.

Retreating from globalization at this time would be particularly bad news for the poor, who would suffer its demise most acutely. The gains of lifting numerous people out of dire poverty and creating a nascent global middle class could be quickly reversed. I hope that in the preceding pages it became apparent that my principal purpose for writing this book was to begin thinking through, as a Christian moral theologian, how a preferential option for the poor could be best exercised in our current circumstances. This preference grows out of the belief that attending to the material well-being of people is a central conviction of Christian faith, a way of expressing neighbor love. Markets have proven to be remarkably efficient in addressing this need, and drying up the streams of capital, trade, and labor will only serve to keep the poor impoverished.

My secondary reason for writing this book comes from my discomfort as an academic. I have spent most of my career in institutions of higher education in which globalization and capitalism are seen, at best, as tawdry affairs best avoided, or at worst, unmitigated evils to be condemned unequivocally. Neither perception is true. Globalization and capitalism are replete with a number of troubling issues that need to be addressed, but they also have their benefits that need to be acknowledged and strengthened. An important task of the scholar is to help the publics he or she serves to understand and respond thoughtfully and appropriately to challenging questions and disputes. This task is not accomplished by ignoring complexity that is lost in sweeping and simplistic denunciation. Globalization is a highly complex phenomenon in which tough questions such as those of efficacy, freedom, and justice must be identified, debated, and resolved. Sorting through such thorny issues requires informed, measured, and sustained deliberation and discourse.

Accomplishing this task is particularly pressing for scholars who, at least in part, serve the church. The theology of the cross teaches, among other things, that we must deal with the thing as it is and not as we might prefer it to be. The "thing" at hand to be dealt with is a globally integrated economy in which the vast majority of Christians participate on a daily basis. If all theological scholarship can do is to echo populist denunciations, then it effectively has nothing of value to say: no useful or credible guidance to offer followers of Jesus Christ on living faithfully in the world as it is. Rather, the more pressing challenge is to offer theological resources that might inform a more just ordering of globalization and its underlying capitalism in ways that facilitate the material well-being of all competitive participants in the global marketplace. I hope this book has made some modest contribution toward pursuing this task.

Bibliography

Allen, Charlotte. "Silicon Chasm: The Class Divide on America's Cutting Edge." *The Weekly Standard*, December 2, 2013.

Althusius, Johannes. *Politica*. Translated by Frederick S. Carney. Indianapolis, IN: Liberty Fund, 1995.

Angell, Norman. *The Great Illusion: A Study of the Relation of Military Power to National Advantage*. New York and London: G. P. Putnam's Sons, 1910.

Arendt, Hannah. *The Human Condition*. Chicago and London: University of Chicago Press, 1998.

———. *The Origins of Totalitarianism*. San Diego, CA: Harvest Book, 1968.

———. *The Promise of Politics*. New York: Schocken Books, 2005.

Augustine. *Concerning the City of God against the Pagans*. Translated by Henry Bettenson. London and New York: Penguin, 1972.

———. *On the Morals of the Catholic Church*. In *Nicene and Post-Nicene Fathers of the Christian Church*, vol. 4. Edited by Philip Schaff. Edinburgh: T. and T. Clark, 1991.

Barth, Karl. *Church Dogmatics*. Vol. 3, *The Doctrine of Creation*. Edinburgh: T. & T. Clark, 1961.

Beinhocker, Eric D. *The Origin of Wealth: Evolution, Complexity, and the Radical Remaking of Economics*. Boston, MA: Harvard Business School Press, 2006.

Bell, Daniel M., Jr. *The Economy of Desire: Christianity and Capitalism in a Postmodern World*. Grand Rapids, MI: Baker, 2012.

Bernstein, William J. *A Splendid Exchange: How Trade Shaped the World*. New York: Atlantic Monthly Press, 2008.

Bhagwati, Jagdish. *In Defense of Globalization*. Oxford and New York: Oxford University Press, 2007.

Biéler, André. *Calvin's Economic and Social Thought*. Geneva, Switzerland: WCC Communications, 2005.

Biggar, Nigel. *In Defence of War*. Oxford and New York: Oxford University Press, 2013.

Blickle, Peter. *The Revolution of 1525: The German Peasants' War from a New Perspective*. Baltimore, MD, and London: Johns Hopkins University Press, 1981.

Bobbitt, Philip. *The Shield of Achilles: War, Peace, and the Course of History*. New York: Knopf, 2002.

————. *Terror and Consent: The Wars for the Twenty-First Century.* New York: Knopf, 2008.
BP Statistical Review of World Energy, June 2014. http://www.bp.com/content/dam
    /bp-country/de_de/PDFs/brochures/BP-statistical-review-of-world-energy-2014-full
    -report.pdf.
Brooks, Arthur C. *Gross National Happiness: Why Happiness Matters for America—and How
    We Can Get More of It.* New York: Basic Books, 2008.
————. "Love People, Not Pleasure." *The New York Times,* July 18, 2014.
Brown, Peter. *Through the Eye of a Needle: Wealth, the Fall of Rome, and the Making of Chris-
    tianity in the West, 350–550 AD.* Princeton, NJ, and Oxford: Princeton University
    Press, 2012.
Bruni, Luigino, and Stefano Zamagni. *Civil Economy: Efficiency, Equity, Public Happiness.* Bern
    and Oxford: Peter Lang, 2007.
Brunner, Emil. *The Divine Imperative: A Study in Christian Ethics.* London: Lutterworth
    Press, 1937.
Brynjolfsson, Erik, and Andrew McAfee. *The Second Machine Age: Work, Progress, and
    Prosperity in a Time of Brilliant Technologies.* New York and London: Norton,
    2014.
Camp, Richard L. *The Papal Ideology of Social Reform: A Study in Historical Development.*
    Leiden: Brill, 1969.
Cavanaugh, William T. *Being Consumed: Economics and Christian Desire.* Grand Rapids, MI,
    and Cambridge, UK: Eerdmans, 2008.
Challies, Tim. *The Next Story: Life and Faith After the Digital Explosion.* Grand Rapids, MI:
    Zondervan, 2011.
Christoff, Peter, and Robyn Eckersley. *Globalization and the Environment.* Lanham, MD, and
    Plymouth, UK: Rowman and Littlefield, 2013.
Chumley, Carol K. "RFK Jr. Wants Law to Punish Global Warming Skeptics." *Washington
    Times,* September 23, 2014.
Clement of Alexandria, *Who Is the Rich Man That Shall Be Saved?* In *Ante-Nicene Fathers,* vol.
    2. Edited by Alexander Roberts and James Donaldson. Peabody, MA: Hendrickson,
    1994.
Coil, David. "True Cost of Electricity Generation." http://www.groundtruthtrekking
    .org/Issues/OtherIssues/True-Cost-Electricty-Generation.html.
Cosgrove, Charles. *Appealing to Scripture in Moral Debate: Five Hermeneutical Rules.* Grand
    Rapids, MI: Eerdmans, 2002.
Credit Suisse Research Institute. *Global Wealth Databook 2013.*
Curry, Judith. "The Global Warming Statistical Meltdown." *The Wall Street Journal,* Octo-
    ber 9, 2014.
Cyprian. *On the Lord's Prayer.* In *Ante-Nicene Fathers,* vol. 5. Edited by Alexander Roberts
    and James Donaldson. Peabody, MA: Hendrickson, 1994.
De Soto, Hernando. *The Mystery of Capital: Why Capitalism Triumphs in the West and Fails
    Everywhere Else.* New York: Basic Books, 2000.
DeYoung, Rebecca Konyndyk. *Glittering Vices: A New Look at the Seven Deadly Sins and Their
    Remedies.* Grand Rapids, MI: Brazos, 2009.
Donnan, Shawn, Ben Bland, and John Burn-Murdoch. "Fragile Middle: 2.8bn People on the
    Brink." *Financial Times,* April 13, 2014.
Dooyeweerd, Herman. *A Christian Theory of Social Institutions.* La Jolla, CA: Herman
    Dooyeweerd Foundation, 1986.

———. *A New Critique of Theoretical Thought.* Vol. 3, *The Structures of Individuality of Temporal Reality.* Philadelphia, PA: Presbyterian and Reformed Publishing Co., 1957.

Dorr, Donal. *Option for the Poor and for the Earth: Catholic Social Teaching.* Maryknoll, NY: Orbis, 2012.

Dunn, James D. G. "The Household Rules in the New Testament." In *The Family in Theological Perspective.* Edited by Stephen C. Barton. Edinburgh: T. & T. Clark, 1996.

Easterbrook, Gregg. *Sonic Boom: Globalization at Mach Speed.* New York: Random House, 2009.

Easterly, William. *The Tyranny of Experts: Economists, Dictators, and the Forgotten Rights of the Poor.* New York: Basic Books, 2013.

———. "Western Vanities That Do Little to Help the World's Poor." *Financial Times,* January 24, 2014.

The Economist. "Faith, Hope—and How Much Change? Pope Francis's First Year." March 8, 2014.

———. "Flatlining: A Ray of Hope in the Debate about Climate Change." March 21, 2015.

———. "In the Depths: As More Countries Turn against Coal, Producers Face Prolonged Weakness in Prices." March 28, 2015.

———. "Let the Sun Shine: The Future Is Bright for Solar Power, Even as Subsidies Are Withdrawn." March 8, 2014.

———. "The Onrushing Wave: The Future of Jobs." January 18, 2014.

———. "Parenting in America: Choose Your Parents Wisely." July 26, 2014.

———. "Poverty: Not Always with Us." June 1, 2013.

———. "Special Report: Mobility." April 12, 2008.

———. "The Third Industrial Revolution: The Digitisation of Manufacturing Will Transform the Way Goods Are Made—and Change the Politics of Jobs Too." April 21, 2012.

———. "The Tragedy of Argentina: A Century of Decline." February 15, 2014.

———. "Two Billion More Bourgeois: The Middle Class in Emerging Markets." February 12, 2009.

———. "Unilever: In Search of the Good Business." August 9, 2014.

———. "Wealth without Workers, Workers without Wealth: The Digital Revolution Is Bringing Sweeping Change to Labour Markets in Both Rich and Poor Worlds." October 4, 2014.

Elshtain, Jean Bethke. *Just War against Terror: The Burden of American Power in a Violent World.* New York: Basic Books, 2003.

Elumelu, Tony O. "Africa Is Open for Business, Ready for Investment." *The Wall Street Journal,* July 31, 2014.

Epstein, Alex. *The Moral Case for Fossil Fuels.* New York: Penguin, 2014.

Estes, Douglas. *SimChurch: Being the Church in the Virtual World.* Grand Rapids, MI: Zondervan, 2009.

Ferguson, Andrew. "Speed Reading the Pope." *The Weekly Standard,* December 23, 2013.

Ferguson, Niall. *The Ascent of Money: A Financial History of the World.* New York: Penguin, 2008.

———. *The Great Degeneration: How Institutions Decay and Economies Die.* New York: Penguin, 2013.

Fernandez, Jose W. "Bridge to Somewhere: Helping U.S. Companies Tap the Global Infrastructure." *Foreign Affairs,* November/December, 2013.

Finn, Daniel K. *Christian Economic Ethics: History and Implications*. Minneapolis, MN: Fortress Press, 2013.

———. *The Moral Ecology of Markets: Assessing Claims about Markets and Justice*. Cambridge, UK, and New York: Cambridge University Press, 2006.

Fisher, David. *Morality and War: Can War Be Just in the Twenty-First Century?* Oxford and New York: Oxford University Press, 2011.

Friedman, Thomas L. *The World Is Flat: A Brief History of the Twenty-First Century, Further Updated and Expanded*. New York: Picador / Farrar, Straus and Giroux, 2007.

Fukuyama, Francis. *Political Order and Political Decay: From the Industrial Revolution to the Globalization of Democracy*. New York: Farrar, Straus and Giroux, 2014.

———. *Trust: The Social Virtues and the Creation of Prosperity*. New York: Free Press, 1995.

Gates, Bill, and Melinda Gates. "Three Myths on the World's Poor." *The Wall Street Journal*. January 17, 2014.

Goldin, Ian, and Mike Mariathasan. *The Butterfly Defect: How Globalization Creates Systemic Risks, and What to Do about It*. Princeton, NJ, and Oxford: Princeton University Press, 2014.

Gore, Al. *An Inconvenient Truth: The Crisis of Global Warming*. New York: Viking, 2007.

Grabil, Stephen J., ed. *Sourcebook in Late-Scholastic Monetary Theory*. Lanham, MD, and Plymouth, UK: Lexington Books, 2007.

Grant, George. *English-Speaking Justice*. Notre Dame, IN: University of Notre Dame Press, 1985.

———. *Lament for a Nation: The Defeat of Canadian Nationalism*. Montreal and Kingston: McGill-Queen's University Press, 2000.

———. *Philosophy in the Mass Age*. Toronto: University of Toronto Press, 1995.

———. *Technology and Empire: Perspectives on North America*. Toronto: House of Anansi, 1969.

Gregg, Samuel. *The Commercial Society: Foundations and Challenges in a Global Age*. Lanham, MD, and Plymouth, UK: Lexington Books, 2007.

———. *Economic Thinking for the Theologically Minded*. Lanham, MD, and Oxford: University Press of America, 2001.

Griffiths, Brian. *The Creation of Wealth: A Christian's Case for Capitalism*. Downers Grove, IL: InterVarsity Press, 1984.

Gutiérrez, Gustavo. *A Theology of Liberation: History, Politics, and Salvation*. Maryknoll, NY: Orbis, 1988.

Handy, Robert T., ed. *The Social Gospel in America, 1870–1920: Gladden, Ely, Rauschenbusch*. New York: Oxford University Press, 1966.

Hayek, Friedrich A. *The Road to Serfdom*. Chicago: University of Chicago Press, 2007.

———. "The Use of Knowledge in Society." *American Economic Review* (35:4), September 1945.

Hengel, Martin. *Property and Riches in the Early Church: Aspects of a Social History of Early Christianity*. Philadelphia, PA: Fortress Press, 1974.

Innes, Stephen. *Creating the Commonwealth: The Economic Culture of Puritan New England*. New York and London: Norton, 1995.

International Housing Coalition (IHC). "Adapting Climate Change: Cities and the Urban Poor." August 2011.

International Labour Organization. *Global Employment Trends 2014*. Geneva: International Labour Office, 2014.

James, Harold. *The Creation and Destruction of Value: The Globalization Cycle*. Cambridge, MA, and London: Harvard University Press, 2009.

Jardine, Lisa. *Worldly Goods: A New History of the Renaissance.* New York and London: Norton, 1996.

Kapur, Devesh. "Western Anti-Capitalists Take Too Much for Granted." *Financial Times.* July 23, 2014.

Khosla, Simrah. "This Chart Shows Which Countries Produce the Most Electricity from Renewable Energy." *Global Post.* June 23, 2014.

Kilner, John. *Dignity and Destiny: Humanity in the Image of God.* Grand Rapids, MI, and Cambridge, UK: Eerdmans, 2015.

Koonin, Steven E. "Climate Science Is Not Settled." *The Wall Street Journal.* September 19, 2014.

Lane, Patrick. "A Sense of Place: Geography Matters as Much as Ever, Despite the Digital Revolution." *The Economist.* October 27, 2012.

Langholm, Odd. *Economics in the Medieval Schools: Wealth, Exchange, Money and Usury according to the Paris Theological Tradition 1200–1350.* Leiden and New York: Brill, 1992.

Lewis, C. S. *Beyond Personality: The Christian Idea of God.* London: Geoffrey Bles, 1944.

Lindberg, Carter. "Luther on Poverty." In *Harvesting Martin Luther's Reflections on Theology, Ethics, and the Church.* Edited by Timothy J. Wengert. Grand Rapids, MI, and Cambridge, UK: Eerdmans, 2004.

Long, D. Stephen. *Divine Economy: Theology and the Market.* Abingdon, UK, and New York: Routledge, 2000.

———. *The Goodness of God: Theology, Church, and the Social Order.* Grand Rapids, MI: Brazos, 2001.

Lopez, Robert S. *The Commercial Revolution of the Middle Ages, 950–1350.* Englewood Cliffs, NJ: Prentice-Hall, 1971.

Luther, Martin. *Against the Robbing and Murdering Hordes of Peasants.* In *Luther's Works,* vol. 46. Edited by Robert C. Schultz. Philadelphia, PA: Fortress Press, 1967.

———. *The Freedom of a Christian.* In *Luther's Works,* vol. 31. Edited by Harold J. Grimm. Philadelphia, PA: Muhlenberg Press, 1957.

———. *Ordinance of a Common Chest.* In *Luther's Works,* vol. 45. Edited by Walther I. Brandt. Philadelphia, PA: Fortress Press, 1962.

———. *Temporal Authority.* In *Luther's Works,* vol. 45. Edited by Walther I. Brandt. Philadelphia, PA: Fortress Press, 1962.

———. *Trade and Usury.* In *Luther's Works,* vol. 45. Edited by Walther I. Brandt. Philadelphia, PA: Fortress Press, 1962.

Mandelbaum, Michael. *The Road to Global Prosperity.* New York and London: Simon and Schuster e-book, 2014.

Markus, R. A. *The End of Ancient Christianity.* Cambridge, MA, and New York: Cambridge University Press, 1990.

Maslin, Mark. *Climate Change: A Very Short Introduction.* Oxford: Oxford University Press, 2014.

Maurice, F. D. *Social Morality.* London: Macmillan and Co., 1869.

McAllister, Ted V. *Revolt against Modernity: Leo Strauss, Eric Voegelin, and the Search for a Postliberal Order.* Lawrence: University Press of Kansas, 1995.

McClay, Wilfred M., and Ted V. McAllister, eds. *Why Place Matters: Geography, Identity, and Civic Life in Modern America.* New York and London: Encounter Books, 2014.

McKibbin, Bill, ed., *The Global Warming Reader: A Century of Writing about Climate Change.* New York: Penguin, 2011.

Meadows, Donella H., et al. *The Limits to Growth: A Report for the Club of Rome's Project on the Predicament of Mankind*. New York: New American Press, 1972.

Meeks, M. Douglas. *God the Economist: The Doctrine of God and Political Economy*. Minneapolis, MN: Fortress Press, 1989.

Meilaender, Gilbert. *Friendship: A Study in Theological Ethics*. Notre Dame, IN, and London: University of Notre Dame Press, 1985.

———. *The Theory and Practice of Virtue*. Notre Dame, IN: University of Notre Dame Press, 1984.

Micklethwait, John, and Adrian Wooldridge. *The Fourth Revolution: The Global Race to Reinvent the State*. New York: Penguin, 2014.

Mommsen, Theodor E. "St. Augustine and the Christian Idea of Progress: The Background of the City of God." *Journal of the History of Ideas* 12:3 (June, 1951).

Moyo, Dambisa. *Dead Aid: Why Aid Is Not Working and How There Is a Better Way for Africa*. New York: Farrar, Straus and Giroux, 2009.

Muller, Jerry Z. "Capitalism and Inequality: What the Right and the Left Get Wrong." *Foreign Affairs*. March/April, 2013.

———. *The Mind and the Market: Capitalism in Modern European Thought*. New York: Anchor Books, 2003.

Murdoch, Iris. *The Sovereignty of Good*. London and New York: Routledge, 2001.

Nelson, James B. *Embodiment: An Approach to Sexuality and Christian Theology*. Minneapolis, MN: Augsburg, 1978.

Niebuhr, H. Richard. *The Responsible Self: An Essay in Christian Moral Philosophy*. Louisville, KY: Westminster John Knox Press, 1999.

Niebuhr, Reinhold. *Moral Man and Immoral Society: A Study in Ethics and Politics*. Louisville, KY, and London: Westminster John Knox Press, 2001.

Novak, Michael. *The Catholic Ethic and the Spirit of Capitalism*. New York: Free Press, 1993.

———. *The Spirit of Democratic Capitalism*. Lanham, NY: Madison Books, 1991.

O'Donovan, Oliver. *Common Objects of Love: Moral Reflection and the Shaping of Community*. Grand Rapids, MI, and Cambridge, UK: Eerdmans, 2002.

———. *The Desire of the Nations: Rediscovering the Roots of Political Theology*. Cambridge, UK: Cambridge University Press, 1996.

———. *The Just War Revisited*. Cambridge, UK: Cambridge University Press, 2003.

———. *Resurrection and Moral Order: An Outline for Evangelical Ethics*. Grand Rapids, MI: Eerdmans, 1986.

———. *The Ways of Judgment: The Bampton Lectures, 2003*. Grand Rapids, MI, and Cambridge, UK: Eerdmans, 2005.

Olson, Jeannine E. *Calvin and Social Welfare: Deacons and the Bourse française*. Cranbury, NJ, and London: Associated University Presses, 1989.

On Riches. In *Pelagius: Life and Letters*, by B. R. Rees. Woodbridge, UK, and Rochester, NY: Boydell, 1991.

Pieper, Josef. *The Four Cardinal Virtues*. Notre Dame, IN: University of Notre Dame Press, 1966.

———. *Leisure: The Basis of Culture; Including "The Philosophical Act."* San Francisco, CA: Ignatius Press, 2009.

Piketty, Thomas. *Capital in the Twenty-First Century*. Cambridge, MA and London: Belknap Press, 2014.

Putnam, Robert D. *Bowling Alone: The Collapse and Revival of American Community*. New York: Simon and Schuster, 2000.

Rachman, Gideon. "Growth and Globalization Cannot Cure All the World's Ills." *Financial Times*. January 27, 2014.

Rauschenbusch, Walter. *Christianity and the Social Crisis.* Louisville, KY: Westminster/John Knox Press, 1991.

———. *A Theology for the Social Gospel.* Louisville, KY: Westminster John Knox Press, 1997.

Rhee, Helen. *Loving the Poor, Saving the Rich: Wealth, Poverty, and Early Christian Formation.* Grand Rapids, MI: Baker, 2012.

Ricardo, David. *On the Principles of Political Economy and Taxation.* Indianapolis, IN: Liberty Fund, 2004.

Ridley, Matt. "Smart Aid for the World's Poor." *The Wall Street Journal.* July 25, 2014.

Rieger, Joerg. *No Rising Tide: Theology, Economics, and the Future.* Minneapolis, MN: Fortress Press, 2009.

Rodrik, Dani. *The Globalization Paradox: Democracy and the Future of World Economy.* New York: Norton, 2011.

Ross, Michael. "Transcendence, Immanence, and Practical Deliberation in Simone Weil's Early and Middle Years." In *The Christian Platonism of Simone Weil.* Edited by Jane E. Doering and Eric O. Springstead. Notre Dame, IN: University of Notre Dame Press, 2004.

Rubin, Jeff. *The Big Flatline: Oil and the No-growth Economy.* New York: Palgrave Macmillan, 2012.

Ryan, John A. *Economic Justice: Selections from Distributive Justice and a Living Wage.* Louisville, KY: Westminster John Knox Press, 1996.

Schneider, John. *Godly Materialism: Rethinking Money and Possessions.* Downers Grove, IL: InterVarsity Press, 1994.

———. *The Good of Affluence: Seeking God in a Culture of Wealth.* Grand Rapids, MI, and Cambridge, UK: Eerdmans, 2002.

Schumpeter, Joseph A. *Capitalism, Socialism and Democracy.* New York and London: Harper Perennial, 2008.

Scruton, Roger. *How to Think Seriously about the Planet: The Case for an Environmental Conservatism.* Oxford and New York: Oxford University Press, 2012.

Seabright, Paul. *The Company of Strangers: A Natural History of Economic Life.* Princeton, NJ, and Oxford: Princeton University Press, 2004.

Sheffield, Carrie. "Skills-Based Education Can Help Solve the Inequality Puzzle." *Forbes.* December 18, 2014.

Shell Energy Scenarios to 2050. Shell International BV, 2008.

Sider, Ronald J. *Rich Christians in an Age of Hunger: Moving from Affluence to Generosity.* Dallas, TX: Word, 1997.

Sirico, Robert. *Defending the Free Market: The Moral Case for a Free Economy.* Washington, DC: Regnery, 2012.

Smith, Adam. *An Inquiry into the Nature and Causes of the Wealth of Nations.* Indianapolis, IN: Liberty Fund, 1981.

———. *The Theory of Moral Sentiments.* Indianapolis, IN: Liberty Fund, 1982.

Song, Robert, and Brent Waters, eds. *The Authority of the Gospel: Explorations in Moral and Political Theology in Honor of Oliver O'Donovan.* Grand Rapids, MI, and Cambridge, UK: Eerdmans, 2015.

Spaemann, Robert. *Persons: The Difference between 'Someone' and 'Something.'* Oxford and New York: Oxford University Press, 2006.

Stayer, James M. *The German Peasants' War and Anabaptist Community of Goods.* Montreal and Kingston: McGill-Queen's University Press, 1994.

Stiglitz, Joseph E. *Globalization and Its Discontents.* New York: Norton, 2002.

———. *Making Globalization Work.* New York and London: Norton, 2007.

Strauss, Leo. *On Tyranny*. Chicago and London: University of Chicago Press, 2000.

SugarCane.org. "Brazil's Diverse Energy Mix." (http://sugarcane.org/the-brazilian -experience/brazils-diverse-energy-matrix).

Thernstrom, Samuel. "The Next Shale Revolution? The Astonishing Promise of Enhanced Oil Recovery." *The Weekly Standard*. December 29, 2014.

Thomas Aquinas, *Summa theologiae*, 2-2, q.77, a.1. Kindle e-book. The Complete American Edition, translated by the Fathers of the English Dominican Province.

Tett, Gillian. *Fool's Gold: How the Bold Dream of a Small Tribe at J. P. Morgan Was Corrupted by Wall Street Greed and Unleashed a Catastrophe*. New York: Free Press, 2009.

Tillich, Paul. *The Socialist Decision*. New York: Harper and Row, 1977.

Tverberg, Gail. Our Finite World. ourfiniteworld.com.

"UN and Climate Change." http://www.un.org/climatechange/.

Van Doosselaere, Quentin. *Commercial Agreements and Social Dynamics in Medieval Genoa*. Cambridge, UK, and New York: Cambridge University Press, 2009.

Van Rooy, Alison. *The Global Legitimacy Game: Civil Society, Globalization, and Protest*. Houndmills, UK, and New York: Palgrave Macmillan, 2004.

Waters, Brent. *Christian Moral Theology in the Emerging Technoculture: From Posthuman Back to Human*. Farnham, UK, and Burlington, VT: Ashgate, 2014.

———. *The Family in Christian Social and Political Thought*. Oxford: Oxford University Press, 2007.

———. "Two, or Perhaps Two-and-a-half Cheers for Globalization." *Anglican Theological Review* 92:4 (Fall 2010).

Weber, Max. *The Protestant Ethic and the Spirit of Capitalism*. London and Boston, MA: Unwin, 1985.

Weil, Simone. *Waiting for God*. New York: HarperCollins, 2001.

White, Ronald C., and C. Howard Hopkins, eds. *The Social Gospel: Religion and Reform in Changing America*. Philadelphia, PA: Temple University Press, 1976.

Wolf, Martin. *Why Globalization Works*. New Haven, CT, and London: Yale University Press, 2004.

———. "Why Inequality Is Such a Drag on Economies." *Financial Times*. September 30, 2014.

Wong, Kenman L., and Scott B. Rae. *Business for the Common Good: A Christian Vision for the Marketplace*. Downers Grove, IL: InterVarsity Press, 2011.

World Bank. *Economics of Adaptation to Climate Change: Synthesis Report*, 2010.

World Energy Council. "Energy Trilemma Index." http://www.worldenergy.org/data /trilemma-index/.

Yergin, Daniel. *The Quest: Energy, Security, and the Remaking of the Modern World*. New York: Penguin, 2011.

Zieba, Maciej. *Papal Economics: The Catholic Church on Democratic Capitalism, from Rerum Novarum to Caritas in Veritate*. Wilmington, DE: ISI Books, 2013.

Index

229

charity, 36, 37, 38, 39, 103–5, 116, 132
  beneficial targets for, 104, 112n36
  in Christian theologies, 25, 25n39, 37,
    109–10, 139, 191
  vs. exchange, 109–10
  vs. investment, 11–12
  limits of, 105
  and love, 93, 94–95, 97, 109, 112, 113,
    116
  mismanaged, 114, 126, 199, 200
  redistribution of wealth through, 199
  in Roman Empire, 36
  self-serving, 103–4, 199
  sources of, 103
China
  automobile manufacturing in, 107,
    107n28
  economic growth and pollution in, 130,
    212, 213
  poverty in, 3
  renewable energy in, 214
choice, 187
  consumer, 121
  freedom restricting, 183
  individual, as priority, 66
  mistaken or irrational, 123, 187
Christianity
  eschatological orientation of, 151
  and loyalty to states, 73–74
  rise of, 35–39
  wealth condemned by, 19–28, 80, 86,
    109
church, 141, 142
  adaptability of, 73–75
  communication and, 79, 149
  creative destruction of, 13
  diversity within, 76–77
  as gathering community, 150, 157
  as global, 78–79
  imperial privileges of, 36
  as largest employer, 39
  as model, 15, 79, 149, 150–51, 155–56,
    159–60, 167–68
  as non-coercive, 149–50, 149n16
  as non-territorial, 151
  not based on charity, 150
  reciprocity in, 165–67, 201

universal cohesion provided by, 38–39,
    151, 154–55
  virtual presence of, 160n31
  as voluntary organization, 12
City of God vs. City of Man, 74–75, 151
civil society, 141–43, 163–82, 199
  affluence strengthening, 88–89, 157–59
  capital investment and, 44
  communicative associations and, 159
  competition promoting, 46, 55, 88–89
  continuity provided by, 141–42
  cooperation promoting, 55
  definition of, 137, 137n26, 138, 141,
    147, 163–64
  and enkaptic relations, 146, 147
  growing out of place and people, 147
  and political ordering, 166, 167–73
  replacing private and public spheres,
    201
  and the state, 58–59, 158, 162
  state coercion and, 170–72
  and Trinitarian thought, 141
Clement of Alexandria, 30
climate change, 204, 209–17
  adapting to, 211, 215
  poverty and, 210, 211, 211n29
  and transition from fossil fuels, 214–17
clothing industry, 173, 173n26
Club of Rome, 205–6, 207
coal, 212, 212n30, 213, 214
coercion, state, 45, 133, 135, 136, 137,
    162, 170
  becoming less effective, 70
  and capital investment, 54
  vs. consent, 172–73
  displacing communication, 152
  vs. God's mercy, 74
  limits to, 144
  principles of, 170–71
collective action, 142
collectivism, 66, 67
colonialism, 2
communication, 15, 115, 144–62, 167, 184
  church and, 79, 149
  definition of, 145
  and enkaptic relations, 146
  freedom of, 186

communication (*continued*)
    as goal of exchange, 16
    markets necessary for, 148, 164
    state, markets, and, 155–62
    stewardship and, 217
    See also association
community chests, 25, 25n39, 31
comparative advantage, principle of, 8,
        42–43, 53, 104, 175, 175n28
competition, 40, 45–54
    badly managed, effects of, 56
    and capital investment, 51–52
    and cooperation, 54, 186, 216
    employment and, 48–51
    freedom to engage in, 184, 186
    and human associations, 140
    human enjoyment of, 46
    as ideology, 27
    innovation, productivity, and, 47–48
    leading to poverty, 58
    against machines, 50
    pricing and, 48
    regulation and, 53–54, 56
    wealth creation and, 52–53
    winners and losers in, 46, 47, 50, 51, 52,
        191
compulsion, 187. *See also* coercion, state
conflict
    environmental regulations and, 130–31
    immigration restrictions causing, 8, 128
consent vs. coercion, 172–73, 186–87, 189
Constantine, 36, 37
consumerism, 14
    and human associations, 161
consumers, manipulation of, 153
consumption, 66–67
contextualization, 33–39
contracts, 88, 173
controversial judgments, 169–70
conversions, forced, 149n16
cooperation, 40, 54–58, 140, 147, 164, 216
    competition and, 54, 186, 216
    between employers and employees, 57
    labor specialization and, 55, 55n25, 57
    in lending, 58
    between sellers and buyers, 57
Copenhagen Consensus Center, 104

corporate tax rates, 175–76
corporations, multinational, nation-states
        displaced by, 2
corruption, 194
Cosgrove, Charles, 34
cost of living, 99
courts, 166, 166n7
creation
    beauty of, 204, 217
    as blessing, 90
    development of, xi, 91–92, 111, 203,
        204, 217
    enjoying, 89–91, 217
    goodness of, xi, 89–90
    human dominance over, 203
    natural resources and, 42, 43–44, 111,
        130–32, 204–17
"creative destruction," 61, 69, 108, 159,
        163
    of church, 13
    Holy Spirit and, 77–78
Credit Suisse Research Institute, 52n21
cross, theology of, 220
Cyprian, 21

Dalits, 105
debt, 7
    slavery, 34
delight in creation, 90–91, 97, 111
dependency, 86, 112, 113
    aid creating, 11
    on fossil fuels, 205, 208, 212, 213
    injustice of, 192
desires
    disordered, 96, 188
    as irrational, 123
    prioritizing, 126–27
    satiating, 64
De Soto, Hernando, 193
developing countries, 99
Didache, 21
direct foreign investment (DFI), 102,
        102n10
disabilities, people with, 127–28, 198
disciples leaving their livelihoods, 20
discrimination
    in hiring practices, 170n21

CPSIA information can be obtained
at www.ICGtesting.com
Printed in the USA
BVHW030608140122
626195BV00013B/123